MW01038462

ep;phany

a literary journal

www.epiphanyzine.com

ep;phany

Editor	Willard Cook
Managing Editor	Chuck Mindenhall
Fiction Editor	Elizabeth England
Nonfiction Editor	Karol Nielsen
Poetry Editor	Jeffrey Gustavson
Editorial Assistant	Adam Levy
Readers	Jennifer Cooke, Amy Dana, Vivian Eyre, Maureen Hope, Pat Ludwig, Deb McAlister, Martha Mortenson, Susie Lilly Ott, W. "RP" Raghupathi, Ph.D., Josh Ralske, Betsy Weis
Design	Rebecca Mindenhall
Web Master	Eric Iversen

Epiphany is published bianuually by Epiphany Magazine, Inc. a nonprofit 501c3 corporation.

For submission guidelines please visit our web site at www.epiphanyzine.com

Donations and gifts to *Epiphany* are tax-deductible to the extent allowed by law.

A one-year subscription is $10; a two year subscription is $18. A donation of $500 and over makes the donor a Friend of *Epiphany* and is good for a lifetime subscription. Make checks payable to Epiphany Magazine and send to: 71 Bedford Street, New York, NY 10014 or visit our website at www.epiphanyzine.com

The ISBN number is 0-9749047-1-6
The ISSN number is

THE FALL/WINTER 2007-2008 ISSUE WAS PRINTED BY:
McNaughton & Gunn Inc. 960 Woodland Drive Saline, MI 48176
Ph: 734-429-8728 Fax: 734-429-8740

All rights reserved. No part of this publication maybe reproduced, transmitted in any form or by any means, electronic, mechanical photocopying, recording, or otherwise without prior written consent of Epiphany Magazine, Inc.

SUBSCRIPTION ADDRESS CHANGES SHOULD BE SENT TO:
Donna Moore, VP of Michigan Operations Publishers Storage and Shipping Corp.
660 S. Mansfield, Ypsilanti, MI 48197 Office 734-487-9720 ext.130
dmoore@psscmi.com • Website: www.pssc.com

Bookstore distribution is through Ingram periodicals. www.ingramperiodicals.com

MISSION STATEMENT

Epiphany publishes fiction, nonfiction, poetry and visual media from both established and emerging writers and artists. We believe continuous study, practice, collaboration, and careful editing all lead to good writing. Epiphany supports and honors the determination of writers and artists by publishing work that is accessible, entertaining, and even life-changing.

FURTHER STATEMENT OF PURPOSE

Epiphany, established in 2003, is a nonprofit literary journal that publishes twice a year: once digitally and once in hard copy. The publication of each issue will coincide with readings, panels, and socials that will help build a strong literary arts community. *Epiphany* promotes its writers and artists by showcasing their work at readings, in mailers, through outreach readings and workshops at organizations like Women in Need, Greenwich Village Seniors Center and Baruch College Campus High School and Elizabeth Irwin High School.

Epiphany is a proud member of CLMP.

HUNGER MOUNTAIN

and Vermont College of Union Institute & University

are pleased to announce the fifth annual

RUTH STONE PRIZE IN POETRY

One $1,000.00 prize winner and two honorable mentions
will be selected for publication in *Hunger Mountain*
by judge Nance Van Winckel, author of *Beside Ourselves*.

GUIDELINES

- $15 entry fee, payable to "Hunger Mountain" - includes a copy of the Spring 2008 Issue of *HUNGER MOUNTAIN*.
- Submit up to three poems per entry, not to exceed six pages total.
- Poems must be original, written in English, and previously unpublished.
- Entries must be postmarked by December 10, 2007 - late entries will be returned unread.
- Entries must be typed, one side only.
- Once submitted, entries cannot be altered.
- Name or address should not appear anywhere on poems.
- Enclose one standard index card with poem titles, name, address, phone number, and email address.
- Enclose a self-addressed stamped envelope for notification of winners.
- Use a paper clip or send unbound - no staples.
- No simultaneous submissions, artwork, or translations.
- Multiple entries allowed - each entry must include a separate entry fee.
- Enclose a postage-paid postcard for acknowledgement of entry (optional).
- No entries will be returned.
- Electronic or faxed entries will not be accepted.

DEADLINE:
postmarked by
DECEMBER 10, 2007

ENTRY FEE:
$15.00, includes the
Spring 2008 Issue of
HUNGER MOUNTAIN

MAIL TO:
Ruth Stone Prize in Poetry
Hunger Mountain
Vermont College
36 College Street
Montpelier, VT
05602

Winners Announced
Spring 2008

www.hungermtn.org

FIND YOUR VOICE ON THE COAST OF MAINE

Stonecoast M.F.A.
in Creative Writing

For more information on this low-residency program, please visit our Web site

www.usm.maine.edu/stonecoastmfa

Director: Annie Finch

To apply, call **(207) 780-4386** or
e-mail: **gradstudies@usm.maine.edu**

Scholarships available

usm UNIVERSITY OF SOUTHERN MAINE

FACULTY
Kazim Ali, Poetry, Experimental Fiction
Tanya Maria Barrientos, Nonfiction
Jeanne Marie Beaumont, Poetry
David Chan, Fiction, Experimental Fiction
Joan Connor, Fiction, Nonfiction
Alan Davis, Fiction
Ted Deppe, Poetry, Coordinator, Stonecoast in Ireland
Boman Desai, Fiction
David Durham, Fiction, Pop Fiction
Annie Finch, Poetry
Jeffrey Harrison, Poetry
Richard Hoffman, Nonfiction, Poetry
Nancy Holder, Pop Fiction
Ann Hood, Fiction
Barbara Hurd, Nonfiction
Gray Jacobik, Poetry
James Patrick Kelly, Pop Fiction, Multimedia
Michael Kimball, Pop Fiction
Kelly Link, Pop Fiction
Charles Martin, Poetry, Translation
Shara McCallum, Poetry
Clint McCown, Fiction, Writing for Stage/Screen
Carol Moldaw, Poetry
Lesléa Newman, Fiction, Young Adult
Dennis Nurkse, Poetry
Lewis Robinson, Fiction
Elizabeth Searle, Fiction, Pop Fiction
Tim Seibles, Poetry
Julia Spencer-Fleming, Pop Fiction
Suzanne Strempek Shea, Fiction, Nonfiction
Michael C. White, Fiction
Baron Wormser, Nonfiction, Poetry

UNIVERSITY OF CALIFORNIA, RIVERSIDE
PALM DESERT GRADUATE CENTER

MFA in Creative Writing and Writing for the Performing Arts

Fiction • Screenwriting • Television Writing
Nonfiction • Poetry • Playwriting

UCR | PALM DESERT GRADUATE CENTER

www.palmdesertmfa.ucr.edu
760-834-0926

FACULTY
Chris Abani
Eric Barr
Charles Evered
Fern Field
Tod Goldberg
Seth Greenland
Juan Felipe Herrera
Stu Krieger
Leila Lalami
Goldberry Long
Tom Lutz, Director
Paul Mandelbaum
Rachel Resnick
Maurya Simon
Susan C. Straight
Lance B. Taylor
Lisa Teasley

RECENT VISITORS
Janet Fitch
Kate Gale
Larry Gelbart
Jessica Hendra
Tim Z. Hernandez
Michelle Huneven
Elena Karina Byrne
Aimee Liu
Ruben Martinez
Robert McKee
John Rechy
Christopher Rice
Margarita Luna Robles
Antonio Sacre
Shelly Saltman
Eric Stoltz
David St. John
Robert Thomas
Michael Tolkin
Al Young

Rolling Admissions

Low Residency option currently pending University approval

Dear *Epiphany* Reader:

We can't thank you enough for picking up this copy of our magazine; our gratitude truly knows no bounds. What good is a work of art without an audience? What's the use of a magazine without readers? Without your intelligence, curiosity, fineness of discrimination, fairness of judgement, and aversion to cant, our efforts to find and print the work of the literary artists gathered here would be worse than meaningless. When I read these stories and poems, I experience the strong feeling that if only *everyone* would read them, the world would change for the better. I can almost persuade myself that, contrary to W.H. Auden's well-known lament, Poetry makes *everything* happen. Language is older than time and more powerful than an atom bomb, I tell myself. And it's clear that you agree, to a greater or lesser extent, with an attitude like that. You know how much work it takes to do anything worthwhile. You know the price, both tangible and intangible, that must be paid to strike out in an untried direction. What I love about literary magazines is that they tell us the truth, but tell it "slant," as Emily Dickinson wrote. A story or a poem digs around for a personal truth or revelation and spins it in a way different from how the writer would speak if he or she were talking to someone in real life; instead, they speak to some abstract ideal listener, some improbable living breathing assemblage of all the qualities and traits that millennia of trial and error have taught us to think of as human—in other words, as Derek Walcott says in one of his poems in this issue, to "You, my dearest friend, Reader." Literary magazines are the medium of choice for giving us access to this kind of spin; in a media-saturated age of blasé impatience, they are still the best equipped of any format to tell the truth slant.

—Willard Cook

CONTENTS

Erica Ciccarone

PIT

The pit came the summer Shelley was pregnant. It arrived at night while I was sleeping and I heard it howling behind the house, in our dirt-and-weeds yard. Morning came and I was making the coffee—strong, because Jared liked it muddy, though I didn't—and I heard something outside. Probably my strays waiting for breakfast, one of them jumping from the fence onto the trash can. A dozen or so lived under the house and in the yard. I had named them after cities in New Mexico, where I'm from—Santa Fe, snow-white Santa Rita, jet-black Estancia, long-haired Roswell, a shy tabby called Pueblo Bonita. I lugged out the big Wal-Mart bag of cat food and unbolted the back door. Roux, my ten-year-old calico, came running up from the other end of the shotgun. She rubbed against my legs and I cooed at her as I opened the door. Then she screeched and leapt up onto the fridge, and something tore up from under the house.

The pit was so skinny I could see its nasty spine arching. Black and brown with a white diamond on its hollowed chest. It had match-stick legs, a short, pointy tail. Yellow bat eyes and a nose smashed into its face. A horrible mouth full of teeth.

I slammed the door and bolted it. For a moment, I thought I'd imagined the whole thing. One of those delusions Jared's been talking about. Something seen in another dimension, out of my invisible eyes. *Am I loco, Lima?* I cracked the door and peeked. *No lemons no melon.* Its snout poked at the screen.

I crept up through the house to the front porch with my coffee, afraid the animal would hear me. It didn't—the kitchen was all the way in the back.

Shelley came out on her side of the double, where she lived with her mother. Shelley was nineteen, and eight and a half months pregnant, but you wouldn't know it if you saw her from the back. She had narrow hips and a little ass, and when she turned sideways it was like an optical illusion. She walked across the porch wearing nothing but an old pair of black elastic shorts and a neon-pink sports bra, her hand holding up her back. As if it could do such a thing. Her huge belly hung over the waistband, striped with light brown and pink stretch marks, her belly button popped out. Shelley's hair was half done, braided into a weave, that blood orange color that only a black woman can pull off. At seven-thirty, she was already sweating.

"Lord," she said.

"Hush," I said. "A dog got into the backyard."

Shelley nodded. "Barked all night. Didn't get a bit of sleep. Wild packs been all over Napoleon."

"It's a pit bull. Nasty one."

"My dad used to raise pits for fighting. Mean, mean." She sat on the porch floor and leaned back on her hands. Sitting is an effort when you're pregnant. "You got a cold-drink inside?"

The living room was dim. I heard Jared snoring, his ragged breath filling the house like heat in an oven. The squat forms of his drums huddled together, his guitar cases reclined in the corner. I stroked the head of a mannequin as I walked past, jingled the strands of beads from last year's Mardi Gras that hung around the doll's neck. In the bed, Jared was long and hairy, his mouth open. Some people look beautiful when they sleep, children, their easy dreams spinning above their damp heads. I grabbed a can from the fridge and got back out.

"That man of yours came in late last night," Shelley said, popping the tab on the can of diet Sprite. "Thank you." She held it up and toasted my coffee mug.

"He had a gig downtown."

"Till four in the morning?" She swatted at a mosquito. "No-good man."

"He does have his moments." I dumped the dregs of the coffee into the weeds. "I've got to get going. Careful out back. I'll make sure he takes care of it."

"If he ever wakes up." She looked off toward Tchoupitoulas and the river.

"I'll be stopping by the store later. You need anything?"

"Sure," Shelley said. "A husband."

I left ten bucks and a note for Jared on the counter. *To idiot.* I worked at a daycare center. The Uptown mothers dropped their kids off early, some of them by seven. It was Friday, payday, and I planned to buy Shelley some baby clothes, those sweet little onesies that button on the bottom, some miniature caps and socks.

I tried to call home during my lunch break, but the machine picked up. He never checks the messages. When I got home, the house was empty except for Roux sleeping in a stripe of sunlight on the floor. She looked up when I dropped the grocery bag on the table. I stood at the back door and pressed my cheek to it. I listened. I didn't hear a thing. Roux cried to be let out and kept under my feet as I tried to cook. I made pork chops and mashed potatoes, corn and salad. The salad was for me. Jared came in just as it was ready, black boots getting closer on the old wood floor. He had a Pet Stop bag and a huge sack of dog food slung over his shoulder. "Surprise!" he said. "I bought you a puppy!"

He took out a heavy metal bowl, a red studded collar, a chain-link leash. *Gods send a madness: dog.*

"Baby," I said, "that's no puppy."

"You're gonna love him," he said, advancing toward the back door.

"We've already met."

The pit sprung from the bottom of the steps and crashed into the screen, barking and snarling. "Monica," my husband said, "meet Star."

The yellow eyes squinted and the snout poked the screen as the pit threw itself against the door. Its nails tore at the aluminum. Roux fled toward the bedroom, knocking a potted plant off the countertop. *God damn! Mad dog!*

"Fine," I said. "Your dog."

A month ago, there had been the old moped he tinkered with for a few days, then left in the alleyway in a heap of rusty parts. Before that, a how-to taxidermy book. Maybe this was his way of learning to nurture, and he was caught up in the excitement of having a pet, like a child. Once, that was what I loved about him.

"Go ahead, go play with it," I said. "Hope it bites your damn hand off."

He slid outside and I shut the door behind him. I could hear him saying, "Get it, Star, fetch!" Then, "Down bitch, *down!*" He came in, sat and waited to be fed. "He just needs breaking in. We'll have him fetching that stick in no time."

"No devil lived on," I said, and made my way out to the front porch.

I needed a walk, knowing after the walk I'd need an excuse for the walk that was not the dog. He'd say, *Why'd you walk out on me?* or *What's your problem?* or *This isn't about the dog.* But it was about the dog. My anger found a cold point of focus, a small white light on the dog's forehead. Rounding the corner, I spotted Shelley in the Missus Bubbles, pulling clothes out of the dryer. When she saw me, she straightened up, squinted into the setting sun behind me.

"What's this hell?" she said. I was still in my work clothes, denim overalls covered with little green handprints, and a Saints T-shirt. My hair had fallen out of the ponytail when I was cooking; my glasses were smudged with grease. I took over pulling the clothes out, and she sat down as I dumped them onto the table. "Your face looks about hotter than these sheets," she said.

"It's *his* dog."

"Lord have mercy."

"He named it Star."

"Monica," Shelley said, her eyes huge and bold. "Can't have a killer dog at the home I bring my child to."

"Of course not."

"What are you going to do?" she said, her eyebrows raised now, her lips pursed in judgment, and I knew this was one of those times Shelley seemed ages older than me.

"He's just looking for attention. So I'll hold out on him."

"He'll just go looking for it from someone else. My baby-daddy lives the same way. No-good man."

Shelley's baby's father was in prison. When I'd asked her what he was in for, she had said, "For being ignorant," and had looked off in a way that told me not to ask again.

"Give me a hand?" I threw her the end of a bed sheet. "Promise you won't worry."

"Fine. One week I won't worry. Got enough trouble with this child looking to burst out of me." As we folded the sheet together, she went, "Ooh!" and put her hand to her belly. "Kicked me."

At home, Jared was gone, the dirty dishes piled in the sink. I opened the back door and peeked outside. It was there in the dirt. Sitting on its haunches, staring at the door, growling. I was getting worried about my strays. In this neighborhood, cats hung around like swamp weed. But now, it was as if the pit sent them hiding.

I went out front and sat on the porch. We lived by the levee, across from the Seventh Street Wharf. I heard a ship docking; the crash of it shook the house for a moment. Jared complained that it was bad for the foundation. But we were renting, and it seemed to me it was nice to be close to the river and feel the ships shake the earth. Our street was bordered by shotgun houses like ours, most of them restored and painted in bright colors. The unrestored houses, like ours, were weathered by hurricanes and by twenty or thirty summers, the paint faded and peeling, the shingles curled like dried leaves. That was the plan when we moved here, restoring the house. We lived in a neighborhood of families and old people, kids who played basketball in the street. Mr. Ameile next door sat watch with his oxygen tank, the tubes coming out of his nose like the tusks of a walrus. Most of my neighbors had potted plants on the porches, or little gardens in their small front lawns. In their backyards, they had barbeques, kiddie pools, slip-n-slides. We had lived here for two years. When I met him, Jared was playing a djembe in a drum circle on Mardi Gras, dressed in an elephant costume. When I told him my name, he said, "Har-Monica," handed me a beer from a cooler beside him, gave me a look that came right up from under me. Something practiced, it seemed, but it worked.

The dog barked behind the house. I reached above the lintel of the door and found half a cigarette I had left there, lit it. Two puffs and I saw our Dodge Ram pull around the corner. I snuffed the cigarette out in the empty diet Sprite can and smiled at him as he hopped down. "You gigging tonight?" I said, hoping he'd have the boys over to play. He was in several bands and drum circles, and my favorite times were when they came over and sat around on the porch; the music could be heard throughout the neighborhood, the kids gathered around to dance. We hadn't done that in a long time.

"Nope," he said. "Got something to take care of." He leapt up the steps, kissed me on the cheek, and went into the house. I rested my foot on the porch railing and it moved. The wood was rotting. I kicked at it.

The gate behind the house slammed, and he came up through the alleyway, the dog biting at the chain-link leash as if trying to tear it apart. Jared lifted it up by the scruff of its neck and threw it into the covered back of our truck—my truck, actually—got in and waved to me with a flick of two fingers and drove off. So good, he was doing something right.

I cleaned up and did a few crossword puzzles. Usually my *Wordsmith* magazines had a soothing effect, like some people get from watching television. Television never made me feel that way. Turn one on and suddenly the room was crowded with quibbling, hungry mouths. The only peace for me was in words, working out solutions with the old dictionary. But that night, I kept looking outside, listening for the truck. What was taking so long? The SPCA was just so far away. Maybe he had a friend who wanted the pit, someone big who was into scaring people.

But by nine, I was panicking. Was he angry? Drunk? Off somewhere in the Quarter, letting some woman slip her hand into the waistband of his jeans, where there was just enough room for slim fingers? I dug into my top drawer and found the blue sock where I kept the pills. Lorisat 7s and 10s mostly, Xanax, and four precious purple Percocets—whatever I could get from the part-time college girl at the center who had been hit by a streetcar on her bicycle and had to live with back trouble, the anxiety of it happening again. I shook out one of the 7s, then thought what the hell, and added a 10. *I did, did I?* Washed them down with a cold can of Miller High Life, started a bath. In the water, my thoughts started slowing down and my body began to feel light and floaty. The black spaces crept up between my thoughts. I turned the A/C up to high and crawled into bed, burrowed into the quilt.

S unday morning, I woke up to find Jared gone and the dishes done. The coffee canister empty except for a few grounds. I knocked *shave and a haircut* on the wall and heard Shelley's screen door swing open and slap against the side of the house. I stepped out the back door. "You got any coff—" and I saw it. Over in the rear corner, chained to the fence pole, crouched in the dirt. It came at us, the chain pulled taunt, the dog fell to the ground.

Shelley waddled down her steps, over to my side.

"I thought he got rid of it," I said.

The pit looked different. Its face was puffed up, as if it had been hit with something. It had cuts on its jowls that hadn't begun to scab. One ear was torn and pointed down, and one eye was swollen shut.

"He been fighting it," Shelley said. She shook her head. "It's a fighting dog. That's why he got it." She looked down at the weeds and her eyes widened. "You get yourself inside." But I'd seen it. *Was it a cat I saw?* Must have been Albuquerque, because the nose was half black and half white and the staring kitten eyes were blue. One ear had been torn off, the neck shredded and gnawed to white bone, a heap of fur and something red and gooey that I couldn't look at. Blood in the weeds.

I had liked Albuquerque because once he had come into the kitchen and darted around terrified as Roux watched from her perch on the sink. I had scooted him out with my foot and left an open can of tuna outside. Ever since, we'd been friends.

The pit kept charging at us, getting pulled up by the leash, strangling, falling, getting up shaking.

"Tough little fucker." Shelley led me by both hands into the kitchen and closed the door.

I leaned against the wall and breathed and the room closed in around me. *Lonely Tylenol. We panic in a pew. Did Mom poop? Mom did. Go a hang a salami I'm a . . . Go hang a salami I'm a. Lasagna hog.*

I looked at the situation backwards and forwards, and everything was wrong both ways. Where would you even *go* to fight a dog? Under the highway overpass far down on Claiborne Avenue where the teenagers glared at you as you drove past? Did he get the dog with this intention? And why did he present it as a gift? The dog seemed to have a cruel power. It would destroy itself to get at me.

"Your *present* killed one of the strays," I said to him when he got home.

"One less burden." He opened a can of beer.

"Dog doesn't look good. Where'd you two go last night? Hit the town? Pick up a couple bitches?"

"None of your goddamn business." He chugged the beer and his Adam's apple throbbed. I had lost track of how long it had been since we'd done it. He smacked his lips. "How about that?"

"Shelley's baby's due any day now. The dog's gotta go. Throw it in the river for all I care. I don't want to see it."

"Don't you get it? It's not your decision."

"What?" I said. "Last I checked we were in a marriage. A partnership."

He said, "You've got to let me have some room to breathe. Besides, you got that cat, sheds all over the goddamn place. A man needs a pet of his own."

"What a man needs," I said, "is something to do with his sorry-ass life."

"Fucking delusional. Why don't you pop a lorry and go to hell." He went outside to get the pit.

I borrowed Shelley's shovel and dug a deep hole in the yard for Albuquerque. It felt good to be digging. I sweated, and smelled myself, earthy in the heat. When we were first married, we would fight like this at night and wake up in the morning crying with forgiveness. He liked to say we operated on a crazy frequency. Couldn't predict when it would kick in or tune out. But things settled. He had his music, and I had my job, Shelley, my dream of dressmaking, the cats. He once had a lucky streak with four-leaf clovers. He'd bring me one every Friday. But it turned out there was a patch of fakes behind a cigar shop on Charters Street, a fact he confessed to me during a fight. I lowered the cat into the hole with the shovel, covered it up, and made a cross out of sticks and wire. In the dirt I wrote: *Step On No Pets.*

I went on speaking strike. Didn't speak for three days outside of work, not even to Shelley. My silence made the house pulse with noise. Coffee dripping. Roux's pads on the floorboards, her tongue lapping at the sink drip. Everything breathed: the mannequins took on the knowing expressions of judges; the dolls huddled together murmuring their secrets. I cleaned. I scrubbed the floors and polished them and the rooms smelled like lemon rind and wax and ammonia. I emptied the wooden carnival Doubloons out of the vases and washed them. I strung the Mardi Gras beads onto the porch railing so I could hear them out there tinkling their melody in the breeze. I opened the windows and turned off the air conditioning, took the piece of plywood out of the bedroom window from a storm six months ago, installed the glass myself. I hung the flutes from the ceiling on a clothesline and listened to the air blowing through them, to the rustling rhythms of the mannequins' crinoline skirts.

Jared occasionally would pick up a drum and start tapping out a beat, but the music of the house eluded him, a melody he couldn't pick up.

I found myself going into the sock more often, swallowing down two, three pills at a time. I tried to keep my mind occupied, and I stayed out of the kitchen as much as possible. I didn't want to think about the circle of crouching men, the animals darting at each other under the streetlights, teeth bared. I had discovered a new type of word: capitonyms. Words with the same spelling but different pronunciations and definitions when the first letter is capitalized. The example in the magazine was Polish and polish. I came up with basil and Basil, a swamp town outside Lafayette. August and august. Lima and lima. And then there was the soothing balance of the palindrome, the perfect mirror of letters that holds up strong against all odds.

F ourth day, I woke to the pit bull's howling. I smashed a pillow over my head and dreamed that there was a baby growing inside me with a smashed-in nose, yellow eyes rolling around in its head.

Nothing righteous in the world. I shook myself awake and got up to make the coffee.

I was getting into my truck when Miss Avery, Shelley's mother, came out of the house. When she called out to me from the porch in her bathrobe, I knew it right away by the look of her—no sleep, and joy.

On my lunch break I went straight to the hospital. Shelley was sitting up in bed, her orange hair bright in the dim room lit only by a muted talk show. At first, I didn't see the baby in her lap, hidden in a blanket.

"Hey, you," she said. Her face glowed, and her eyes, turned down at the corners, sparkled under their long lashes. "So glad this child is a girl." She turned the bundle toward me and the baby's face peeked out the blanket. "Jade Shenell Avery."

"Sounds like a famous jazz singer." I peered at her face. "How do you feel?"

"About run down by a train," she said and laughed. "Nurses say I need to sleep, but I can't stop watching her. You want to hold her?"

Jade looked like a plump raisin under her pink cap. Her tiny lips parted to reveal her tender pink mouth, and her eyelids were delicate flower petals with purple veins. She had Shelley's broad nose and high cheekbones. Jade gurgled and squirmed for a moment, then slept on. She felt so light in my arms, like a bundle of rags. Her fists were no bigger than chestnuts.

I thought of Jared, and the pit.

I headed back down Louisiana Street, then thought better of it and pulled onto Magazine, then right on Third. In the bar, I called in to work and told them I was sick. I ordered a gin and tonic. The long wooden bar looked dull in the sunlight, the posters worn and faded, everything yellowed by cigarette smoke. An Irish bar, walls cluttered with pride slogans and jokes: PARKING FOR IRISHMEN ONLY; RED SOX FANS FINISH FIRST.

The bar was empty except for a couple watching a baseball game. The man had graying sideburns, a lazy shadow of a beard. His glasses were sliding off his nose, and he leaned on the bar as if it had been holding him up for decades. He had a coarse handsomeness about him, like a man who had always inhabited bars and lounges. The woman—much younger, early twenties, I guessed—sat up straight. She wore a denim skirt and a floral blouse that looked like an old lady's wallpaper. She kept her legs crossed at the ankles on a rung of the stool.

"This guy's a madman," the man would say. Or "He can't hit curveballs." Or "Keep watching that shortstop." She nodded. They never touched, but they had an intimacy about them. As if they had experienced something that showed them each other's righteousness. I drained my glass before I knew it and ordered another.

The girl was not beautiful. She had small, dark eyes, a gap in her front teeth, her hair in two long braids with flyaways stuck to her forehead. The acne on her cheeks was made more visible by the foundation meant to cover it up. But she was striking. She glowed in the sunlight by the man's side, as if it were his presence illuminating her. She could not hide her contentment or her innocence. They gulped pints of Guinness and smoked. If she had trouble keeping up with him, she didn't show it. Their team—the Angels—was losing by two runs in the ninth. The man cursed the team and the coach loudly in an accent that was not quite

New Orleans, like he had lived here for a long time but had come from someplace else. He took her cigarette from time to time and dragged on it, gave it back.

I think it was the impossibility of them that struck me. She so young, and waiting, practically dying with love for him, on that bar stool. He, august in her presence, his eyes moving between her and the game and the clock—as if time were running out for all of it and they could not control it or understand it, nor did they want to.

I looked up at the television just as the batter popped the final out. The phone rang and the bartender muted the volume. Fan whirring, video poker machine bleating. The team sulked in the dugout, the crowd already pouring in a flood out of the stadium. The man shook his head and drank his beer, staring past himself in the mirror. The girl got up and strode over to the jukebox with quarters clicking in her hand. I didn't know the song. It sounded like ice cream truck music, only sadder; then the accordion. The song was something about love or ceasing to, the moon, cats and dogs and fish growing legs. For a moment, I felt as if it were the last hours before Ash Wednesday, when the people you love feel closest to you, and the world is full of thanks. The girl returned to the man's side, swaying to the music as the bartender poured two more drafts. The man nodded toward me, and the bartender brought me a third drink. The girl pushed her pack of cigarettes down the bar. I took out a smoke, lit it with her red lighter, pushed them back.

The girl said, "You all right, miss?" She had one of those sleepy Southern accents. "That song always makes me sad too, but he likes it. Sort of makes the rest of your life dim away, don't it?"

The man was looking at her and smiling, only his smile came with difficulty, as if pulled up from memory.

"I met my husband on Mardi Gras." I couldn't tell you why I said it. I knew I was trying to re-create the music in the junk of my life, in the thin music of my house. I thought of the baby and of Shelley's expectations for her life, the brief moments of certainty she'll wait for like the arrival of parades. The promise of their distant drumming.

I came out of the bar into the clear blue day, my thoughts rushing. I knew I had to move fast to beat Jared back home. It took me ten minutes to find the number in the stupid blue pages with Roux batting at the thin sheets of paper. I dialed and sat down at the table. Listened to the menu—"If your child has been bit by a rabid dog, press *star* now"—until I got the option for the operator.

A woman answered after many rings. They could pick up the dog next Thursday, no sooner. Unless I could bring it there myself.

I picked up Roux and shut her in the bedroom. Then I walked toward the back door.

The pit was chained to the fence pole, the chain-link leash clipped to its spiked collar. It was asleep, but as I stepped outside, it lifted its head off its paws and regarded me. I jumped back into the house and waited behind the screen, heart beating, stomach feeling empty and tight. It groaned and closed its eyes.

I crept out again. The thing looked pitiful. One ear was completely gone, a mangled stub. One eye drooped like a basset hound's, revealing a red wound underneath. The nose split in the middle. The skin hung off the body like wet clothes. It looked like

23

the remains of another animal, something feral. *Late fetal.* It tried to get up but whined and favored a back leg, balked in place, growling at me in a tight voice.

I picked up a stick and brandished it, thinking the dog was about to come at me. Its chest heaved and it let out a high, strained whine that seemed to me like a last warning. I backed up, and then it collapsed. Its head thumped to the ground, the neck stretched and throbbing as if waiting for an ax.

I approached it. The water bowl was tipped over, so I rinsed it and filled it with the hose. The dog slowly lifted its head off the ground and tucked its paws under its chest. It drooled something thick and yellow, leaned over, sniffed the water, put its head on its paws again and closed its eyes.

When I think back about it, I still don't understand what he was trying to find in that dog, or why he had to make it suffer before he could leave me. Maybe he was brimming with that kind of violence when I met him, and I was too blind to see it. Or maybe he was lost in his aimless energy, constantly failing to find the right beat. Anyway, he didn't come back. And I thought, My God, the things you have to go through to lose people.

I knelt before the dog and let my hand hover above its head. Stroked its ear as it whimpered and glared at me, as if it would kill me if it could only get up. But I whispered things to it that I didn't know I knew, called it Star-darling, Star-love. I sang something to it, but don't ask me what it was. The animal's cloudy eyes glazed over and it put its head down again on its folded paws and went to sleep.

I took the quilt from the bed and fashioned it into a hammock with knots and brought it out into the yard next to the pit. Come, little one, I said. *Pull up if I pull up.* I inched the dog onto the quilt. It groaned, and sniffled, spraying blood onto my blouse. I lifted the hammock by the tied loop and crossed it over my chest, the knot resting at the nape of my neck. It was lighter than I expected, and warm against my stomach. I walked carefully out through the alleyway to the truck. I put him on the front seat and drove off. ✦

WRITER'S PROCESS:

Erica Ciccarone

It took me three years to write *Pit*. Although it is about a dog, it started with the stray cats that lived underneath my Uptown shotgun in New Orleans. There were, in fact, a dozen of them, and I named them after Southern states.

It is a valuable story to me, because it taught me more about the writing process than any undergraduate or MFA class ever could have. *Pit* went through more revisions, titles, and character names than I can remember. I knew I wanted to write about a trapped woman, and I knew I wanted to capture the music of my neighborhood in New Orleans. It wasn't until I left New Orleans, weeks before the hurricane, that I really was able to figure out the story's heart. What that is, I can't tell you. I think that when you finally finish a good story, the way it works eludes you as much as faith does. But it's the process that you remember. It's the process that you can repeat.

It was said in a workshop that the story does not go outside the narrator's mind. Some people wanted me to slice it apart, to remove the palindromes because I couldn't explain a reason why they were there, to turn Monica into some sort of dog fighting stalker. Not to say that the three workshops I put it through didn't help; it's just that it taught me how to tunnel criticism into the story in a way that doesn't break it apart—which is not to say that I didn't crack it open, write and rewrite and delete abusive love and rape scenes, demonize the Jared character (first called Jeb), go overboard with the palindromes and name Monica Hannah. I think that writing this story taught me how to get advice from other writers while still remaining true to the characters in the story. Monica, Shelley,

Jared, and that couple in the bar create a tension that I think speaks to the many forms and ways of loving and loyalty that Monica struggles with.

When I lived in New Orleans, my sister would write palindromes on bar chalkboards. Later, after she moved to Chicago, we would send lists of them to each other. I remember reading the dictionary with a boyfriend on a hot New Orleans afternoon, looking for capitonyms, the words relieving all of the things we couldn't say. I think this story is partly about the weird way language can soothe and nourish us, abet and distract us, distance and occupy us. It also made me very conscious about all of the language in the story, and I knew that I had to make each word count. Nothing could be superfluous, no throw-aways. Working the palindromes into the story came very late in the process. I felt that I needed a way to define Monica outside of her destructive marriage and drug habit, something to get really into her thinking beyond her external surroundings. To my surprise, it felt organic to her. As a character in desperate want of motherhood, neighboring a teenaged, single soon-to-be mom, slamming doors shut on her emotional and moral pulses, Monica is not exactly a heroic character until the last page of the story. I realize as I'm writing this that as much as Monica is a "dynamic" character in the sense that she does change in the denouement of the story, she only changes in the moment on the page. I will never know what happens to her and I will never stop wondering.

The biggest question I get from readers is the same question I ask myself: Where do those barflies come from? In a story that took so much revision, so much articulation, so much giving up and giving in again, the bar couple was a joyous surprise to me. I wrote the scene and revised it only once in three years. The story started to revolve around this scene, around this unlikely pair, around this sort of frozen-in-time mirage. It's these surprises that make all the work worth it, that make all the cruel workshops and line-cutting teachers dim away. It's these surprises that we wait for as writers, as readers, that nourish and sustain us. Without the help of Daniel Menasche and David Gates, this story never would have found a home.

Martin Edmunds

ANNO DOMINI 1999

I.
Imagined Rome,
and the scum
from Alexandria
swirled through
her outskirts,
the bald heads
of her triumvirs
burned for lime,
your loves, Catullus,
Cavafy, smudging
the shrunk grove
and the queen-
less hive.

The Nile's
fertile green
muck dried
to a cake
on the spine
of an old campaigner,
the felled oak,
this obelisk
rotting on its side.

The sacred
rivers dead
or beheaded,
the old gods,
dust in rut,
the stone
gone, the sun
blind.

Ash
falls like a snow
of salt in the wounds
of the windrows.

✦

Romans!
Your new god's flock thins
to a handful
of bystanders and these
armed men who come
to draw down his father
with him
plucked and bloodied and strung
up live
as bait
for the hawk
in a forest
of weeping trees.

✦

And what of that tawny
queen whose thighs
ached to encumber
Rome with the Ptolemies'
incestuous offspring,
with the ten plagues
and the twelve tribes?

Her life the stuff
of opera, her aria,
a venomous vein
complaining
in the vulgar tongues:
Coptic, demotic, Italian.

These are her gifts, small
everlastings: river
sickness, cholera, malaria,
the needled mosquito
and the industrious flies.

Isaiah, shall she have
the last word,
penned by the bloody
stings of your scribes?

II.
Through charred sockets, I watch
the torched wasp's nest
of the Colosseum,
blown sands hissing
over hot stones re-echo
the fawn-colored Sibyl's whisper
of the Sirocco, mocking
Cato's immortal
hatred of Dido:
*delenda est
Carthago.*

The flames of her suicide pyre
lap at the tawny
flank of the Tiber.
His fountain shut,
his green scales drying
duller in the sun,
Sahara is what
the dying Triton
sucks from his
conch-shell horn.

*Ovid could say the Black Sea isn't black,
its salt not bitter, his sun-blistered neck
ready to bear the cross-straps of the war-pack
and drudge for Caesar, but he can't come back.*

The stumps of Dodona
petrify in the Forum,
the Senate's filibuster drones on.
An iodine wind approximates the sea,
without the relief of the sea.
Homo lupus homini.

Noon. Out at Fiumicino,
the ceiling falls to zero:

time
shifting its sands
from hand to hand.

In the sun's
air space over Santa
Maria *sopra* Minerva,
a barn owl guts
a pigeon. Keats
weeps. Gibbon
opens his notebook and writes.

Three nuns in dark glasses and wimples
greedily widen their lips
for their *priest stranglers*
drowning in *marinara*.

A wipe. A slow dissolve.
Federico cries *Lights!*
as the room goes and the dark
engulfs what he loves.
Sexless, the vestals cannot strike a spark.

We pay with the faces pressed in our palms for the right
to walk through airless, expensive halls.
The Renaissance is *In Restoration*, but
a classical beauty with her jaw wired shut
points us through the filtered dimness where
the state museum puts on display the state's
greatness, how Greece and Egypt were raped
repeatedly, easily. Again, the Pope escaped
this hell from Mecca in his summer home.
The sands of the arena seem reserved
for all the stray cats of Rome.

✦

Come dusk, the sexual
purr of a solitary

desert leopard
multiplies

and the topaz
orbs of her eyes
flash from the headlamps of Vespas
out prowling the piazzas.

Where is the wolf bitch
who suckled the twins
cast on her breast
in bronze?

Some stone age goddess
who took pity on
these weakling human infants,
not her own.

Their milky mouths already
rounding the O
of *Omertà*, it is a silence
they imbibe.

Her scalding, black milk jets
into our speechless, lean-
lipped mouths from the she-wolf's teats
of a cappuccino machine.

✦

A live bee sips
at a chiselled calyx
in a cemetery waiting
for rain.
The lockjaw wrought-
iron gates rusted
shut, a mossy silence cropping the carved
Etruscan legend running the length of the lintel:

Fummo come voi. Sarete come noi.

Honeycombed marble
sarcophagi
of the Popes' tombs,
(excellent cadavers!)
and these dead,
anonymous because
they refuse to give
even their own names.

I, whose mother's
patronym is Caia,
from which I derive
to fall, to fall silent,
am startled by
the throbbing of the hive.

We were like you.
You will be like us.

The same. The same
death corrects
our indiscretions.

Clapperless, the swung
bell does justice
to us, who,
when called upon to witness,
swallow our tongues.

Come. Stand
under the shade
of this tower that is
an inverted well,
a poured-out cauldron
scalding the faithful,
this iron-age
flower, that hangs
by a tendril,
with its petals in heaven
and its root in hell—

until the nib of this pen split
like the tail of the scarab's shell

and a drop distilled from the night
runs onto the page.

III.
The best that I wrote was only a paraphrase
of the light that exacts compassion for these dead.
Look, Isaiah: *The Rainbow. Redemption. Revenge.*
As if the Biblical prophets had pirated
the names of ships from my tongue's imperial days.

QUILOMBO

My legs are in chains,
my hand, crushed
in the cane press
of memory.
How can I hold a pen
even to write your name
until you come back again,
until our dawns and sunsets
are the same?
I am a slave
until you are free
to walk through the spirit gates,
male and female, with me,
into Palmares.

If I have to wait,
to squat in the dirt by the gate
for an age, by turns burnt
by the sun and wet by the rain,
or beg for a year on my knees
from each chance passerby
some word of the way you went,
then dust on the tongue
will be my sacrament.
This waiting, too,
is Palmares.

And if they cut out my tongue,
char the stump with a brand
at the old Portuguese fort
for having conversed with Iansã,
for being Pomba Gira's consort,
the mate of my drunken dove,
or simply for wanting you,
my fate, my life, my love,
still, the women can read
your name in the lines of my hand—
that is my letter of transport,
my visa to Palmares.

Sleeping by day in trees
to throw off the shagging hound,
like all who came before me
I got here on the run
from everything I had
and hadn't done.
Only to find it gone.
Moved off somewhere else.
A handful of mud
huts, ash
fluttering unfledged wings,
a nest of blackened stones.
Where, now, is Palmares?

I refuse to credit its ruin.
But what ranks could I join
here where flesh comes in
all the colors of earth,
like earth, harrowed, furrowed, flailed,
branded, and scarred
under the millwheel of sun,
the cane blade of the moon?
The only white thing is the far
cotton headcloths of breakers
in endless procession
arriving from Benin,
Angola, Côte d'Ivoire,
and the white gloves of their black-
clad undertakers,
and the scattered
teeth of the stars.

Was it a mirage? Trees
waver and fade
in the day, an armored
conquistador, the chameleon
gallops away
into the underbrush;
perched in his howdah,
above it all, crossing
these anthill Alps,
the landsnail, Hannibal,

cares nothing for the jungle
trampled in his path.
Gladiators enter
on the double-quick
into the Hippodrome
of a hoofprint, the Greek
chorus of *ventiladors*,
Anopheles, punctuate
the emperor's pleasure,
the snake with his coil of rope,
the spider with her net,
the Jesus lizard, staked
to the whipping post
of a thorn, the mace-
tailed scorpion,
whose flail,
motionless, hangs
over the harvest. Sun-struck, I will go
on all fours, a lunatic
chewing my spoon of clay.
I will close ranks with the moon.
I will join the revolution of rain
overtaking Palmares.

I am alone in this land
of *Eros* and *mineiros*,
of slaves run free,
a republic—eh, Zumbí?—
with a king, padres who fathered
their flocks, half-
Indians hunting Indians,
a viceroy temporarily
replaced by the roy-
to-be, a hanged, drawn and
quartered pull-tooth tax-
rebel, Tiradentes, hero
of men who extracted
gold from the mouth
of the rivulet Tripui, his head
stuck on a spike
for all to see, a failed
popular empery,
and, after,

the ants, the army...
The only royalty here
are the palms, and they wear
not last season's gorgeous court clothes
packed in camphor from Lisbon,
but the feathered headdress
of the *caboclos*—
the green
crown of Palmares!

Across the sea, the king's
columned chamber is only
a cricket's grass-barred cage
and a matchbox throne.
If you listen closely, you can hear
his grave counselors chirping
over Palmares.

But at night I hear the sound
of big drums coming
from everywhere at once,
beating like your bare
heels on the ground,
beating in my chest,
beating in my own pulse—
the drums of Palmares.

I am at home with those
who have everything
or nothing left to lose.
Enfranchise me.
Set the seal of your eyes
on my brow for all to see.
Then, when I pass like a flame
in daylight, a wraith
of steam after rain,
a ghost on your ochre roads,
that brand will be my freedom
in the streets of Palmares.

The road ends
and begins here.
I am not listening for your step

behind me. Face me.
Your eyes will show me
the way.
Come. Open your arms
and close them around me.
They are the borders
of that country.
Open your arms, my love.
Don't you know your heart
is my Palmares?

OPIUM

Old ghost, live in me, eat
what I leave on the plate.

✦

Poppy moon-
dome, feathered
like the iris
of an eye,
slashed, healed, held,
razored open, milked
for venom, and glued
shut, sight-slit
beaded with semen,
the pearl sap of sleep.

✦

Cobra hiss
of the primus
breathes this breathing space.

Infinite peace.

Tarbutter
bloodbubble:
a new planet

spins & spins & spins.

✦

Ether-whore,
sip the smoke
you'd trade your soul
and this world for the gold-
rosy glow of the bowl

for.

✦

Silk smoke-
skin bitch,
where is the corpse of Morpheus, beautiful youth?

Not this ashflesh
scattered with pigfood
on the mudbed under the hut.

✦

Squat there, Succubus, fix
your eyes on dinner, suck
the black teeth
your tribe finds beautiful.

BOCA NEGRA

Little lizard, little lizard,
with your eyes sewn open
and your lips stitched tight,
was it the sun you struck
with your tongue and swallowed
or was it the night?

Your puttysack gut slung
down like a truncheon,
a blackjack, a sock
weighted with pesos
to whack the heads off jimson
or bribe the border guard.

The ignition
coil of your tail
twitched, and you moved
like a lit fuse through
these hills the slow
explosions ripped apart.
Cold-blooded, you
proved earth
held fire in its heart.

Sun-arrow,
earth-dart,
your work was murder,
enforcing
a no fly zone.
Deep cover
black ops
master sergeant,
unseen, all-seeing
from your stakeout
in the schist,
under the chips
of obsidian, above

the pumice, your eye
petrified, a drop
of fossil water
from the Pleistocene.
Dead, you commune with these
mortal enemies:
it is the flies
who tithe
your measly feast.

O Boca Negra,
O my black-tongued bell
mouth soldered shut,
once, your wedge-head cut
a neat cuneiform
you had to erase with your tail:
livewire, whipstock-swipple,
lash of the sandstorm.

Quicksilver digit,
O my morning star,
your little, mimic
hands have traveled far
to end up where
you are, where
the hours are sanded down,
where the blood pulse trips
the sun's hoofs
over the rooftop
of these cratered acres
where nothing moves.

Little lizard, little lizard,
with your eyes sewn open
and your lips stitched tight,
who staked you to your shadow
on the sand?
What carbon visions dripped
to your brain pan
as your pupils widened
and the light
shuddered out?

Gorge on your silence, lizard.
Be bitter, but
be quick about it, since
you can't complain.

✦

Still with me,
lizard? Look:
someone scratched the basalt's
desert varnish, limed
the markings, a map
of their passing, and yours:

an open palm, a spiral,
a star. Someone gouged
a shallow basin, carved
to catch the rain
that never comes, or came
too late for you.

Your death
stains what it touches
a pre-Cambrian ochre
sunset glow.

And now that smutch
is on the corn.
The mothers gather,
the black mouth calls you home.

Listen: cicada:
flute of the ruins.

Touch:
pulse of the sun.

Shake
the beetle's rattle carapace

and watch
how the clouds come.

✦

O little pinstripe lizard, slit
from groin to chin,
gutted, stuffed with leaves to keep
the magic in,
did no one teach you shun
the sparse
snakebush, its green
too lush for you?

Did no one ever say:
that empty
sky is the sign of plenty, this
is the bowl of the skull,
these are the hands that hold
the eye of the thistle open
and close the doors of the rain?

✦

Listen, lizard.
There was a woman
who appeared
when I was dead inside.
Her tribe
descended the star-
studded cedar
ladder of the sky,
her hair
fanned out
against the pillow
like the night, her hands
cupped water falling
through my dreams of dry
riverbed and winterkill.

Drink,
or let it fall?

I saw
myself
doubled in the pupils of her eyes.
Two of a kind.
You and I, lizard,
we left our skins there.

✦

Little lizard, little lizard,
with your eyes sewn open
and your lips stitched tight,
quick! Before they drop us down
some chimney into hell:

what did you see? What did you say?
What did you threaten to tell?

Little lizard, liquid sybil,
sip the bitter quill
of forgiveness,
bathe with me in this
abysmal water, lava
font of the dawn.

✦

What could free us?
The wind tries.
Death tries.
Life tries.
Braided or unbraided
like her hair.

✦

Drink, or be damned!
Water is life, lizard.
It can't be denied.

Elena Ferrante

AN EXCERPT FROM

THE LOST DAUGHTER

(translated by Ann Goldstein)

I had been driving for less than an hour when I began to feel ill. The burning in my side came back, but at first I decided not to give it any importance. I became worried only when I realized that I no longer had the strength to hold onto the steering wheel. In the space of a few minutes my head became heavy, the headlights grew dimmer; soon I even forgot that I was driving. I had the impression, rather, of being at the sea, in the middle of the day. The beach was empty, the water calm, but on a pole a few meters from shore a red flag was waving. When I was a child, my mother had frightened me saying, Leda, you must never go swimming if you see a red flag: it means the sea is rough and you might drown. That fear had endured through the years, and even now, although the water was a sheet of translucent paper stretching to the horizon, I didn't dare go in: I was anxious. I said to myself, go on, swim: they must have forgotten the flag, and meanwhile I stayed on the shore, cautiously testing the water with the tip of my toe. Only at intervals my mother appeared at the top of the dunes and shouted to me as if I were still a child: Leda, what are you doing, don't you see the red flag?

In the hospital, when I opened my eyes, I saw myself again hesitating for a fraction of a second before the flat sea. Maybe that was why, later, I convinced myself that it wasn't a dream but a fantasy of alarm that lasted until I woke up in the hospital room. The doctors told me that my car had ended up against the guardrail but without critical consequences. The only serious injury was in my left side, an inexplicable lesion.

My friends from Florence came, Bianca and Marta returned, and even Gianni. I said it was drowsiness that had sent me off the road. But I knew very well that drowsiness wasn't to blame. At the origin was a gesture of mine that made no sense, and which, precisely because it was senseless, I immediately decided not to speak of to anyone. The hardest things to talk about are the ones we ourselves can't understand.

2

When my daughters moved to Toronto, where their father had lived and worked for years, I was embarrassed and amazed to discover that I wasn't upset; rather, I felt light, as if only then had I definitively brought them into the world. For the first time in almost twenty-five years I was not aware of the anxiety of having to take care of them. The house was neat, as if no one lived there, I no longer had the constant bother of shopping and doing the laundry, the woman who for years had helped with the household chores found a better-paying job and I felt no need to replace her.

My only obligation with regard to the girls was to call once a day to see how they were, what they were doing. On the phone they spoke as if they were on their own; in reality they lived with their father, but, accustomed to keeping us separate even in words, they spoke to me as if he didn't exist. To my questions on the state of their lives they answered either in a cheerfully evasive manner, or with an ill humor full of irritable pauses, or in the artificial tones they assumed when they were in the company of friends. They called me often, too, especially Bianca, who had a more imperiously demanding relationship with me, but only to know if blue shoes would go with an orange skirt, if I could find some papers left in a book and send them urgently, if I was still available to be blamed for their rages, their sorrows, in spite of the different continents and the spacious sky that separated us. The telephone calls were almost always hurried, sometimes they seemed fake, as in a movie.

I did what they asked, reacted in accordance with their expectations. But since distance imposed the physical impossibility of intervening directly in their lives, satisfying their desires or whims became a mixture of rarefied or irresponsible gestures, every request seemed light, every task that had to do with them an affectionate habit. I felt miraculously unfettered, as if a difficult job, finally brought to completion, no longer weighed me down.

I began to work without regard for their schedules and their needs. I corrected my students' papers at night, listening to music; I slept a lot in the afternoon, with earplugs; I ate once a day and always at a trattoria next door. I changed rapidly, my habits—my mood, my very physical appearance. At the university I was no longer irritated by the students who were too stupid and those who were too smart. A colleague I had known for years and whom occasionally, rarely, I slept with, said to me in bewilderment one evening that I had become less distracted, more generous. In a few months I regained the slender body of my youth and felt a sensation of gentle strength; it seemed to me that my thoughts had returned to their proper speed. One night I looked at myself in the mirror. I was forty-seven years old, I would be forty-eight in four months, but by some magic years had fallen from me. I don't know if I was pleased; certainly I was surprised.

It was in this state of unusual well-being that, when June came, I felt like taking a vacation, and I decided that I would go to the sea as soon as I had finished with exams and the annoying bureaucratic formalities. I looked on the Internet, studied photographs and prices. Finally I rented a small, fairly inexpensive apartment on the Ionian coast, from mid-July to the end of August. In fact, I didn't manage to leave until July 24th. The drive was easy, the car packed mainly with books that I needed for preparing next year's courses. The day was beautiful; through the open windows came a breeze full of parched summer scents, and I felt free and without guilt at my freedom.

But halfway there, as I was getting gas, I felt suddenly anxious. In the past I had loved the sea, but for at least fifteen years being in the sun had made me nervous, exhausted me instantly. The apartment would surely be ugly, the view a distant slice of blue amid cheap, squalid houses. I wouldn't sleep a wink because of the heat and some night club playing music at high volume. I made the rest of the journey with a faint ill humor and the sense that I would have been able to work at home comfortably all summer, breathing the air-conditioned air in the silence of my apartment.

When I arrived the sun was setting. The town seemed pretty, the voices had a pleasing cadence, there were good smells. Waiting for me was an old man with thick white hair who was respectfully cordial. First he bought me a coffee at the bar, and then, with a mixture of smiles and unmistakable gestures, he prevented me from carrying even a single bag into the house. Loaded down with my suitcases, he climbed, panting, to the fourth and top floor, and put them down in the doorway of a small penthouse: bedroom, tiny windowless kitchen that opened directly into the bathroom, a living room with big picture windows, and a terrace from which one could see, in the twilight, a rocky, jagged coast and an infinite sea.

The man's name was Giovanni; he wasn't the owner of the apartment but a sort of caretaker or handyman; yet he wouldn't accept a tip, in fact, he was almost offended, as if I hadn't understood that he was merely following the rules of a proper welcome. When, having been assured many times that everything was to my satisfaction, he left. I found on the table in the living room a big tray of peaches, plums, pears, grapes, and figs. The tray shone as if in a still-life.

I carried a wicker chair out to the terrace, and sat for a while to watch the evening descend on the sea. For years every vacation had revolved around the two children, and when they got older and began traveling the world with their friends I always stayed home, waiting for their return. I worried not only about all kinds of catastrophes (the dangers of air travel, ocean voyages, wars, earthquakes, tidal waves) but about their fragile nervous systems, possible tensions with their traveling companions, sentimental dramas because of affections returned too easily or not returned at all. I wanted to be ready to cope with sudden requests for help, I was afraid they would accuse me of being what in fact I was, distracted or absent, absorbed in myself. Enough. I got up, went to take a shower.

Afterward I was hungry and went back to the tray of fruit. I discovered that under the beautiful show figs, pears, prunes, peaches, grapes were overripe or rotten. I took a knife and cut off large black areas, but the smell disgusted me, the taste, and I threw almost all of it in the garbage. I could go out, look for a restaurant, but I gave up on eating because I was tired, I wanted to sleep.

In the bedroom there were two large windows. I opened them and turned off the lights. Outside, every so often, I saw the beam of a lighthouse explode out of the darkness and strike the room for a few seconds. One should never arrive in an unknown place at night, everything is undefined, every object is easily exaggerated. I lay down on the bed in my bathrobe, my hair wet, and stared at the ceiling, waiting for the moment when it would become white with light. I heard the distant sound of an outboard motor and a faint song that was like a meow. I had no contours. I turned drowsily and touched something on the pillow that felt cold, something made of tissue paper.

I turned on the light. On the bright-white material of the pillowcase was an insect, three or four centimeters long, like a giant fly. It was dark brown, and motionless, with membranous wings. I said to myself: it's a cicada, maybe its abdomen burst on my pillow. I touched it with the hem of my bathrobe, it moved and became immediately quiet. Male, female. The stomach of the females doesn't have elastic membranes, it doesn't sing, it's mute. I felt disgust. The cicada punctures olive trees and makes the sap drip from the bark of the mountain ash. I cautiously picked up the pillow, went to one of the windows, and tossed the insect out. That was how my vacation began.

3

The next day I put in my bag bathing suit, beach towels, books, xeroxes, notebooks, got in the car, and went in search of beach and sea along the county road that followed the coast. After about twenty minutes a pine wood appeared on my right. I saw a sign for parking, and stopped. Loaded down with my things, I climbed over the guardrail and set off along a path reddened by the pine needles.

I love the scent of resin: as a child, I spent summers on beaches not yet completely eaten away by the concrete of the Camorra—they began where the pinewood ended. That scent was the scent of vacation, of the summer games of childhood. Every squeak or thud of a dry pinecone, the dark color of the pine nuts reminds me of my mother's mouth: she laughs as she crushes the shells, takes out the yellow fruit, gives it to my sisters, noisy and demanding, or to me, waiting in silent expectation, or eats it herself, staining her lips with dark powder and saying, to teach me not to be so timid: go on, none for you, you're worse than a green pinecone.

The pinewood was very thick, with a tangled undergrowth, and the trunks, which had grown up leaning under the force of the wind, seemed on the point of falling over, fearful of something that came from the sea. I took care not to stumble on the shiny roots that crisscrossed the path and controlled my revulsion at the dusty lizards that left the patches of sun as I passed and fled in search of shelter. I walked for no more than five minutes, then the dunes and the sea appeared. I passed the twisted trunks of eucalyptus growing out of the sand, took a wooden walkway among green reeds and oleanders, and came to a tidy public bath house.

I liked the place immediately. I was reassured by the kindness of the dark man at the counter, by the gentle young beach attendant, who, tall and thin, unmuscular, in a T-shirt and red shorts, led me to an umbrella. The sand was white powder, I took a long swim in transparent water, and sat in the sun. Then I settled myself in the shade with my books and worked in peace until sunset, enjoying the breeze and the rapid changes of the sea. The hours slipped away in such a gentle mixture of work, daydreams, and idleness that I decided I would keep going back there.

In less than a week it had all become a peaceful routine. Crossing the pinewood, I liked the squeak of the pinecones opening to the sun, the scent of small green leaves that seemed to be myrtle, the strips of bark peeling off the eucalyptus trees. On the path I imagined winter, the pinewood frozen among the fogs, the broom that produced red berries. Every day on my arrival the man at the counter greeted me with polite satisfaction; I had a coffee at the bar, a glass of water. The attendant, whose name was Gino and who was surely a student, promptly opened the umbrella and the lounge chair, and then withdrew into the shade, his full lips parted, his eyes intent as he underlined with a pencil the pages of a big volume for some exam or other.

I felt tender as I looked at that boy. Usually I dozed as I dried off in the sun, but sometimes I didn't sleep; with half-closed eyes I observed him with sympathy, taking care that he wouldn't notice. He seemed restless, contorting his handsome, nervous body, running the fingers of one hand through his glossy black hair, worrying his chin. My daughters would have liked him, especially Marta, who fell in love easily with lean, nervous boys. As for me, who knows. I realized long ago that I've held onto little of myself and everything of them. Even now, I was looking at Gino through the filter of Bianca's experiences, of Marta's, according to the tastes and passions I imagine as theirs.

The young man was studying, but he seemed to have sensors independent of sight. If I merely made a move to shift the lounge chair from the sun to the shade, he would jump up, ask if I needed help. I smiled, shook my head no, what did it take to move a lounge chair. It was enough to feel myself protected, without deadlines to keep in mind, nothing urgent to confront. No one depended anymore on my care and, finally, even I was no longer a burden to myself.

4

The young mother and her daughter I became aware of later. I don't know if they had been there since my first day on the beach or appeared afterward. In the three or four days following my arrival I hardly noticed a rather loud group of Neapolitans, children, adults, a man in his sixties with a mean expression, four or five children who fought fiercely in the water and on land, a large woman with short legs and heavy breasts, nearly forty, perhaps, who went back and forth between the beach and the bar, painfully dragging a pregnant belly, the great, naked arc stretched between the two halves of her bathing suit. They were all related, parents, grandparents, children, grandchildren, cousins, in-laws, and their laughter rang out noisily. They called each other by name with drawn-out cries, hurled exclamatory or conspiratorial comments, at times quarreled: a large family group, similar to the one I had been part of when I was a girl, the same jokes, the same sentimentality, the same rages.

One day I looked up from my book and, for the first time, saw the young woman and the little girl. They were returning from the water's edge to their umbrella, she no more than twenty, her head bent, and the child, three or four years old, gazing up at her, rapt, holding a doll the way a mother carries a child in her arms. They were talking to each other peacefully, as if they alone existed. From the umbrella, the pregnant woman called out with irritation in their direction, and a fat gray woman in her fifties, fully dressed, who was perhaps the mother, made gestures of discontent, disapproving of I don't know what. But the girl seemed deaf and blind, she went on talking to the child and walking up from the sea with measured steps, leaving on the sand the dark shadow of her footprints. They, too, were part of the big noisy family, but she, the young mother, seen this way, from a distance, with her slim body, the tastefully chosen one-piece bathing suit, the slender neck, the shapely head and long, wavy, glossy black hair, the Indian face with its high cheekbones, the heavy eyebrows and slanting eyes, seemed to me an anomaly in the group, an organism that had mysteriously escaped the rule, the victim, now assimilated, of a kidnapping or of an exchange in the cradle.

From then on I got into the habit of looking every so often in their direction.

There was something off about the little girl, I don't know what; a childish sadness, perhaps, or a silent illness. Her whole face expressed a permanent request to her mother that they stay together: it was an entreaty without tears or tantrums, which the mother did not evade. Once I noticed the tenderness with which she rubbed lotion on her. And once I was struck by the leisurely time that mother and daughter spent in the water together, the mother hugging the child to her, the child with her arms tight around the mother's neck. They laughed together, enjoying the feeling of body against body, touching noses, spitting out streams of water, kissing each other. On one occasion I saw them playing with the doll. They did it with such pleasure, dressing her, undressing her, pretending to put suntan lotion on her; they bathed her in a green pail, they dried her, rubbing her so that she wouldn't catch cold, hugged her to their breast as if to nurse her, or fed her baby food of sand; they kept her in the sun with them, lying on their towel. If the young woman was pretty herself, in her motherhood there was something that distinguished her; she seemed to have no desire for anything but her child.

Not that she wasn't well integrated into the big family group. She talked endlessly to the pregnant woman, played cards with some sunburned youths of her own age, cousins, I think, walked along the shore with the fierce-looking old man (her father?), or with the boisterous young women, sisters, cousins, sisters-in-law. It didn't seem to me that she had a husband or someone who was obviously the father of the child. I noted instead that all the members of the family took affectionate care of her and the child. The gray, fat woman in her fifties accompanied her to the bar to buy ice cream for the little girl. The children, at her sharp cry, interrupted their squabbling and, though they grumbled, went to get water, food, whatever she needed. As soon as mother and daughter went out a little way from the shore in a small red-blue rowboat, the pregnant woman cried Nina, Lenù, Ninetta, Lena, and hurried breathlessly to the water's edge, alarming even the attendant, who jumped to his feet, to keep an eye on the situation. Once when the girl was approached by two young men who wanted to start a conversation, the cousins immediately intervened, with shoving and rude words, nearly provoking a fistfight.

For a while I didn't know if it was the mother or the daughter who was called Nina, Ninù, Ninè, the names were so many, and I had trouble, given the thick weave of sound, arriving at any conclusion. Then, by listening to voices and cries, I realized that Nina was the mother. It was more complicated with the child, and in the beginning I was confused. I thought she had a nickname like Nani or Nena or Nennella, but then I understood that those were the names of the doll, from whom the child was never parted and to whom Nina paid attention as if she were alive, a second daughter. The child in reality was called Elena, Lenù; the mother always called her Elena, the relatives Lenù.

I don't know why, I wrote those names in my notebook, Elena, Nani, Nena, Leni; maybe I liked the way Nina pronounced them. She talked to the child and her doll in the pleasing cadence of the Neapolitan dialect that I love, the tender language of playfulness and sweet nothings. I was enchanted. Languages for me have a secret venom that every so often foams up and for which there is no antidote. I remember the dialect on my mother's lips when she lost that gentle cadence and yelled at us, poisoned by her unhappiness: I can't take you anymore, I can't take anymore. Commands, shouts, insults, life stretching into her words, as when a frayed nerve is just touched, and the pain scrapes away all self-control. Once, twice, three times she threatened us, her daughters, that she would leave, you'll wake up in the morning and won't find me here. Every morning I woke up trembling with fear. In reality she was always there, in her words she was constantly disappearing from home. That woman, Nina, seemed serene, and I felt envious.

5

Nearly a week of vacation had already slipped away: good weather, a light breeze, a lot of empty umbrellas, cadences of dialects from all over Italy mixed with the local dialect and the languages of a few foreigners who had come for the sun.

Then it was Saturday, and the beach grew crowded. My patch of sun and shade was besieged by coolers, pails, shovels, plastic water wings and floats, racquets. I gave up reading and searched the crowd for Nina and Elena as if they were a show, to help pass the time.

I had a hard time finding them; I saw that they had dragged their lounge chair closer to the water. Nina was lying on her stomach, in the sun, and beside her, in the same position, it seemed to me, was the doll. The child, on the other hand, had gone to the water's edge with a yellow plastic watering can, filled it with water, and, holding it with both hands because of the weight, puffing and laughing, returned to her mother to water her body and mitigate the sun's heat. When the watering can was empty, she went to fill it again, same route, same effort, same game.

Maybe I had slept badly, maybe some unpleasant thought had passed through my head that I was unaware of; certainly, seeing them that morning, I felt irritated. Elena, for example, seemed to me obtusely methodical: first she watered her mother's ankles, then the doll's, she asked both if that was enough, both said no, she went off again. Nina on the other hand seemed to me affected: she mewed with pleasure, repeated the mewing in a different tone, as if it were coming from the doll's mouth, and then sighed: again, again. I suspected that she was playing her role of beautiful young mother not for love of her daughter but for us, the crowd on the beach, all of us, male and female, young and old.

The sprinkling of her body and the doll's went on for a long time. She became shiny with water, the luminous needles sprayed by the watering can wet her hair, too, which stuck to her head and forehead. Nani or Nile or Nena, the doll, was soaked with the same perseverance, but she absorbed less water, and so it dripped from the blue plastic of the lounger onto the sand, darkening it.

I stared at the child in her coming and going and I don't know what bothered me, the game with the water, perhaps, or Nina flaunting her pleasure in the sun. Or the voices, yes, especially the voices that mother and daughter attributed to the doll. Now they gave her words in turn, now together, superimposing the adult's fake-child voice and the child's fake-adult one. They imagined it was the same, single voice coming from the same throat of a thing in reality mute. But evidently I couldn't enter into their illusion, I felt a growing repulsion for that double voice. Of course, there I was, at a distance, what did it matter to me, I could follow the game or ignore it, it was only a pastime. But no, I felt an unease as if faced with a thing done badly, as if a part of me were insisting, absurdly, that they should make up their minds, give the doll a stable, constant voice, either that of the mother or that of the daughter, and stop pretending that they were the same.

It was like a slight twinge that, as you keep thinking about it, becomes an unbearable pain. I was beginning to feel exasperated. At a certain point I wanted to get up, make my way obliquely over to the lounge chair where they were playing, and, stopping there, say, That's enough, you don't know how to play, stop it. With that intention I even left my place, I couldn't bear it any longer. Naturally I said nothing, I went by looking straight ahead. I thought: it's too hot, I've always hated crowded places, everyone talking with the same modulated sounds, moving for the same reasons, doing the same things. I blamed the weekend beach for my sudden attack of nerves and went to stick my feet in the water.

6

Around noon something new happened. I was napping in the shade, even though the music that came from the bath house was too loud, when I heard the pregnant woman calling Nina, as if she had something extraordinary to announce.

I opened my eyes, noticed the girl pick up her daughter and point out to her something or someone behind me with exaggerated cheerfulness. I turned and saw a heavy, thickset man, between thirty and forty, who was coming down the wooden walkway, his head completely shaved, wearing a tight-fitting black T-shirt that held in a substantial belly above green bathing trunks. The child recognized him, made signs of greeting, but nervously, laughing and coyly hiding her face between her mother's neck and shoulder. The man, with a serious expression, gave a faint wave. His face was handsome, his eyes sharp. In no hurry, he stopped to greet the manager, gave an affectionate pat to the young attendant, who had immediately come over, and at the same time an entourage of large jovial men in bathing suits also stopped, one with a backpack, one with a cooler, one with two or three packages, which, to judge from the ribbons and bows, must be gifts. When the man finally reached the beach, Nina came up to him carrying the child, again stopping the little procession. He, still serious, with composed gestures, first of all took Elena from her embrace; she hugged him, arms around his neck, giving his cheeks small anxious kisses. Then, still offering his cheek to the child, he seized Nina behind the neck, almost forcing her to bend over-he was at least four inches shorter than she was-and fleetingly touched her lips, with restrained, proprietary command.

I guessed that Elena's father had arrived, Nina's husband. Among the Neapolitans a kind of party started up immediately, and they crowded around, right up to the edge of my umbrella. I saw that the child was unwrapping presents, that Nina was trying on an ugly straw hat. Then the new arrival pointed to something on the sea, a white motorboat. The old man with the mean look, the boys, the fat gray-haired woman, the girl and boy cousins gathered along the shore, shouting and waving their arms in signs of greeting. The motorboat passed the line of red buoys, zigzagged among the swimmers, crossed the line of white buoys, and arrived, its motor still running, amid children and old people swimming in the shallow water. Heavy men with worn faces, ostentatiously wealthy women, obese children jumped out. Embraces, kisses on the cheek, Nina lost her hat: the wind carried it off. Her husband, like a motionless animal that at the first sign of danger springs with unexpected force and decisiveness, grabbed it in midair, despite the child in his arms, before it ended up in the water, and gave it back to her. She put it on more carefully; suddenly the hat seemed pretty, and I felt an irrational pang of unease.

The confusion grew. The new arrivals were evidently disappointed by the arrangement of the umbrellas; the husband called Gino over, and the manager came, too. I got the impression that they all wanted to be together, the resident family group and those who were visiting, forming a compact wedge of loungers and chairs, and coolers, of children and adults having a good time. They pointed in my direction, where there were two free umbrellas, with a lot of gestures, especially the pregnant woman, who eventually began asking her neighbors to move, to shift from one umbrella to another, just as at the movies someone asks if you would please move over a few seats.

A game-like atmosphere was created. The bathers hesitated, they didn't want to move, with all their belongings, but both the children and the adults of the Neapolitan family were already cheerfully packing up, and finally most of the bathers moved almost willingly.

I opened a book, but by now I had a knot of bitter feelings inside that at every impact of sound, color, odor became even more bitter. Those people annoyed me. I had been born in a not dissimilar environment, my uncles, my cousins, my father were like that, of a domineering cordiality. They were ceremonious, usually very sociable; every question sounded on their lips like an order barely disguised by a false good humor, and if necessary they could be vulgarly insulting and violent. My mother was ashamed of the rude nature of my father and his relatives, she wanted to be different; within that world, she played at being the well-dressed, well-behaved lady, but at the first sign of conflict the mask cracked, and she, too, clung to the actions, the language of the others, with a violence that was no different. I observed her, amazed and disappointed, and determined not to be like her, to become truly different and so show her that it was useless and cruel to frighten us with her repeated "You will never ever ever see me again"; instead she should have changed for real, or left home for real, left us, disappeared. How I suffered for her and for myself, how ashamed I was to have come out of the belly of such an unhappy person. That thought, now, amid the confusion on the beach, made me more anxious and my disdain for the habits of those people grew, along with a thread of anguish. ◆

Matthew Rohrer

NINE ÉTUDES

I.

In a field, near Lake
Stanley Draper—he
smoked sumac. Nothing
happened . . . then he drank
some vodka . . . then a gentle
bombardment
commenced in the distance
and a faint sweet taste
in the back of the air force base.

II.

Artemisia smoked. Goskel
Kartal over. Roar overhead
all night. Imagine
a command center
where they can see every bad thing
that enters the city,
but can do nothing about it.
That is what it is like to be
at war with yourself.

III.

Chairs—they never move.
I have to move them
myself. They sit there
forever. Until the house
gets soft and falls down,
and they fall through
the floor. I drove them all
the way here from Iowa

where they were enslaved.
Sing my praises when I'm gone
in a little chapbook

IV.

I remember you threatened
to lurk in the forest
naked to scare people.
You had to urinate
the entire time you were
in Puerto Rico. I screwed
my wife in a hotel.
Tarpaulins flapped
in the dark. The cloud
forest dripped and cried.
And the pressure of the night
changed, everyone
felt different.
But no one felt scared.

V.

I sat on the top
of the ziggurat and watched
while people climbed towards me
in the shapes of their animals.
Beads of light.
The pressure on the base
of the skull that pinned me
to the lichens. Crow of death
in the sky. A buzzard
circle. There is something wrong
with the great cities
of our people,
they do not dream.
They make faces
at their reflections.

(They are reflected in lakes
and sometimes against the clouds)

(How they are reflected against the clouds
is a mystery)

(Now I think I cannot
inhabit you any longer)

VI.

He stood on a promontory
twirling a stick.
Bats fell from his hat.
I played the acoustic guitar
badly. And my long hair
dragged in the duckweed.
He always wanted to take
his clothes off and stand
like a tree. The moonlight
swept across our feet.
A stir of breeze,
a cicada in the ear.
And vast grasslands
whose little voices I couldn't hear.

VII.

The charismatic religions
where the people jump around
are visible from space

the I Ching needs only a small
space to do its mischief—
in the backseat of a car

The cloak of muddling draped
itself across the windshield
and I saw truly astonishing things—

I saw the light of existence
split by dark fingers
rotating all around me
This was the light of faith

and the Angelus sat beside me
in the passenger seat

He spoke a blessing—the congregation
was waiting for us on the lawn where the summer
night unrolled its carpet.

The Angelus
is hiding behind that name
because I let him

And he is safe

In life he is plain to look upon

VIII.

I woke up with a headache
and made pancakes
and sausages for everyone.
I had no idea where he was
who he was with.
The last time we talked
he was drunk and stood
wrapped up in a stiff
blanket like Geronimo.
America. Kinked-out sea-
green automobiles.
I'm going to throw away
the *Artemisia capillaris,*
I won't smoke it anymore,
I have to write a letter
to the wizard, I can't face him
about it. The animals
that surround him
and swarm him on the steps
of the pyramid. He's busy
with them, I will leave
him there,
I will not get caught up
in their star-in-a-circle.

IX.

You were my hero

and so you think you have the upper hand

but I have the upper hand

you fade away as I piss in the rusty bowl

as I button my jeans

you climb a tree and you never come down

you climb into the sunshine, into the lake

I tried to shoot you one night when you were set on shooting me

but you couldn't do it

you rose up into the night

to rain down on me

but you got tangled in the rigging

Joe Tully

WAITING FOR MR. HASKELL

T he summer of 1949 had been unusually hot and oppressive on Long Island. The still air and humidity seemed to hang like a moist towel over the whale-shaped sliver of land. There were no breezes off the Atlantic or the Sound; we could have been in Kansas.

Billy, Mike, and I found some relief from the stifling heat in the cool basement where I showed off my model trains. Being friends with Billy and Mike didn't come easily to me. I was about to turn nine and most days I isolated myself because I wasn't like other boys. I wasn't good at the sports they all seemed to enjoy; I didn't understand their jokes, and I didn't get their growing curiosity about girls.

My model trains were what I used to gain and retain their friendship. But having the best model train collection in the neighborhood wasn't enough to hold Billy and Mike's interest very long that day, and they quickly tired of watching my silver diesel engine pull its string of cars around the artificial landscape. We climbed back up the steps and reentered the hot, still air where I hoped we would find another diversion to hold their interest and occupy the time.

Scrappy, my six-month-old puppy, had been sprawled spread-eagle on the cool tile at the top of the stairs, but as we stomped up the steps, he jumped up, begging for attention. His tail wagged in a blur, and he nervously began to pee, missing the newspapers that had been placed on the floor to paper-train him. He was a cute little black dog, half spaniel and half setter, that we had adopted while on vacation in Pennsylvania earlier that summer.

My mother was in the kitchen preparing dinner, and despite the heat and the small fan that failed to offer any relief, she looked perfectly groomed, crisp and cool in a black-and-white print dress and starched apron. As she poured each of us a glass of cold lemonade from a pitcher made of cobalt-blue glass etched with white sailboats, I could smell the faint scent of lavender powder she had used after her bath.

"Now, don't spill any on my clean floor, boys," Mom said while handing me a paper towel to wipe up the puddle Scrappy had left. Billy and Mike eyed my mother cautiously as they grasped the sweating glasses. She was fastidious about the house, almost as fastidious as my brother was fanatical about baseball. It was nothing short of a miracle that she had let me have a dog. I quickly wiped up the small puddle.

We gulped down our cold drinks and, hoping for a breath of cool air, the three of us made our way outside, Scrappy running behind. The screen door slammed shut as Billy and Mike took the lead, choosing a spot to sit under the thin shade of a young maple tree on the freshly mown grass of the front lawn. The three of us looked like characters from *Huckleberry Finn* in our shorts and shaggy hair that had resisted cutting all summer. We pulled at plantains, small weeds with buds at their tips that had somehow escaped my father's mower. We bent the stems around to make miniature rockets and aimed them at each other as Scrappy rolled around on his back, happy to be outside. He quickly picked up a scent, probably from a squirrel, and followed it to the backyard, where my father sat, reading the afternoon paper, a bottle of cold Rheingold in his hand. Choruses of cicadas echoed through the neighborhood, sounding like miniature lawn mowers.

I hoped as we sat there, shooting the miniature rockets at each other, that our neighbor Mr. Haskell would come home drunk again in his red Chevrolet truck. Over the past few weeks, I had watched him swerve from one side of the street to the other, ignoring the new stop sign that had been installed at our corner after many cars had collided there. One of those collisions resulted in a car landing in my mother's favorite pink azaleas while we ate breakfast one morning, totally unaware that a car was resting inches from the living room window.

When I told Billy and Mike about Mr. Haskell, their eyes grew wide with interest. Mine did too, only because if the afternoon played out the way I hoped it would, my house would be front row center to all the action.

"Do you think he might do that today?" Mike asked excitedly, bending another plantain stem while Billy shielded his face from Mike's oncoming attack.

"Maybe," I said, hunching my thin shoulders.

Len and Roberta Haskell lived diagonally across the street, between the Loudons and the Hoopers, two families with whom they battled constantly over one petty thing or another.

They were a strange couple that always seemed to be yelling at each other. He usually barked at her with a trace of a Polish accent, and she usually snapped back with a voice that was a cross between a screech owl and a crow.

On any given day, their disagreement with the neighbors could be about the Loudons' hedges, a few branches of which might have protruded onto the Haskells' property, or their maple tree, which was casting too much shade. Or, it might be the Hoopers' unkempt lawn and their crabgrass that made Mrs. Haskell furious, their weeds invading and flawing her otherwise perfect lawn.

Most days, like this afternoon, she could be seen on all fours, picking away at her lawn, searching for stray blades of crabgrass, an old apple basket by her side. Dressed in trousers and an old plaid shirt, her mousy brown hair under a large straw hat shading a prominent chin and hooked nose that did nothing to compliment her scowling face, she took great pleasure in yelling at a careless child who might stray off the walk and onto her lawn. I can't say that I ever remember walking or riding my bike in front of her house. She was the Wicked Witch of the West, and she scared the hell out of me.

The only time Mrs. Haskell seemed to take a break from her war on wanton crabgrass was on Sunday mornings, when she would drive to church to attend Mass. Backing her old blue Dodge sedan out of the garage, she would let the car "warm up"—whether it was ten degrees or ninety. The car would sit there, coughing and sputtering in the driveway, a cloud of exhaust filling the morning air, while she closed the garage door behind her and picked at a blade or two of crabgrass on the way. The blue finish of the old car had oxidized, and patches of the surface had turned purple, making the Dodge look as if it had a nasty sunburn. Eventually, she would roll the car slowly into the street and head to the intersection at no more than fifteen miles per hour. Frustrating drivers unfortunate enough to come up behind her while she hesitated at the stop sign for a car that might be blocks away, she often yelled a few choice words in reply if they so much as gave her a disgusted look or blew their horns. Even when she was going to church, she managed to be as unpleasant as possible.

My father often said that Mrs. Haskell was obsessed with her lawn because Mr. Haskell was always drunk, and it was probably the only interest she had. In truth, I think Mr. Haskell drank because his wife cared more about her lawn than she did about him. However the scale was tipped, they were downright peculiar. They didn't have any friends, their grown son and daughter rarely visited, and none of the neighbors bothered with them. We often heard their frequent squabbles through the open windows on summer nights, accompanied by the crashing of a plate or two, a car door slamming, and the gunning of an engine as Mr. Haskell raced off down the street in his truck.

She would scream after him as he escaped to McCann's Tavern, where he would toss back a few too many and probably tell his cronies how miserable his life was. Dad said it was hard to believe that he could hold down his job as a plasterer, much less plaster a wall properly. But in the years following World War II, there was a shortage of tradesmen in the construction industry. Houses seemed to pop up almost overnight, as more and more people fled the city, wanting a patch of land and a small house "in the country." Builders had to use all the resources they could find.

"Joseph, it's almost suppertime," my mother announced from the front door, hands on hips: her standard pose when she was trying to be serious.

"Okaaaay," I said in the irritated tone that I had perfected.

"You should come in and wash up for dinner soon."

She usually called me Joey, but when my mother was being serious and assertive, Joey became Joseph. It came out sounding more like Jozev, and I hated the formality of the way it sounded, especially in front of Billy and Mike as I tried to be one of the boys. And I knew she was really trying to divert my attention from what I hoped might be afternoon entertainment. As much as she thought the Haskells were peculiar, she didn't like it that I found pleasure in watching Mr. Haskell make a fool of himself.

"We had a letter from your brother today," Mom continued, trying to entice me. "You can read it when you come in."

I watched her open the screen door, pinch off a dead bloom from the geraniums on the front step, and toss the faded blossom behind the yew bush. Stepping back inside, she disappeared, returning to the kitchen. I was happy that we had heard from my brother Roger, who had joined the Navy earlier that year, but the letter was going to have to wait. I thought of the hot air inside the house being pushed around by the small fan. It was better on the lawn as we waited for Mr. Haskell.

Refreshed after his cold beer, my father returned to the front of the house and began sweeping grass cuttings from the driveway. Mrs. Haskell saw him as she was picking up her basket of crabgrass. She waved. Dad waved back, wiping the beads of sweat from under his straw hat with his handkerchief, his white T-shirt clinging to his sweating back. He was the only person who was even moderately friendly with her, which I always thought was a bit out of character for a cool, stoic Irishman like him. But Dad always seemed to get a kick out of unusual people, and Mrs. Haskell seemed to fit that category perfectly.

Accepting my father's offer of friendliness, Mrs. Haskell darted across the street, probably to vent her frustrations with not having a lawn worthy of a page in *Better Homes and Gardens*. She looked left and right, and with her back hunched and a sneaky kind of walk (undoubtedly fearing her husband's red truck coming down the street), she joined Dad in the driveway.

"I don't know why you bother with her, she's nuts," my mother would say after she had observed one of Dad's frequent exchanges with Mrs. Haskell from the living room window, watching from behind the curtains like a nervous mother robin.

Mom was a jealous woman who guarded and protected her home and family. Maybe it was because her first husband had walked out on her when my brother was only five. Why she was abandoned we never knew, but Mom always perceived any woman who showed an interest in my father as a potential threat. When Mom thought Mrs. Haskell's conversation with him had gone on long enough, she would do my father a favor and rescue him.

"Hon, you have a telephone call," she would say, her voice rising and falling musically from behind the front door, careful not to make any eye contact with Mrs. Haskell. Probably enjoying the conversation, Dad would whirl around, acting surprised by my mother's voice, as though he had never expected it. But he would excuse himself, and Mrs. Haskell would wander back across the street to her waiting lawn.

"What does she want now?" Mom would say, irritated, as Dad hurried in the back door.

"The usual. You know. Her lawn. The neighbors. Did someone call?" thinking perhaps there just might have been a phone call this time.

"No one. You know I don't like you talking to her. There's something about her I don't like. I don't trust her."

"Aw, for chrissake, she's harmless," he would say, brushing my mother off with a wave of his hand and returning to his chores. She would stand there, shaking her head in annoyance, but with a sense of satisfaction, knowing that she had successfully sent Mrs. Haskell back across the street and away from my father.

Billy, Mike, and I heard a screech of wheels and the sound of metal hitting metal. We jumped to our feet as we saw a red truck coming down the street, weaving from one side to the other as a garbage can that had been hit tumbled across the pavement.

"Is that Mr. Haskell?" Billy asked in a breathless soprano as he rushed toward the curb for a better view, with Mike and me right behind him. It *was* Mr. Haskell, and the truck seemed to be going faster than ever as it jumped onto the sidewalk and flew through the intersection, knocking down the stop sign at the corner where Mrs. Hooper was about to cross the street. Mrs. Hooper had been the talk of the neighborhood since one of her pendulous breasts got tangled in the wringer of her Bendix washing machine earlier that summer. All the neighbors heard about it, courtesy of New York Telephone's party line, when she phoned Mr. Hooper to tell him what had happened. And the unfortunate incident had become the butt of Mr. Haskell's mocking humor whenever he saw her.

Mrs. Hooper dropped her grocery bags as the red truck streaked by, only yards away. She stood there, her mouth open, nervously fussing with her hair. Billy, Mike, and I shrieked like three little girls, first with excitement and then with a bit of fear, as we watched the red truck jump the curb across the street and fly up onto Ethel Loudon's lawn, snapping in half the little plum tree that she had planted that spring. The truck ploughed ahead erratically and mowed down her hedges as Mr. Haskell took aim at his wife's carefully tended lawn. Patches of sod, grass, and dirt flew everywhere as the red truck came to a stop in front of his house, resting in his wife's rhododendron bushes, the remains of the little plum tree twisted pitifully under the wheels.

"There'll be hell to pay tonight," my father muttered as he walked over to join Billy, Mike, and me.

Mrs. Haskell tore out of the front door, shrieking at her husband as he stumbled out of his truck, looking very confused after hitting his head on the windshield and falling on his wife's now gouged and disgraced lawn.

"I'm calling the police! You're a goddamn bastard. Look at my lawn."

He rolled around on the grass in his white overalls and painter's hat, spattered with blood, looking like a squirrel that had been hit by a car. Continuing to scream and ignoring her husband's injuries, Mrs. Haskell disappeared back into the house. She really did sound like Margaret Hamilton, I thought, riding off with Toto in her bicycle basket, screeching like a madwoman.

Within minutes, two police cars and an ambulance raced down the street from the local precinct, a few blocks away. With sirens wailing and red lights flashing, a tall, red-faced cop with a crew cut jumped out of his car, as did a shorter, chubby one who looked as if his diet contained too many doughnuts. I thought it looked a bit like a scene from *Dick Tracy*, but there was no handsome detective or Tess Trueheart anywhere. My mother came to the front door wiping her hands on her apron, urging my father not to get involved as she joined the neighbors who were quickly gathering, whispering, astonished at the scene. Ethel Loudon crossed the street to talk with Mom, shaking her head as she looked at the big gap in her hedgerow and her plum tree that was no more, lying under Mr. Haskell's truck.

"I want him arrested. He destroyed my lawn!" Mrs. Haskell shrieked to the two cops as she reappeared at her door. Mrs. Loudon joined in, wanting to press charges against Mr. Haskell for destroying her property as well. Billy, Mike, and I retreated to the safety of the front steps as the crowd grew, and passing cars stopped to see the show that was quickly unfolding.

Mr. Haskell was arrested for drunk driving, driving without a license, and reckless endangerment. A small bandage was taped to his head by a medic, and the police ushered him into one of their squad cars.

"Good riddance!" we heard Mrs. Haskell shout as they drove away. She retreated to the house once again, slammed her door shut, and tightly closed her blinds. One by one, everyone trickled back to their houses and their waiting dinners, the red truck sitting on the Haskells' lawn, looking like a child's toy that had been cast aside in a fit of anger. The street returned to a sense of normalcy, and the cicadas could be heard once again. Billy and Mike went home, saying it was the best excitement of the summer and, feeling satisfied, I finally went in and washed up for dinner. We ate on the back porch that night, hoping for a cool breeze; my father agreeing with my mother that the Haskells were probably just a trifle nuts.

Mr. Haskell did not come home until the middle of September, having landed in the county jail for thirty days. While her husband was behind bars, Mrs. Haskell would still wander over to chat with my father, her routine proceeding as if nothing had happened, and my mother still watched them from behind the curtains. As I eavesdropped on their conversation one afternoon while I sat on the front step with Scrappy, I heard Mrs. Haskell say that she had no intention of visiting Mr. Haskell. She was glad he was in jail, out of her hair, and away from the lawn that had taken her weeks of careful tending to restore to its former, pristine condition.

September brought cooler weather. Billy, Mike, and I had finally got our haircuts and returned to school. Windows were closed to ward off the early chill, so we couldn't hear any arguments from across the street. In fact, things seemed relatively quiet. Mrs. Haskell continued to pick at her crabgrass, as she would until snow fell. She still yelled at anyone who might stray onto her lawn or, heaven forbid, toss a cigarette butt on the walk in front of her house. Now she was telling people that they couldn't park their cars in front of her house if they were visiting nearby.

Two days before Halloween, as Mom was setting the table for dinner, sirens shattered the calm of the early evening. "There are police cars in front of the Haskells again," she said excitedly, parting the café curtains over the kitchen sink, taking care not to disturb her African violets. Flashing red lights lit up the kitchen. Scrappy's nails clicked on the tile floor as he scrambled to get out of our way while we hurried to the front door for a better view. My father reached for his wool shirt and cap and strolled across the street to see what was going on. As he did, an ambulance pulled up behind the two police cars.

"Oh my God, what happened now?" Mom said. My father walked over to the familiar red-faced police officer with the crew cut, who had started to fill out a report in the harsh light of the squad car as two medics pulled out a stretcher from the back of the ambulance. Mom returned to the kitchen, turned down the heat under the stew, put on her sweater, and handed me a jacket from the cedar closet in the front hall. Scrappy thought he was going for a walk and danced around. I put on his leash and shut the front door, the Indian corn Mom had tacked up that morning rustling behind us. We followed my mother as she joined the gaggle of neighbors gathering once again to see what had happened. The air was chilly, and it smelled sweet with the scent of newly fallen leaves as we made our way down the walk. Colder weather wasn't far off. A large orange moon was rising in the sky, and from across the street, the flicker of Ethel Loudon's jack-o'-lantern and the flashing red lights from the police cars and ambulance cast an eerie glow into the night. I wished that Billy and Mike could see all the excitement, but they lived on another street and couldn't hear the sirens or see the lights from the police cars.

The medics and police, their flashlights casting long beams of light in the darkness, gathered in front of the Haskells' house. My father spoke to the police officer, who told him it looked as if Mrs. Haskell's car had rolled over Mr. Haskell as he lay drunk in the driveway. The neighbors gasped.

"I bet she tried to kill him," Ethel Loudon said, turning to my mother, while some of the other neighbors nodded their heads in agreement.

It didn't look good. The police were going to arrest Mrs. Haskell for aggravated assault and take her into custody. It looked as if she had intentionally tried to run her husband over with her ugly old Dodge. Mr. Haskell was placed on a stretcher and rolled into the mouth of the waiting ambulance. The doors slammed shut, and it quickly disappeared down the street, red lights flashing, sirens screaming in the crisp October air.

Mrs. Haskell was struggling with the police as they tried to usher her into the back seat of a waiting police car.

"To hell with him. To hell with you all," we heard her muttering behind the windows of the squad car as it rolled by the astonished faces of the neighbors. It moved slowly down the street, and paused briefly at the newly replaced stop sign. But I felt sorry for Mrs. Haskell as I saw her slumped there in the darkness, a bit like a rag doll that had been tossed in the back seat, while gory visions began to whirl in my young head of what the old blue Dodge had done to Mr. Haskell. Had it been moving fast enough to really hurt him? Did the car bounce as it hit? Was he dead?

A grand jury would later charge Mrs. Haskell with attempted murder. Mr. Haskell never recovered from the crushing weight that his wife's blue Dodge had inflicted on him. His condition deteriorated, and he died a few months later. The charges against Mrs. Haskell were changed to second-degree manslaughter, and she was sent to the county jail without bail to await trial. Following the almost daily reports in the local paper, we learned that she had been found mentally unstable and unable to withstand a trial. She was sent for treatment to a psychiatric hospital in the piney woods of eastern Long Island. We never saw her again.

Spring came. Mrs. Haskell's beloved lawn had grown tall and was overrun with crabgrass and other weeds. Her son and daughter returned and listed the house with a real estate broker. It quickly sold to a young couple with two young children. From a house where we had heard only fighting and screaming, laughter now resonated, as children played on the grass that had been Mrs. Haskell's obsession.

The next summer, Billy spent two months with his grandparents in Pennsylvania, Mike went to camp in Maine, and I started taking piano lessons. When Billy and Mike returned, and we were together for a couple of days in the few weeks before school started, it was clear that we had grown apart. The previous summer I had used my model trains and a performance by Mr. Haskell to sustain our friendship. But after weeks of fishing in lakes and camping in woods, Billy and Mike weren't interested in what I had learned on the piano or that my first recital was coming up.

And, except for brief encounters in school, we didn't see much of each other anymore. It seemed as if our friendship had evaporated into the humid summer air. ◆

D. Nurkse

SACRIFICE

How angry we were
at the stuffed rabbit
for making us love it
night after night.

We ripped off an ear,
tore out the stuffing,
scattered it in handfuls,
prized out an eye
to roll in our palms.

The back, that we had never seen,
shone just as bright
as the staring pupil.

We licked our fingers
and teased the empty socket.

Night fell.
We listened for footsteps.

When they came
they were the same as ever,
just the blood beating in the mind,
but the silence was utterly new.

We entered it
as you might sneak through a door,
answered it, as if it were a voice—

yet it was just silence
and we could no longer change it
by laughter, tears,
or any silence of our own.

THE ABSOLUTE

We passed a bent sign—
Manzanilla State Park—
a schematic picnic hamper,
a board dangling from a pine,
a fish silhouette
outlined in nailheads.

We pulled in a dirt road
roofed with interlacing branches
of pale flashing mountain ash.

We came to gouged tables.
One date crisscrossed another.
The entire surface was chiseled,
bevels marked the intersections
of nicknames and initials.

There we found the clearing
where the child runs sideways
under the tilting red Frisbee,
the child flails at a Wiffle ball,
the child rocks a doll
made of parched leaves, and sobs—

we drove so slowly
the needle barely climbed.
We parked by a dusty rope.

We changed in the prefab log cabin,
sheets of tin nailed over the windows,
you at the south end, I at the north.

We entered that freezing lake,
forgot who we were,
tiptoed past our depth,
and swam to the line of floats.

The child teetered on a plank
to mime diving from a great height,
the child skipped stones, rapt

then tormented by a record score,
the child launched a beech-leaf boat
freighted with a dead bee,
the child doubled up in terror
at Venus in reflection.

When we emerged from that silence
we were dappled and translucent.
We missed each other,
happy but too cold to feel it.
We resented the ecstatic cricket.

We groped our way into the forest,
found a mossy bank, lay together,
but the child had followed
to call us soft airy names
and toss a beech pod,
a double-winged maple key,
a glistening cloud of pollen.

You, You, You . . .

Where that child was
we could not know
though we shouted
command after command
to the vase-crested elm,
black-banded birch, ladder-branched spruce—

for answer, birdsong as always
sounding deeply faked,
too fluent to be real,
echoes charged by deep water,
maniacally suppressed laughter.

The child was hiding in the future.

Elizabeth Macklin

IT SOUNDED LIKE DOVES OR GALLON JUGS OR BOTTLES

Let's say that after dinner at their end of the table the two of them

break away from the general hubbub and amuse themselves

or don't amuse themselves making hand-to-mouth birdsong.

Hands to mouth, making up callings as they go along,

sounding like doves or gallon jugs or bottles.

Or one does first. Later the other starts up, to go along.

The one, though clearly audible, has been invisible, when the song

suddenly—which bird?—magnifies the same and, not by himself,

the first makes harmony, in the eyes of the other an answerable question.

SOME HOW

It became a habit,
I picked up this bad
habit of falling in love
to avoid the war.

The way the eyes go
shiny for a new reason,
nothing to avert from
yet still seeing.

So like that pop song
that went, *I was lost*
and you've rescued
me some how—

what was it called?
Oh, of course:
Unbelievable.
And how, and how

TRANSLATION

The poet was trying to teach me
the flavor of a pending word,
a word for a dangling kind

of awaiting, contained, he said,
in the very sound of the word,
for which we had nothing easy.

Casting about, casting out and finding
only an orange, bobbing; another;
a purple for which we had no rhyme.

This kind was not "impatient"; no Southern
biding. A slow fast toward food. Wasted no time.
And so I had to find another way of conveying

a long, long moment of waiting
alert to catch a slight sign, any day
the whole length of our wait.

THE SMALLEST TRANSACTION

Learn it as you would a poem, learn it as you would
a poem or a song, and say or sing it that way,

the way we learned to sing the bosom of Abraham,
every one, or "I was glad when they said to me

let us go to the house of the Lord,"
or daytime and nighttime should not cease.

That way you could have it by heart
and be able to improvise at need.

IN OUR LANGUAGE

By an accident of speech,
hearing and *listening*
were the same word.

Our silence made them
exactly the same.

Let's go back to the basics
of what made a human race
flick God into Heaven

for the whole species, stars
in seeming ellipses

above us, moon pulling
round to light the face
of the other party.

For the sake of the air
leaving the window open,

we opted for taking the way
of greatest resistance,
leaning in close to speak,

the outlines of where we are,
of where we were

when it happened, the lull
come upon us just
as we needed to do our part.

NECESSITY IN *PARIS, TEXAS*

When she's in her cubicle
telling him, telling him
what sex is, both of them
facing the one way

and not each other,
disembodied
above the waist
in polarized glass,

she's telling him all that
he'd missed seeing
even though he was there.
You can see

the raw insulation
on her side,
all the bare wood around her
explicating,

Whatever doesn't need
to be finished
can be left unfinished
as a matter of course.

"They hurt each other
too much to start again.
That house burning
was a *true sight*."

DESPITE THE TEMPTATION

I wasn't allowed to write the poem
about the asparagus, fattest white asparagus,
trying to open the can of asparagus
without a can-opener, where he was finally

down on the floor on his knees with hammer & chisel,
at which point he said I was not allowed
to write a poem about any of this.
And yet ever after I was tempted

to say how I'd loved the experience (*you
in the experience*). At least he'll know now
we all know about the asparagus, & will
guess that, despite explicit orders,

I did 'love' him. Or maybe the can of asparagus,
fattest white asparagus, & opening the can
of asparagus without a can-opener. And yet
look how well we did with the tools at hand.

Cynthia Weiner

THE WATCHER

In a daze, the morning after her mother's sudden, and fatal, heart attack, Kate Ehrlich had agreed to nearly all the Jewish burial customs the funeral director recommended, even though neither she nor her mother had ever been the least bit religious. *Better safe than sorry,* he'd said, and Kate had let him check the boxes for a plain pine coffin, a ritual cleansing, and a Watcher—a man who would stay with her mother's body until she was safely in the ground, keeping her emerging soul company as he read from the Book of Psalms. Now it was several hours later, close to midnight, and Kate was alone with the Watcher in a small, candle-lit room on the third floor of the West End Memorial Chapel. She stood in the doorway, across the room from the coffin, while he slouched in an armchair a few feet away and read aloud from his prayer book. He was in his early sixties, thirty years older than Kate: her mother's age. His face was haggard, scattered with gray stubble and damp with sweat. In the air between them was the musky odor of bourbon. "I am weary with my moaning," he moaned. "All night I make my bed swim." He looked at her, and even as she looked away, Kate was sure his gaze was lingering on her breasts. She shivered, horrified that this leering, drunken man had been entrusted with the care of her mother's soul, but each time she felt his glance, her heart jumped and her body swayed in his direction. She was sweating as heavily as he was, under her arms, down the backs of her thighs.

In the candlelight, everything in the room had a feverish shine.

Vials of smelling salts shimmered. A vase of roses flashed sparks as if the stems inside had ignited. The tan carpet was the wet, rich brown of quicksand. The Watcher's mouth was the slick purple of plums. Kate stared straight ahead. She'd been standing here for nearly half an hour, holding two shopping bags full of her mother's things that she'd brought to put in the coffin. This morning, the funeral director had suggested the traditional burial garments, a loose linen gown, a little white cap, booties for the feet, but Kate had imagined her mother's appalled expression—*you're going to make me parade around for eternity dressed like an infant?*—and shaken her head. Her mother's greatest pleasure had been her clothes, collected over a lifetime and tended to like flowers. She had a stack of diaries going back forty years, a daily chronicle of what she'd worn where: the poodle skirt to a high school dance, the velvet-trimmed tweed suit to visit her father at Sloan-Kettering, the picture hat with the big satin bow to watch Charles and Diana's wedding on the BBC. Kate couldn't remember a time when her mother hadn't flinched as she looked her up and down, Kate's indifferent jeans and T-shirts, or stared at her in a stricken way and said, "Do you have any idea how that shirt makes me feel?" or kept a little distance between them as they walked together down the street—but that didn't mean she'd send her mother off wearing something she'd hate.

A few hours ago, Kate had dropped off a more dignified gray wool skirt and white silk blouse at the funeral home. But as the day wore on, she'd become more and more uneasy. She'd forgotten a sweater. She'd forgotten shoes and underwear. She'd forgotten a watch, a handbag, her mother's glasses. After a while, she couldn't even be sure that she'd dropped off the skirt and blouse she thought she had. Rummaging through her mother's closets, she'd been dizzy and nervous and she'd gone a little blind; it was entirely possible that in her anxiety she'd in fact grabbed something absurd and inappropriate, a decades-old pleated skirt and middy blouse, maybe, or denim overalls and fringed suede top from a years-ago Wyoming dude ranch vacation. By nighttime, the image had become intolerable: all the other mothers decked out in the pretty outfits their daughters had selected with tenderness, and taste, while Kate's stood off to the side, cold and squinting, barefoot and braless, dressed like a sailor or a cowgirl.

November 3, 2010, she'd write in her diary—*what was Kate thinking?*

June 28, 2040—what was Kate thinking?

Now, in the lurching flames of the candles, the coffin's shadow twisted and turned as if her mother were squirming impatiently inside. It was past midnight and Kate had to get home, work on the eulogy for tomorrow's service—*Good morning*, was as far as she had gotten, *thank you for being here*—but the lid of the coffin was down and Kate had no idea how she'd get it open to put in the things she'd brought. She'd need a crowbar, or maybe a saw, neither of which she or her mother owned. It was too late to go to a hardware store. She thought about calling her father, but knew she'd be in for a half hour of convoluted, evasive chatter that boiled down to the same thing it had been boiling down to for the twenty-five years since the divorce: *thank God she's your problem, not mine.*

The Watcher turned the pages of the prayerbook. Kate could see that they were dogeared and underlined. "My heart is like wax," he read. "It is melted"—he glanced up at her—"in the midst of my bowels." Surely it was against Jewish law to pry open a coffin, but at least he didn't seem the type to try to stop her.

"Can you help me?" she asked. "I just need to put in a few things."

He regarded her over the top of his prayerbook, his eyes unreadable. In his black suit and black hat, he was hardly visible in the candlelight. "It hasn't been sealed yet," he said.

She crossed the room to the coffin, her stomach cramping with a mix of relief and apprehension. He pushed himself up from the armchair and came to stand beside her, so close she could feel his breath on her neck. She shut her eyes and breathed in the scent of bourbon and cigars. Her heart was pounding too hard; it seemed to have swelled to twice its size, flooding her body with heat. Sweat pooled in the small of her back. Beneath her jacket, her shirt stuck to her skin. She wondered what would happen if she asked him to hold her, to hold her down.

She heard her mother's voice in her head: *Over my dead body.*

She stumbled backward a little, slamming her hip into the edge of the coffin. The Watcher put out his hand but she took another step away from him. What *was* she thinking? "I'm all right," she said. She made her voice as cool as she could, imperious as her mother's when people she thought ought to know better tried to get too familiar. ("Last name?" a maitre d', or the receptionist at the dentist's, might ask. "Ehrlich." "First name?" "*Mrs.*") "Please," Kate said to the Watcher, "proceed." She looked deliberately at her watch. "I won't be but a moment."

He nodded and reached for the lid, pushing it back until it was propped against the wall. Here was her mother, her jaw rigid and her lips a thin, severe line. She did have on the gray skirt and the silk blouse, but her uncovered legs looked too pale against the dark wool. The veins stood out like they'd been shot through with black ink. Her bare breasts showed through the flimsy top. Without her glasses, her face seemed vacant as the moon. Kate felt the frames of her own glasses digging into her temples. Her hands started to shake. The shopping bags banged against her legs, and she let them fall to the ground.

The smell of bourbon rising from the Watcher was making her feel reckless, drunk off the fumes. Kate had hardly touched her mother even when she was alive—certainly not her face, not since she was a child—but now she laid her hand on her cold, unyielding cheek. She raised her other hand to her own face. Her fingers, still trembling, were warm and slippery with sweat. Beneath them, she could feel her muscles twitching, the lunge of her pulse in her jaw. She drew her thumb across her mother's cheekbone. She'd heard that the dead often appeared angry, the muscles stiffening as death set in, but she hadn't expected to feel her own, answering anger. A current of helpless, dry-eyed rage was rocketing up her spine—even in the candlelight, her hand on her mother's face was a bright, almost incandescent white. A roar filled her ears, a gust of fire crackling with all the ugly sounds she'd ever heard, the grubbiest profanities, the cruelest insults, the iciest silences. There were cries and complaints and accusations. There were glasses shattering and doors crashing shut. She yanked her hand off her mother's face, but still her ears burned.

Beside her, the Watcher took a wrinkled handkerchief from his pants pocket and dabbed at his cheeks and neck. His shirt was damp around the collar. Kate felt her own blouse damp around her throat, the collar so tight it seemed to have shrunk. Standing like this over her mother reminded her of nights twenty years before when she was in high school and still living at home, how on the way to her own bedroom after she'd been out at a bar or a club, she'd stop in the doorway of her mother's bedroom—her father was already gone—and stand there for a minute in the dark watching her mother sleep. Kate had been a little wild then and she might be drunk or high, or something frightening might have happened out in the night, the way somebody had looked at or touched her, but standing amid the familiar smells of face cream and tissues, the TV remote on the night table beside a glass of water and the shape of her mother beneath the chenille bedspread, she'd feel reassured by the ordinary blandness of it all, and soon she'd be yawning and ready for sleep. Until one night her mother opened her eyes and said acidly, "What the hell are you staring at?"

The Watcher began reading again from the tattered pages of his prayerbook. Kate's head still blazed with noise, but his voice was loud and insistent, and she heard "hot displeasure" and "thy hand presseth me sore" and "my groaning is not hid from thee." The darkness around him glittered with candlelight. His hair was shining silver and his eyes were gleaming gold. "For my loins are filled with burning," he said. Kate looked down at her mother's face. It was blank and white as bone. Where was her soul? Had it emerged yet? Was it here with them, in this room? Kate felt another wave of heat surge through her. She wedged two fingers into the collar of her blouse and pulled it away from her body. Her glasses fogged up, and the room went patchy. Behind her now, the Watcher had started to rock in time to the cadence of his prayers. He was breathing hard; Kate inhaled a cloud of bourbon. He gripped his prayerbook with both hands. "My heart panteth," he said. "My strength faileth me." Kate took a step back and allowed the Watcher to press himself against her, as her mother lay before them, silent and still. ✦

B.J. Buckley

FIRST CUTTING

Even the Buddha could not dwell
in ceaseless epiphany.

This spring
when so much rain made dust
miraculous with grass

the lambs
drowned in stock tanks, that mare
mired in mud
whose heart just quit

were a kind of relief—

something in us recalls
blood bargains

when there's hay cut in the fields
and two days left before we bale.

CALLING OUT OVER
THE GRASS

Kill deer! Kill deer!
and summer falling
from the cottonwoods
into stubbled fields

gravel scrape
where eggs lay

puddled with rain

Kill deer!
bird dragging a slack
bent wing—

followed, leaps
into the air still
calling

out over the fallen
grass

where last night two
does
undisturbed
in their nests

dreamed no dreams of blood

or winter

ADRIFT

In the thermals
a fragment—
ash, burnt paper

Vulture
his dark joy,
covert quietness

How the sunlight dazzles!

Ship with black sails
rudderless
returning

FIVE HORSES

Stopped in the lee
of a billboard
proclaiming

BEST WESTERN MOTELS!

the horses
agree

their small room
of calm

such a wide door
to slam
on the wind

LEAN

Barns
gaunt hulls, no cargo
in their holds

turtle shells
fragile deserted buildings

crows
their echo
deer carcass stripped bare

they tell us the flesh
will rise again

wind

how it sails off the edges
of blue

BROKEN

Fence down
muddy margins
the shrinking stock ponds

criss-cross of hoof-prints—
cattle, deer

And it took his wife
most of the afternoon

(How long
on his back
lined up with the corn rows?)

Sky
with his heart
on its sleeve

FIVE O'CLOCK

Coyote's unweaving the world
again

Lifts his leg

Road-shoulder grass
burned ragged
by salt

Contrails
those long torn seams

Startling and naked
pale skin
the moon

Carla Gericke

FATHER LET ME WALK WITH THEE

"The dorm's not too Orphan Annie," Ma says to Pa in Afrikaans as she jabs the lighter on the dashboard. We're in the Mean Green Flying Machine, Pa's Beemer, racing from Mafikeng to Pretoria.

Ma is referring to St. Albans—pronounced *sint,* not *saint*—where I will now live. Pa has been transferred to Stockholm to become the attaché something or other at the South African Consulate, and Lisbet and I—she's thirteen, I'm almost eleven—will remain in South Africa and attend boarding schools in Pretoria, where Ouma, Pa's Ma, lives. *English* boarding schools. I once asked Pa what it was that he did and he said: "A diplomat is someone who tells you to go to hell in such a way, you look forward to it."

Let me tell you, I'm not looking forward to living at St. Albans, no matter what Pa says. A few weeks ago, Ma and I went on a reconnaissance trip to meet the staff and inspect the facilities: Dormitories with bunk beds, long narrow dark corridors, strange sullen sunken-faced children, and a praying mantis of a matron called Missus Smith. Because Lisbet is older, she's going straight to Pretoria High School for Girls, but I have to spend the next four months at St. Albans while I complete primary school.

St. Albans, Lisbet says, is for the riffraff.

The lighter clicks and Ma lights two cigarettes. Smoke billows over the headrest towards Lisbet. Ma hands one of the ciggies to Pa and takes a deep drag on the other. Lisbet waves her hand in front of her nose and rolls her eyes at me.

Not too Orphan Annie? I kick the back of Pa's seat just hard enough that, if he complains, I can claim I was uncrossing my legs. I bloody-well beg to differ. Last week, lying in my favorite spot under the date tree in the garden in Mafikeng, my head resting on my dog Attila's stomach, I was rereading one of my favorite horror comic books. In it, an entire family gets chopped up by an axe-wielding garden gnome, and Stink Albans looks exactly like the ivy-covered, two-story gray stone building in which they get killed.

Lisbet and I glance at each other. She counts off on her fingers, one, two, three, and we start to yell over the music: "It's the hard-knock life, for us. It's the hard knock life, *for us.*"

Ma glances over her shoulder and when she catches my eye, she winks.

"Instead of treated!" Lisbet shouts.

Pa laughs, fiddles with the cassette player, and turns down the volume.

"We get kicked!" I yell, and kick the back of Pa's seat. My high-gloss Mary Jane leaves a black smudge against the cream leather.

"Instead of kisses!" Lisbet shouts, then stops and says, "No, wait, you're doing it wrong! You're supposed to say 'tricked' first, not 'kicked.'"

"Am not."

"Are so! It's 'tricked,' Ma! Tell her it's 'tricked'!"

Pa glances at me in the rearview mirror, and when he dips his head to look over the rim of his mirror sunglasses, his bald spot moves back. I grin at him. He flips over the tape and says, "Sing this instead, girls," and a voice starts to wail, "It's raining tears from my eyes, over you raining oooooh . . ."

"Ag, Pa, man, we hate this one," Lisbet and I say in unison. "Rewind to 'Summer Nights.' Rewind, Pa, rewind."

A few days after the St. Albans sortie, Pa, Ma, and I were sitting on the stoop after dinner—Lisbet was inside watching *Dallas;* Ma says I'm not old enough—when they started to speak to me in that special way they sometimes do, as though they had practiced their lines. Wouldn't it be "an awful waste of money," Pa said, to buy a new school uniform for only four months, and wouldn't it be "rad," Ma said, if I were the only one wearing a different kind? What? Genuine? A bit like wearing civvies, *nêh?* One of a kind. Unique. Special. *Ja,* special in an especially retarded kind of way. I jumped to my feet and stood in front of them, my fists balled on my hips. Do you even understand the concept of the word *uniform,* I wanted to shout. I stared at them for a long time before shaking my head, as though they were the naughty children and I the disappointed parent. Bloody grumps. First they tell me we have to move, *again.* I mean, what's this? Primary School Number Four, Five? And this time, an English school. A bloody boarding school. And in the middle of the term, *nogal.* Now this? After yesterday? After they told me we're going to have to give the dogs to Uncle Hans? I stared at them for a moment longer, then whipped around. I tried to whistle for Attila but couldn't get the air past the lump in my throat, so I slapped my thigh twice and he bounded in from the darkness of the outer garden. The floodlight tripped on. My new netball post—Pa said we'd have to sell it—stood illuminated in the middle of the lawn. The long metal pipe and hoop cast a spooky shadow, like a crooked monster finger beckoning me. Attila jammed his muddy snout into my palm and, ever loyal, followed close on my heels when I dashed inside. I raced barefoot down the lukewarm slate corridor, skidded into my room, and slammed the door.

Pa has a rule about door slamming: Don't. Once, in a fit of pique after Pa said I would have to stop roller-skating on the tennis court at the Ambassador's house because my skates were cutting grooves into the tarmac—groovy—I did slam my bedroom door. Shortly afterwards, Pa, dressed in the brown-and-red African caftan he always wears around the house, came to my room to explain that "this is not acceptable behavior, girly" and "in order to learn not to slam doors, you'll have to open and close your bedroom door one hundred times without making a sound." Pa bunched up his dress—"It's not a dress," he always insists, "it's a caftan!"—sat down on the floor next to the door, Castle can in one hand, cigarette in the other, ashtray in his lap, and pressed his ear to the wall. If he heard me, I had to start over again from number one. I think I was at twenty-seven, after having started over twice, when he said, "That's enough. You get the picture." Either the floor was getting uncomfortable, or he'd finished his beer. Probably the beer.

But that night, when I slammed my bedroom door and sat listening to the *Dallas* theme song—*tahdatahdahtahdahdadadah*—coming through the wall, no one came to my room. I guess they reckoned making me wear my stupid Afrikaans Hicksville uniform was punishment enough.

Lisbet's new beret is lying face-up on the seat between us. She told me yesterday that the motto on the crest—*Prosit Spes Labori*—was Latin for "Prozzies, Spazzes, and Labor. Like when you have a baby." She'd paused and added, "Life's a bitch and then you die."

I grab her beret and pull it artist-style Oh-là-là-*oui-oui* onto my head. "Aren't you supposed to wear your beret at all times?" I intone in English. Even though I won't be going to Girl's High yet, I've memorized all the rules. "A strict dress code is in place," I say in a frightfully upper-crust English accent. All South Africans can speak at least two languages, usually three or four. Our Ousie, Lena, who lived in the tiny room next to the laundry, can speak Tswana, Sotho, Afrikaans, and English. I can only speak two languages, Afrikaans, fluently—we speak it at home—and English, so-so. I read a lot in English but I dream in Afrikaans.

"School uniforms are to be worn proudly, never varying in time or place," I continue in a nasal voice. "Only regulation items of clothing are permissible. No jewelry of any kind."

Lisbet punches me on the shoulder and says, "Pa! Frankie's got my beret."

"I'm driving here, girls."

"Gerty's going to kill you," I sing-song. Gerty Mulligan, Gertrude Mulligan, Miss Mulligan, is the headmistress of Pretoria High School for Girls. Lisbet says she heard the Matrics say Miss Mulligan is still a virgin at the age of sixty-seventy-something because her fiancé, an R.A.F. pilot, died during the Second World War and she never got over it. Miss Mulligan is what people call "an institution." She requires her all-female staff to wear long black robes to Hall in the mornings. Bare legs are not permissible. Pantyhose, mandatory. Slacks may never be worn, not even during the cold Highveld winters when the frost stretches like Saran Wrap across the hockey fields. And—true as *njannies*—if a teacher wears an even vaguely see-through blouse, she is expected to wear two brassieres—*brassieres*, not bras—underneath. The same rules— and then some—apply to the boarders.

Up front, Ma opens the automatic window and flicks out her cigarette. Hot air punches into the air-conditioned car.

"Don't!" Lisbet and I yell. Once the heat lodges inside the car, it takes ages for it to cool down again. We'd rather have the gross ashtray stink and smoke.

Lisbet is dressed in her apple-green Girls High uniform, an all-in-one dress with a neat collar, two pockets in front, and a belt. Pinned on her right lapel is a plastic nametag with her name printed in yellow tape. Yellow means she's in Standard Six. Next year, my nametag will be yellow and hers will be green. Each Standard has its own color. Matrics are red. Pinned to her other lapel is a small purple button to show she's now part of Selbourne House. Since we're sisters—even though we don't look alike—next year I'll be in Selbourne House, too. Selbourne, Lisbet says, was a Governor-General of the Union of South Africa. She also says Selbourne House will, she knows, suck rat poison in hell.

I'm dressed in my Mafikeng primary school winter uniform: a gray pleated skirt, white shirt, tie, knee-length gray bobby socks, and black polished Mary Jane's. Winter uniforms are snazzier than summer ones, and at least I won that battle.

In Mafikeng, our school—which goes from Grade One through Matric—doesn't have badges or houses or all-girls anything. We have rugby matches and wrestling and athletics and no one wears stockings, ever. In summer, we go to school barefoot. I'm our under-12 100-meter sprint champion. But, get this: at Girl's High, there's no athletics. It's "unladylike." But field hockey? That's allowed. I know, you tell me.

Lisbet snatches her beret off my head and stuffs it between her seat and the car door. The outline of her bra is visible and I lean over and snap one of the straps. She turns around, eyes narrowed, and hisses, "At least I have boobs," then snickers. I fold my arms over my flat chest, lean my head against the window, and stare at the pink scab on my forearm.

Sometimes, Pa tells me I'm adopted, or, even worse, that he

caught me in the hills behind Ouma's house and chopped off my tail. He says that's why I'm all arms and legs and I'm covered in fine blond hairs and don't look like the rest of them. Except, Ma and I both have green eyes. Lisbet and Pa have brown eyes, dark hair, and olive skin. Ma says there's African blood in the Gerbers. Pa says there's African blood in all Africans, including us.

I glance outside. The familiar reds and khakis and spiky thorn trees have changed into *mielie* fields and hairy brown tufts jut from the top of the cobs, like mangled spaghetti. We usually drive this route to visit Ouma, whom Lisbet and I will now stay with every other weekend when we get "Privs."

"Privileges," that's what weekends off are called. Imagine, an honor to go home. Then, at the end of each term, we will fly to Sweden for proper hols with the grumps.

The flashing rows make my head hurt, but I don't look away. Pa changes the tape and Dolly Parton starts to sing. Once in a while, we pass a donkey cart or people walking beside the road with bundles balanced on their heads. When it feels as though my head might explode, I switch from counting corn to counting telephone poles, like Pa taught me to do. He says I can figure out how fast he's driving by counting the poles for a full minute and then extrapolating it. I never get the right answer, all I know is: (a) he drives bloody fast—"Just burning the engine clean, girls"—and (b) it's easier to look over his shoulder at the speedometer than to extrapolate jack-crap. Besides, as Lisbet says, word sums suck.

Pa down-gears to pass a truck and the engine whines. As we zoom past the giant fourteen-wheeler with "Stuttafords Van Lines" stenciled on the side, I'm convinced we are going to die.

After the three tall grain silos, the "almost-there-girls" mark, and with Dolly wailing "Please don't take my man," I look down at my red, green and white striped tie. Uniforms, I decide, and flip over the tie, are all about control. Like in the army. If you're worried about where your regulation hat is or whether your shoes are shined, you're less likely to plan that mutiny.

I study the label sewn on the underside. When Ma and I went to the Indian market to have the labels printed up—so we could sew them onto everything, even my socks and regulation undies—I'd asked her if mine could say "Frankfurter."

"Don't be daft, Francis."

"Daft," I'd muttered at the exact decibel I knew she couldn't hear, "as in you bozos making me wear my old uniform to a new school?"

"Watch it, missy."

I'd forgotten how good she was at reading lips.

In Pretoria, Pa pulls up under a giant jacaranda tree near the ivy-covered wall of St. Albans. The lilac-blue flowers make the branches sag, and I can hear them scrape against the car's roof. Pa jerks up the handbrake—*grtz*—and the sound reminds me the journey is over and a new one is beginning. Usually, this sound fills me with excitement, but today, as I look through the wrought-iron gate towards the boarding school, a snaking, squirming feeling I've never felt before swirls in my stomach. My hands are clammy. I feel dizzy. I close my eyes and the swish-swish-swish of the cornfields rushes across my lids. I need to pee. As we alight from the car, Lisbet hangs on her door and says, "You guys need to hurry, hey. I don't want to be late."

Late-afternoon sunlight spills through the leaves, casting dabbled yellow spotlights on the purple carpet of fallen blooms. People say if a Jacaranda bloom falls on your head, it's good luck. I glance up at the trumpet-shaped flowers and wish one would fall on my head. I walk around to Lisbet's side.

Ma stands in a pool of gold while Pa lifts my suitcase and my brand-new bed-in-a-bag from the trunk. He puts them on the ground, slams the trunk, and rubs his hands. The engine ticks, cooling down.

"Don't let them go with you," Lisbet whispers to me. "It'll make it worse."

"Right then," Pa says, and claps his hands. "Who's ready to roll, eh?"

"O.K., bye." Lisbet pecks me on the cheek. "See you next Friday, right? Ouma'll pick you up at six sharp." She pats my shoulder. "Don't be late. You know she hates to wait. Cheers, hey." She ducks into the car and when I look, she's blowing her nose. Probably her allergies.

"Now, Francis Jakoba Gerber," Ma says, stepping closer. "I want you to promise me that you'll behave yourse—"

"—Ma-ah." I grab the suitcase. I need to get away. I don't want to cry. I won't cry. I'll show them. "Just let Pa take my stuff up and you wait here, alright? He'll be back in a sec." I put the suitcase down between us and reach over it to hug her. I smell Pall Malls and Esteé Lauder. Ma. My heart races. I squeeze my eyes shut and, when I open them, I let go. I take a small step back and tap her arm. I clear my throat and say, "Last touch, nix." I cross my fingers and show them to her. She smiles. Usually, she'd try to touch my fingers to trump my "nix"—the last "nixer" is the winner—but today she lets me win without a fuss. She cups my face and kisses me on the lips. "Be good." I nod, bobbling my head because there's something lodged in my throat.

Fingers crossed, I pick up my suitcase and follow Pa towards the gate. Halfway up the path, he notices I'm lugging the suitcase, elbows bent, walking on my tiptoes so it won't drag on the ground. He's hugging the bed-in-a-bag to his chest. "Gimme that, Pumpkin," he says.

A hand bell starts to clang from deep within the building. *Ca-clang-ca-clank. Ca-clang-ca-clank.* Back in Mafikeng, Ma would call us inside using a cowbell she'd bought in Switzerland. That way, we could play anywhere inside the massive fenced Embassy compound and still know when it was time to go home. When that bell rang, it signaled a phone call from a friend, or the end of a day of play, or yippee-yippee-yippee, grub-time. Now, with every *ca-clang-ca-clank*, my stomach flip-flops. This bell sounds different, like loneliness.

Side by side, Pa and I climb up the last few steps. As we walk across the stoop, the stained-glass front door swings open.

"Ah, there you are," Missus Smith says, and takes the bed-in-a-bag from me. She smells of vegetable soup and chamomile cream. "Just in time for prayers." Oh no, I think. I hope she isn't one of those Jesus freaks Pa's always railing about. Pa and I are atheists, although I'm not supposed to tell Ouma and must still attend church every week, like I used to do with Ma and Lisbet. I'm a non-practicing atheist, I suppose.

"Let's say our goodbyes then, chop-chop"—she clutches me by the shoulder—"and then we'll get this little lady settled in nicely. Prayers first, of course."

I glance at Pa. His shades are propped on his head. I know he's thinking the exact same thing I am. Ohnosweetjesusmotherofgod, not a "royal we," chop-chopping Jesus freak. He grins and I grin back, and for a moment I feel better.

Missus Smith prods me towards the door, saying to Pa, "Just leave the suitcase there, we'll have someone bring it in. Best if we run along now, no?" Pa puts the suitcase down. I turn to wave. He blows me a kiss and mouths, "last touch," pretending to reach for my arm. He shows me his fingers are crossed. I lift my hands in return, showing him that both hands' fingers are now crossed. I lift them higher. Just before Missus Smith leads me into the belly of the building, from the corner of my eye, I see him turn and jog down the stairs. He walks quickly down the garden path, slightly bandy-legged, head down, the way he always walks, away.

The bell stops. Girls of all ages, dressed in civvies since it isn't a Priv weekend, gather in the large foyer. I'm standing next to Missus Smith. My bed-in-a-bag is propped against the upright piano where she put it down. My suitcase is still on the stoop. I hope it's safe. Shoes clomp down the wooden stairs. The room smells like wet swimming towels, Colgate Apple shampoo, and boiled cabbage. Someone yells, "Abigail, shut-up and get in line!" Someone flips a switch and the chandelier above my head sparkles. Dishes clatter in the kitchen. Someone jostles me. A voice says, "Zambezi Mud tonight." Girls cheer. Someone says, "Dibs on your Camel Kotch." Zambezi Mud? Camel Kotch?

"Check it out, man. Fresh meat."

Silence descends. All eyes fall on me. I shrug one shoulder all the way to my ear and let it drop. I try to smile, but I can't open my mouth. I'm scared of what might come out.

"Check it out," the pudgy red-haired girl says again. "Why you wearing a Boy's High tie, hey?" She flicks up my tie with one finger and it snakes through the air, rippling like a tongue before flopping against my skinny chest. "Check it out, man." She nudges the girl next to her, who also points and snorts. "You a boy, or what?"

The girls laugh, elbowing each other. I want to flatten my short hair but look down instead. The redhead has freckles on her legs. A huge purple bruise would go nicely with that. I look up and manage a squint.

"Colleen! That's enough," Missus Smith says. "One more peep out of you and we will not be having seconds, will we?"

Boy's High? I glance down at the tie. Makes sense because I know small-town schools sometimes use bits and pieces from other schools' uniforms to keep their costs down. But, *Boys High*? I'm going to…kill…the grumps.

Missus Smith claps her hands in front of her pointy nose—praying mantis indeed—and Colleen sneers at me before falling in line. Everyone moves in a choreographed fashion, slipping into place.

"Now, young lady," Missus Smith nudges me forward, "you go stand over there with the rest of the Standard Fives."

I look at them. Front or back? From my research—I borrowed the whole Malory Towers series from the library—I know these things matter. I notice Colleen near the back. She's taller than a giant. Front it is, then.

The head girl reads from the Bible. In English. The Dutch Reformed Church we attend is Afrikaans and this Anglican God sounds foreign. Meaner. Real mean for someone who isn't supposed to exist. A girl with humongous boobs sits at the piano. She twists and stares at me. I look down at my hands. They are folded neatly in front of me. My best-behavior hands. The head girl continues to read, and the ache in my heart grows stronger. A crash of cutlery in the dining hall startles me and I look up. The piano player turns towards the upright. I focus on her, trying to distract myself from this thing pinching my heart. Her hands are poised over the keys. When the head girl stops reading, her hands drop and she starts banging out a hymn, using loads of pedal. I recognize the tune, we sing it in church all the time. I open my mouth to join in when I hear the English. I don't know the words in English. I press my lips together and taste a hint of Ma's Lancôme lipstick.

I try to keep the thing pressed down, inside me, but I can feel it welling up. Don't you dare bawl, moron. I clear my throat. I rock up and down on the balls of my feet, watching my socks crinkle. Buck up, bozo. It's Lisbet's voice in my head. Show these bloody Englishmen what a real stiff upper lip looks like. I want to be all grown up, but my lips tremble. I bite my bottom lip, but a tear slips out and rolls down my cheek. I keep my head bowed, my hands clasped, and let it drip off my chin. I don't want these strangers to see me cry. I want to go to the loo. I really, really need to pee now but I can't remember where to go. Besides, "Girls may not be excused during prayers." It's Rule No. 3.

I try to take a deep breath like Lisbet taught me to do so I won't cry in sad movies, but I hiccup instead. I want to cry for being left here amongst strangers. I want to cry for Attila, whom I'll never see again. I want to cry for my old duvet that smelled like Baby Soft, which we gave to Lena for her kids. I want to cry for the people I saw walking next to the road. I want to cry for Pa, for Ma, for Lisbet. But most of all, I sniff and unclasp my hands, I want to cry for me.

I wipe my chin. I peek at the girl next to me. She makes bug-eyes at me. I glance down at my shoes and notice there's a scuffmark from where I kicked Pa's seat. As I study the smudge, I listen to the song swell around me. I take one last look at the scuffmark, then, lifting my foot, I start to polish my shoe against my bobby sock as the girls' voices rise and they sing: Father let me walk with Thee. ♦

A NOTE TO THE READER: Names have been changed, including the narrator's, but the story is true.

Sameer Pandya

M-O-T-H-E-R

In high school and college, Uma Shastri was good at math and economics because she studied hard. But with a field hockey stick or a tennis racquet in her hand, her body slid to all the right places without conscious thought. With her strong thighs, quick feet, and icy insides, she was always the best player on any field. Later, when she was married, she wanted a daughter, but learned to be excited about the boys that came out of her belly. Sure, she could have given a girl the real encouragement in sports she never had, but the boys would be an easier sell. As the years passed, neither boy showed any interest in Little League, tennis, or even Ping-Pong. Instead, they loved chess and, with their sharp memory and an ability to visualize and break down words, were highly skilled spellers. Her husband Arun thought spelling and chess were the only sports worth encouraging. She said they weren't real sports; he said they showed spelling bees on ESPN. Once she realized both boys had genuine interest, Uma decided she'd help them become accomplished, well-known spellers, even though they weren't interested in the competitions.

It was just past six on a Saturday morning and the family was on the road to the state spelling championships, in Sacramento. They'd allotted two hours' drive time and two more just in case. Arun had suggested they drive the night before and stay at a motel, but Uma said no because all the responsibility would fall on her. Arun would pack a few things in a bag five minutes before they were scheduled to leave. She had to pack for herself and the two boys, and deal with food. Her elder son Pankaj was allergic to dairy products and wheat. And so they were on the road at 6 A.M. Both of them liked getting to their destination early, though Uma liked it just a little more.

As soon as they got in the minivan, Pankaj went to the seat all the way in the back and fell asleep. Bankim sat in the first passenger seat. Arun drove, and Uma sat next to him.

Arun and Uma didn't think of driving a minivan as surrendering to a staid domestic life in the suburbs. In fact, they'd actively sought out the life. They spent the first two years of their marriage in Baltimore, where Arun was completing his medical residency. They rented an apartment at a safe distance from the tough neighborhood surrounding Johns Hopkins. Arun spent his days and many nights at the hospital, while Uma had to fend for herself. She had an economics degree, but had trouble finding work. She ended up working at a fabric store for minimum wage. In the first month, a woman in their apartment complex was held up as she was opening the door to the building. This moment haunted Uma for the rest of their time in Baltimore. When she ventured out, she felt uncomfortable until she was safely back inside their apartment. When they left Baltimore and headed west, they agreed that they wanted nothing more to do with urban living. They wanted a place where the parking was easy and where they didn't have to spend the 30 yards before the front entry readying the key so that they could open and close the door in one swift, defensive movement. A large, comfortable car was one small part of the life they'd envisioned.

"Don't you want to get a little sleep?" Uma asked Bankim. "You didn't fall asleep until late last night."

"I'm fine," he said, staring out at the empty freeway. Bankim was good at chess and spelling because he could sit quietly in one place for hours.

"We have plenty of time. Rest your eyes." She felt more nervous than he was. She'd only had a few short stretches of sleep the night before and now her eyes and head felt heavy. A lack of sleep shortened the leash on her temper. She closed her eyes for a few minutes.

Some of Uma's best childhood memories revolved around early mornings. When she was young, she, her mother, and her two older brothers took an early morning train from Bombay into Gujarat to spend time with her mother's family. Uma's mother got them up, dressed, and to the train station while she and her siblings were still half asleep. And then they'd be settled in a train compartment. Even before the train started moving, Uma was fast asleep. She'd wake up a few hours later to a sharp, sunny day, with the countryside moving in a blur of greens and blues. Her mother had a plate of fried snacks and a thermos of hot tea ready. Uma wanted to duplicate the magical sensation of going to sleep in one world and waking up in another, but Pankaj usually slept through all their trips and Bankim never went to sleep.

When they were about half an hour away from Sacramento, Uma called back to Pankaj and woke him up.

Both brothers wore long-sleeved button-down shirts that Uma had ironed for them the night before. Pankaj's shirt was already untucked and completely wrinkled. He didn't do this on purpose. Two years before, when he was 13, Pankaj was pictured on the front page of their local newspaper, with his wrinkled chambray shirt, standing with his shoulders slouched and his back in a C, holding up his plaque: "Local boy wins state spelling bee." At the national bee, he lost in the second round. Both brothers knew that Bankim was expected to win here and then do better at the nationals. They'd be the first set of brothers to win the same state spelling bee. There was a two-year age difference between them, but they looked alike. They wore wire-rimmed glasses, and had bowl cuts, soft hands, bad posture, and slightly protruding bellies. The only difference was that Bankim didn't wrinkle his shirts, and that might have been the advantage the younger had over the elder.

Pankaj climbed out of the back and sat next to Bankim. "Monkey," he whispered.

Bankim started giggling. They were best friends and each other's spelling partner. In between difficult words, they competed over who could come up with the silliest ones.

"Shh," said Arun, looking through the rearview mirror. "Let Bankim concentrate."

"He's concentrating too much," said Pankaj. "He needs to relax."

Arun didn't say anything for a few seconds. "Maybe that's a good idea. We all need to relax a bit." It had been a quiet and tense ride. Uma had tried, but couldn't fall asleep.

"Just sit quietly," said Uma. "We're almost there." She didn't like how Arun let the boys do what they wanted. He was too easily swayed by them. Pankaj had made a good point, but she didn't like how he talked back. He wasn't rude, but he was entering that phase where he no longer assumed his parents were always right. Bankim was impressionable and looked up to his brother.

"Booty," whispered Bankim.

"B-o-o-d-y."

"Stupid. It's b-o-o-t-y."

By 7:30, they reached the high school where the bee was being held. Though the parking lot was nowhere close to full, there were quite a few cars. Uma felt panic, but assumed that people had simply arrived early. Arun and Pankaj stayed in the car while she and Bankim went to register.

Ten minutes later, Uma was taking long strides across the parking lot. Bankim was several steps behind her, trying his best to keep up.

"Arun, it starts at 8:30, not 10." Uma didn't understand how she got it wrong. She never got such things wrong. She was worried that this was a sign of bad things to come. If she couldn't keep up her end of the bargain, how could she expect Bankim to keep up his?

"It's fine," said Arun, looking at his watch. "We still have over half an hour."

Arun's patients and colleagues always commented on how casual and comforting he was in his bedside manner. But this wasn't the time for it. "I asked you to take care of this one thing. I've done everything else. Why can't you help out a little?" She knew she hadn't asked Arun to keep track of the start time. She was just worn out from everything she'd done to insure the smooth movement of the day. The night before, after they'd all gone to bed, she stayed up well past midnight, making fresh samosas for the trip. When she offered them during the car ride, they all dismissively said they weren't hungry.

Pankaj called Bankim into the car, where he was playing his Game Boy.

"We're fine," Arun said. "Let's not do this in front of them now."

Arun walked to the open side of the car and asked, with added cheer, "Are you ready?"

"Sure," said Bankim. "I've been ready for a week."

"Let's go in," said Arun.

"The boy's haven't caten yet," said Uma. "And I don't want to be in the auditorium with all the nervous kids and their parents."

She handed Pankaj his own Tupperware, which had three different kinds of wheat-free and dairy-free snacks. She, Arun, and Bankim ate from a larger container of samosas and pakoras. Samosas and tea before the start of a spelling bee: it was their small version of a tailgate party.

"Are those O.K.?" Uma asked Pankaj. They'd only recently found out about the wheat allergy and she was still figuring out how to work around it.

"They're fine," said Pankaj.

Bankim ate two samosas quickly and was going for a third.

"Slow down," Uma said. "You don't want to get a stomachache up there."

Pankaj looked into the canvas food bag. "Where's the ginger ale?"

Uma looked into the bag. She'd packed a thermos of tea and a bottle of cold, sweetened milk for Bankim. She forgot Pankaj's safe drink for road trips.

"I'm so sorry," she said. "I was running around and I forgot this one thing. I'm really sorry."

"What am I supposed to drink?"

Uma didn't like the tone in his voice. "The tea doesn't have that much milk," she said. Even a couple of tablespoons of milk destroyed Pankaj's digestive system for days.

"That's not funny," replied Pankaj, his voice a little shaky.

"We'll get you a drink inside," said Arun.

She looked at Pankaj, still her little boy with allergies, and thought about apologizing, but didn't feel like it.

They finished eating and went inside.

In the auditorium, they wished Bankim good luck: Pankaj squeezed his shoulder; Arun shook his hand; Uma played with his hair and then combed it through with her fingers. By 8:20, Bankim was in his seat onstage, in the first of five rows of seats. Only a few others kids were seated. Many parents were still standing with their kids in front of the stage, hugging and kissing them. Uma hoped that

Bankim knew that though she wouldn't be so affectionate in public, she'd be there for him long after most of these parents gave up.

She didn't love one son more than the other, but she and Bankim had an unusual connection from very early on. Like his father, Pankaj had an intellect that scared Uma. They both used it to cut people off in conversation. Bankim, on the other hand, had to work a little harder in school. But he was a charmer. Right now, there was a charm in how his glasses always slipped below the bridge of his nose. Since he was very young, Bankim knew how to handle attention. Everyone wanted to play with him, but he'd withhold his interest for as long as he could and then give himself to one or two people, and only for a limited period of time. Mostly, he'd stay attached to Uma's leg. She'd never known love and devotion in the way she felt it from him.

Arun, Uma, and Pankaj found seats toward the back of the auditorium. Uma wanted a place where she didn't have to make small talk with any of the other parents. Once they sat down, she raised her hand and put it down when Bankim noticed. Now that he knew where they were, Bankim would only look for them if he was in trouble.

At 8:30, the main judge came up onstage and explained the rules to the participants and audience. As he was talking, Uma scanned the stage for competition. She recognized several kids from previous bees, but felt confident about Bankim's chances. And then they got started. There were a hundred kids competing and so the first couple of rounds were very slow. The initial rounds got rid of the underprepared and those who were too nervous to perform in front of crowds. One boy broke into tears before he was halfway through *democracy*. Bankim easily got past the first two rounds with *abdomen* and *ostensible*.

By the time Bankim got up for the third round, an hour had passed. Arun read Ludlum; Pankaj had recently gotten into Asimov.

Uma, however, had not taken her eyes off the stage. Arun and Pankaj only looked up when Bankim asked for the word *dungarees* to be pronounced for the second time. In the early rounds, Bankim usually spelled the words quickly, in order to save his energy for the later rounds. But now, he was taking a long time.

"What's he doing?" asked Pankaj. "He knows this word. It's easy."

"Shh," said Uma.

Bankim stood casually at the mike with his hands in his pockets. For about ten seconds, he just stood there. Uma quickly scanned the audience. Except for a few whispers here and there, they were all intently watching her son.

Even from where they were sitting in the back, Uma could clearly see Bankim's eyes as they bulged out and then receded. It frightened her. His head swooned back a little, and with his hands still in his pockets, he stumbled like a drunk, took a few steps sideways, and at the last possible moment, took his hands out of his pockets and used them to break his fall. All the kids leaned forward to look, and there was a collective gasp from the audience. Just as Arun and Uma got up out of their seats, Bankim used his hands to get up. He pushed his glasses up his nose with his thumb and middle finger, walked to the mike, spelled out d-u-n-g-a-r-e-e-s correctly, and went back to his seat, as if nothing had happened. For the first several seconds after he sat down, no one knew what to do. It took the audience that time to decide that Uma's cute but dorky 13-year-old boy had displayed a great bit of courage and strength when, despite the pain and disorientation he must have felt, he got up and took care of the job he'd come to do. He persevered through pain for the sake of a larger purpose. As the audience was thinking about what had just happened onstage, they clapped quietly. But when they finally figured it out, seemingly all at the same time, they went wild with their cheering. Everyone stood up and clapped and kept clapping. As the family walked down the center aisle toward the stage, Uma whispered under her breath, "That's my boy." They were clapping for him, but they were also clapping for her, for raising a child who got up when others would have stayed down.

When the family reached the stage, the bee officials had already taken Bankim to the back. The main judge went onstage and said the competition was temporarily on hold.

"What's wrong?" asked Arun, placing his hand on Bankim's forehead and cheeks.

"Nothing," said Bankim. He was sitting in a chair, his shirt still neatly tucked in. "I just felt a little lightheaded."

"We have a school nurse and she's on her way," said the judge.

Arun was about to say that he was a doctor, but the judge walked away.

"Do you feel tired?" Arun checked his son's pulse and looked at his eyes.

"A little."

Arun asked Pankaj to give Bankim some of the cranberry juice he'd bought earlier from the vending machine. Bankim took several sips. Uma ran her fingers through his hair. "How do you feel?"

"Fine," he said.

The nurse, an older woman in street clothes, arrived a few minutes later, checked Bankim's vitals, and asked him some questions. Arun spoke to her, but didn't say he was a doctor. She said she couldn't see anything outright that was wrong, and that he was fine to go on if he liked. "It's up to you."

Arun and Uma walked to a corner away from the kids.

"What do you think?"

"You know what I think," said Uma.

"Even after what's happened? He's sick. He passed out. We've been pushing him too hard. His body is rebelling against the exhaustion and stress."

"I know you think I'm being selfish, but I'm not. Bankim has worked very hard for this. And he'll want to know why we didn't encourage him to keep going."

"Bullshit," said Arun and looked to see if his kids had heard him. If they had, they didn't turn to look at them. "This isn't encouragement, it's being pushy."

"This isn't about me. I've watched him study." Not only had she watched him, she'd created tests for him to take and study guides for him to use. She'd even found a guy who taught Bankim basic Latin roots. "He doesn't want to lose this opportunity. Look at them. They're going on like nothing has happened." The two brothers were standing around and laughing, as if, indeed, nothing had happened.

The boys were a constant source of disagreement between Uma and Arun. Arun believed in a *laissez-faire* policy of child-rearing. His parents had maintained a distance from their children, but had offered advice and emotional support when needed. Arun thought he'd turned out pretty well: he loved his parents and he'd never cheated on either his wife or his taxes.

"Arun, your father never knew whether your birthday was in April or October," Uma had once said.

"So? He remembered everything that was important."

Arun was comfortable with his father's distance; Uma tried to make up for the distance she had from both her parents.

"And the nurse said he's fine," said Uma. "You said he's fine."

"O.K.," said Arun. "Let's at least ask him."

They called Bankim over.

"Hey, buddy," said Arun. "How do you feel?"

"Fine."

"Do you want to keep going?"

Bankim looked at his mother and then his father and then back to his mother. "Yeah," he said.

"Are you sure?" asked Arun.

This time, Bankim just nodded his head.

Arun and Uma went to find the judge. "I still think this is a very bad idea," said Arun.

When Bankim returned to his seat onstage, the audience clapped again, though this time not as loud. Bankim kept his head down and found his seat. He'd never had this much attention centered on him before. He waited as they went through the rest of the third round. When it was his turn in the fourth, he got up, listened for the word, spelled *regiment* immediately, and returned to his seat, without letting a second pass between each task. And then the words kept coming and Bankim kept spelling them right. *Idiopathic, pharmacology, lumpen, fecundity, odoriferous, pettifog.* The group onstage got smaller and smaller. Uma went to the bathroom when there were still twenty-five kids left and Bankim had just completed a round.

She walked into a stall and sat down. Ever since Pankaj was born, she used the bathroom for a few stolen moments of quiet, which she now desperately needed. She was relieved that Bankim was on track. When she played tennis, she had an uncanny ability to sense when her opponent was feeling nervous. And right at that moment, she'd attack. Bankim was equally good at the mental game. He didn't think about what came before or what would come after. He went from word to word and stayed within the game. But as much as she loved competition, her constitution couldn't quite handle the pressure when her kids were competing.

A couple of women came into the bathroom a minute after her. They washed their hands and fixed their makeup.

"I'll be glad when it's over," said one woman. "Our lives have been crazy."

"I don't know where Sam gets the strength and motivation," said the other. "He's up in the morning before us."

There was a pause for a few seconds.

"I'm glad that little boy is O.K.," said the first woman, her voice a little softer than before.

"He's precious."

Uma was happy to hear this.

"But I can't believe he's continuing on. If I was that mother, I'd get him to a doctor and give him a full checkup. What if there's still something wrong?"

Uma wanted to say that nothing was wrong. Her husband had checked.

"It's just irresponsible. I'd be mad too if, after all the work we've done, Michael had to drop out. But I'd understand."

Uma had seen them on TV: mothers who pushed their kids too far, mothers who fought other mothers over who had the better, brighter, prettier, more athletic child. In the minute she'd been sitting in the stall before they came in, Uma had wondered if she'd gone too far this time. Bankim could take the pushing, though she needed to be careful. But hearing these women articulate her fears made her feel more self-righteous. Who the hell were they? They knew nothing about her or her life. Spelling separated her from parents pushing their children to be better football players and bouncier cheerleaders. She was helping them to be smarter, more successful kids. Who didn't want that for their children? Once she got over the disappointment that her boys weren't interested in physical sports, she realized that encouraging them at spelling was very important. Despite the promise that America made about equality, her boys would never get their backs scratched in the same way their white counterparts would. The only recourse they had was to be the smartest ones in the room. It wouldn't make them equal, but at least it would keep them in the game.

And she encouraged the boys in spelling so that she could spend time with them. She'd gone from a father to a husband. In her boys, she saw a chance to give and receive with some purity. Uma didn't have many friends. She'd lost touch with her school and college friends from India and child-rearing didn't leave time to make new ones. But it wasn't really an issue of time. She didn't know how to relate to adults. She was graceful and wore her saris well, and made small talk when she and Arun had dinner with his colleagues. But she didn't spend time one-on-one with other women. She didn't act childish and she didn't want to be a child. But given the choice, she'd rather spend time with children. Adults disappointed her. They insisted on conversations about their anxieties and failures. They said one thing when they meant another. She found children to be straightforward: they smiled when they were happy, cried when they weren't.

Uma had intended to wait until the two women left the bathroom to come out. But occupied by her thoughts, she opened the stall door. All three made eye contact through the large mirror in front of them. Uma was unmistakable. At 5'10", she was an inch taller than Arun. And they'd all watched her as she ran down the middle aisle when Bankim fell, her single braid whipping up and down like a snake.

Right when she made eye contact with them, Uma felt calm. She wasn't going to say anything. It was not her place or responsibility. They were the ones who'd been talking and they'd have to be the ones doing the talking now. Uma walked over to a sink, washed her hands and wiped them, but still they said nothing. Uma looked at one woman then the other and smiled. "Have a nice day," she said and walked out the door. As she stepped away from the bathroom, she wished she could hear what they were saying now. Her moment of restraint felt like a great victory, as if her restraint, when she had every right to tell them to go fuck themselves, washed away their criticism that she was a bad mother and a bad woman. A bad mother would have insisted on a fight in the girl's bathroom while their kids were outside competing and working hard. No, Uma was a good mother for taking the hit on the chin and moving on.

She walked back to her seat a little tingly, as if things were going to turn out all right.

At the end, there were two: Bankim and an unremarkable young girl named Joan from Stockton who'd not struggled with a single word that day. The auditorium was still full. The audience didn't openly root for one kid over another. But Uma felt that despite what they thought of her, surely they were secretly hoping that Bankim would win. Bankim and Joan went back and forth for seven rounds. Uma couldn't sit and watch. Her stomach was rumbling and she vowed that this would be the last time she was going to come to one of these events. She had a family history of high blood pressure.

A run came up to the little hidden corner behind the last row of chairs where Uma was standing. When she first saw him coming toward her, she was annoyed. They stood together for about five seconds before Uma said she was going back to her seat.

"It's fine," he said. "Pankaj is there. He'll take care of him if he needs it."

She hesitated and then stood there.

Arun stood next to her and instead of saying anything, he held her pinky finger in his hand and kept repeating, "He'll be fine, baby." This was Arun's term of comfort and love, used very sparingly.

With Arun holding her pinky, they got through the rounds. As often happens, Joan got a fairly easy word—*solvent*—wrong. She spelled it with an *a*. According to the rules, Bankim had to spell *solvent* and the next word on the list to win. He began to work it out in his mind. Uma remembered going over the word with him. He knew it. Bankim took his time: he asked for the definition, the origin, and the use of it in a sentence. And then he took a step toward the mike and spelled it correctly. The judge announced the next word: *auteur*. Bankim asked for the definition, kept his head down for about ten seconds, and then spelled the word out correctly.

The applause was long and loud. Arun squeezed Uma's pinky and the two of them stood there for a few seconds. She'd gone to other competitions where the boys had won. But this one felt different, like she'd won as well. They walked up to the stage where the judges and the other participants were congratulating Bankim. The family waited for a few minutes, but when the crowd didn't appear to be thinning, they walked through it. Pankaj slapped Bankim's arm, Arun gave him an awkward hug, and Uma fixed his hair.

They'd been through the aftermath before with Pankaj. Then, it was simply one boy, one victory. There were more story angles this time for the newspapers: Bankim's victory, his perseverance, the brothers' joint victory. Uma filled out the proper paperwork and they stood onstage taking pictures and answering questions from the local newspapers. Uma knew that though the newspapers were only small, stories had the ability to grow bigger with every retelling. She placed most of her hope in the local TV station. If they were there from the beginning, surely they'd captured Bankim's fall and rise. She couldn't wait to see how it looked on film.

The TV reporter asked Uma if he could interview Bankim.

"Of course," she said.

"Do you want your mom to be with you?" the reporter asked.

Without looking at her, he said, "No, I'll be fine."

He asked Bankim how he felt after the fall.

"When I was standing up there for my—what round was it?"

"I think it was the third," said the reporter.

"Right. When I was standing up there for my third word, I felt very dizzy and disoriented. I went blank for a few seconds. That's when I must have fallen. But the second I fell and hit the ground, I felt better. I didn't feel great, but I really wanted to keep going."

Uma thought he'd freeze up in front of the camera, but he was perfectly comfortable. Uma and Bankim had not made eye contact since she got up onstage. She assumed he was overwhelmed and busy.

After Bankim finished with the reporters, the crowd began to disperse. Uma and Arun thanked the judges and the four of them headed back to the car. In the parking lot, Pankaj and Arun were walking ahead, while Uma and Bankim followed about 20 yards behind. She was happy finally to have a word. She wanted to congratulate him for his masterful performance. It was just like they'd planned, but even better. They'd decided that he'd fall at the third word. At that point, there would still be enough participants and audience members to get the best effect. Uma had been thinking about the plan for several months. Spelling bees had some suspense, but they were never exciting. If there was going to be any excitement, something extraordinary needed to happen. Unfortunately, it wasn't going to grow naturally out of the competition. The idea of Bankim falling had just come to her. Even if he didn't win, he'd be the one people would remember. If her boys weren't going to be well-known tennis players, at least they could be well-known spellers. For months, she kept the idea to herself. But the longer she didn't tell anybody and the longer she thought about it, the more she felt like it was a reasonable plan. A month before the bee, she talked to Bankim. She thought he'd tell her she was crazy. But he reacted with neither excitement nor disbelief. He treated it like it was a reasonable request, as if she'd asked him to wear his brown pants instead of the blue ones. And so they practiced. Falls to the left, falls to the right. She taught him to use his hands to break the fall. They practiced after school, before Arun and Pankaj got home. She made him promise not to tell anybody.

And when he finally did it earlier that morning, it was better than all the practice rounds. He used his hands without any hesitation. Uma wanted to know the details of what he was thinking up there and she wanted to know how he did that thing with his eyes. They'd not practiced that. They could talk about all this at home; for now she simply wanted to congratulate him. But right when she turned to him, Bankim picked up his step and went toward Arun and Pankaj.

The second he took that step away from her, she knew he was gone. She knew because mothers can sense these things about their children. Somewhere between their initial conversation and now, Bankim decided that his mother asked him to do something mothers shouldn't ask of their children. Bankim was getting closer, but he hadn't reached Arun and Pankaj quite yet. Uma thought she could catch up with him, and so she picked up her speed. The closer she got to him, the closer he got to Arun and Pankaj. By the time she'd made some ground, Bankim was walking between his brother and father. Right when Bankim reached them, and she saw Arun put his arm around him, she stopped and labored to catch her breath. She felt a tiny, sharp prick behind her right eye, the beginning of a headache she'd been fighting off all morning. There was the boy she loved and craved more than anything else. She kept repeating in her mind that she'd done it for his sake, because if she didn't convince herself, she'd fall right down in that parking lot.

When she reached the car, they were already in their seats.

"Bankim, you choose where we're going to eat," said Arun. "We're celebrating."

"It doesn't matter," said Bankim.

"Of course it matters," said Arun.

Bankim didn't respond. Arun looked at Uma, asking her to say something.

"C'mon, sweetie," said Uma, turning her head to face him. Someone needed to fill the silence. "Pick something."

And perhaps because of the look in her eyes or the way the word "sweetie" rolled off her tongue, Bankim started crying. Pankaj looked at him and Arun watched him through the rearview mirror, but neither said anything. Uma reached back and placed her hand on his knee. He didn't move it away. There was no way for her to recover that part of Bankim she'd ushered away. But she still had that part of him that could break down in the moment when his own confusion about adult life crossed paths with her sweet voice. In that moment, he was still all hers.

"He wants pizza," said Uma and nudged Arun to start driving. ✦

WRITER'S PROCESS:

SAMEER PANDYA

Initially, the idea for M-o-t-h-e-r came from a clip of an actual spelling bee that was on high rotation on ESPN's SportsCenter. In the clip, a young Indian boy falls down in the middle of a word, gets back up and spells it correctly. Not only did he spell it right, but he went back to his chair like nothing had happened. I was of course intrigued by this kid and kept thinking about what motivated him to get up and step back up to the mike. Competitiveness? Confidence? Fear?

As I began thinking about him, I also wondered about his family. Indian kids don't have much of a presence on sports television, except in spelling bees. What motivates these kids, and what role does the family play? In the story, the boy became Bankim, and while I was very interested in him, it was his mother's character that kept scratching away at me. On the one hand, I wanted to explore her life. She is part of a generation of Indian women who were educated in India, came to the United States in their early 20s, and chose to raise children instead of working. The character has some ambivalence about this last decision. On the other hand, I wanted to explore the mother-son relationship, and the particular power that mothers have over their boys. With all the attention paid to father-son obsessions, the mother-son relationship gets a little lonely.

The movement of the plot was set in my mind pretty early in the drafting process. I wanted to show Bankim get up and continue with the competition, and I had a sense that the motivation was his mother. But the real work of the story came in working through Uma. What is her relationship to mothering? Why do the staging? It took a while to understand her, to work through her conflicting motivations, to create a woman I recognized, liked, understood, and feared. But in many ways, I am not sure whether the work of figuring out mothers and their relationship with their sons is ever complete.

Gail Albert Halaban

THIS STAGE OF MOTHERHOOD

The following are untitled photographs from
Gail Albert Halaban's exhibit "This Stage of Motherhood,"
examining the lives of a group of women in New York.

DEREK WALCOTT

"Becune Point, St. Lucia" (1993)

PHOTO: LEONARDO BARRETO

White Egrets
&
Down the Coast

The selection here from Derek Walcott's forthcoming book *White Egrets* begins with four poems from what he's calling the Spanish Series, then moves variously to Caribbean locales and into an interior space where geographic reference seems less central, before concluding with a final wistful poem from Spain.

In "Down the Coast," a work in progress, Walcott addresses his repeated frustrated attempts, over a period of five decades, to make a film taking as its point of departure "Ti-Jean and His Brothers," a play he wrote in 1957, based on a classic tale from French Antillean folklore, in which the title character, a modest, precocious, intelligent boy—who moves through a world of "Midsummer Night's Dream"-like fantasticality, conversing with a frog, a cricket, a firefly, and a Bolom (you'll have to read the play to find out what *that* is)—manages, to make a long story short, to outsmart the Devil. As boys, Walcott and his twin brother Roderick would climb the hills above their home in the Caribbean island of St. Lucia to beg their great-aunt Sidone to tell them the stories in which Ti-Jean figured as the hero. For Walcott writing today, the natural features of the landscape that surrounded him then are scarcely less mythological than the world conjured in those stories his aunt told, and it is his vivid evocation of childhood and youth—that and many other things besides—which makes this piece a tour-de-force.

Derek Walcott

WHITE EGRETS

I

Plod of a hoof in blood-crusted earth.
Clatter of a rivulet over bleached stones.
Black bulls trampling the shade of cork trees,
wind in the high wheat whispering like surf
in Sicily or the opening pages of Cervantes.
Two storks on the bell tower in Alcalá.
The boring suffering of love that tires.
Though you change names and countries, Espagña, Italia,
smell your hands, they reek of imagined crimes.
The cypresses suffer in silence, but the oaks, sometimes,
rustle their foliate lyres.

II

A train crosses the scorched plain in one sentence.
In the cork groves shadows rhyme with their sources.
No name except Andalusia would make sense
from the train window of horses and galloping horses.
Echoes and arches of Spain, the word *campagna*
you smuggled from Italy and its fields of sunflowers;
is there a tilde here for Anna or Anya?
Irises stipple the hot square in passing showers,
shadows pause in the sun's capework, ornate balconies rust,
the sunlight of olive oil slowly spreads in saucers
and loaves that are hard to break have a sacred crust.
Esperanza, cherished Esperanza!
Your lashes like black moths, like twigs your frail wrists,
your small, cynical mouth with its turned-down answer,
when it laughs, it is like a soft stanza
in a ballad by Lorca, your teeth are white stones
in a riverbed, I hear the snorting stallions
of Cordoba in heat, I hear my bones'
castanet, and a rattle of heels like machine guns.

III

Suppose I lived in this town, there would be a fountain,
the tower with two storks, I called them cranes,
and black-haired beauties passing; then again,
I wouldn't be living in a posh hotel. All of Spain's
heart is in this square, its side streets shot
and halved by the August sun. The bullring would be
closed until Sundays, heat
would scorch the park benches, and there would be a lot
of pigeons hopping on the cobbles with their pink feet.
I would sit there alone, an old poet
with white thoughts, and you, my *puta*, would be dead
and only half your name would be remembered
because by then you would have lost power
over my sleep, until all that remains
is the fountain's jet. Storks on the bell tower, or cranes.

IV

For the crackle and hiss of the word 'August,'
like a low bonfire on a beach, for the wriggling
of white masts in the marina on a Wednesday
after work, I would come back and forget the niggling
complaints of what the island lacks, how it is without
the certainties of cities, for a fisherman walking back
to this village with his jigging rod and a good catch
that blazes like rainbows when he shows it to you,
for the ember that goes out suddenly like a match
when the day and all that it brought is finished,
for the lights on the piers and for the first star
for whom my love of the island has never diminished
but will burn steadily when I am gone, wherever you are,
and for the lion's silhouette of Pigeon Island,
and your cat that presumes the posture of
a sphinx and for the long, empty sand
of your absence, for the word 'August,' like a moaning dove.

V

The chessmen are as quiet on their chessboard
as those life-sized terra-cotta warriors whose vows
to their emperor with bridle, shield and sword,
sworn by a chorus that has lost its voice,
echo in that astonishing excavation.
Each soldier was a vow, each gave his word
to die for his emperor, his cause, his nation,
but still to stand still, breathlessly erect
as his own effigy that silence will select
and station like a chessman on a board.
If vows were visible we would see ours,
the way these changeless chessmen stand in the light
vowing eternal fealty to a cause
whose queen you are, vigilant through the night,
and suffering silently from love's deep curse,
that not all the clamour of battle can set right,
only the chessmen's silence, while trees toss
on the lawn outside with the music that is Time's
and vows that die and harden in their loss,
while a sable blackbird twitters in the limes.

VI

This was my early war, the bellowing quarrels,
at the pitch of noon, of men moving cargoes
while gulls screeched their monotonous vowels
in complex curses without coming to blows;
muscular men swirling codfish barrels
and heaving rice bags, who had stunted nicknames,
who could, one-handed, hoist phenomenal rolls
of wire, hoist flapping galvanise with both arms
to pitch it into the hold while hooks and winches
swung nearby. At lunch they ate in the shade
of mountainous freight bound with knots and cinches,
ignoring the gulls with their boulders of bread.
Then one would be terribly injured, one lose a leg
to rum and diabetes. You would watch him shrink
into his nickname, not too proud to beg,
who would roar like a lorry revving in the prime of his drink.

VII

When light fell on the bushes around Soufrière,
it was orderly, it named what it fell on—
hog plum and zaboca, dasheen, tannia and melon,
and between the hills, the orange and vermilion
immortelles that marked the cocoa's boundaries.
We stopped there, driving in prolonged stupor
at perfection framing itself, like the light
that named the town walls of the Marque, the shore
of the nibbling Adriatic, that made me elate
as a windblown chicken hawk, or an eagle's emblem
over Aquila, or where a hidden, guttural brook
recited 'Piton Flore, Piton Flore,' cedar, cypress and elm
speak the one language, the wind, from a common book,
open at summer. I stopped and listened to them.

VIII

We were by the pool of a friend's house in St. Croix
and Joseph and I were talking; he stopped the talk,
on this visit I had hoped that he would enjoy,
to point out, with a gasp, not still or stalking
but fixed in the great fruit tree, a sight that shook him
'like something out of Bosch,' he said. The huge bird was
suddenly there, perhaps the same one that took him,
a sepulchral egret or heron; the unutterable word was
always with us, like Eumaeus, a third companion,
and what got him, who loved snow, what brought it on
was that the bird was such a deathly white.
Now when at noon or evening on the lawn
the egrets soar together in noiseless flight
or tack, like a regatta, the sea-green grass,
they are seraphic souls, as Joseph was.

IX

I hadn't seen them for half of the Christmas week,
the egrets, and no one told me why they had gone,
but they are back with the rain now, orange beak,
pink shanks and stabbing head, back on the lawn
where they used to be in the clear, limitless rain
of the Santa Cruz valley, which, when it falls, falls
steadily against the cedars till it mists the plain.
The egrets are the colour of waterfalls,
and of clouds. Some friends, the few I have left,
are dying, but the egrets stalk through the rain
as if nothing mortal can affect them, or they lift
like abrupt angels, sail, then settle again.
Sometimes the hills themselves disappear
like friends, slowly, but I am happier
that they can come back, like memory, like prayer.

X

All day I wish I was at Case-en-Bas,
passing incongruous cactus which grows in the north
in the chasm-deep ruts of the dry season
with the thunderous white horses that dissolve in froth,
and the bush that mimics them with white cotton
to the strengthening smell of kale from the bright
Atlantic, as the road-ruts level and you come upon
a view that dissolves into pure description,
a bay whose arc hints of the infinite
and Africa. The trade wind tirelessly frets
the water, combers are long and the swells heave
with weed that smells, a smell nearly rotten
but tolerable soon. Light hurls its nets
over the whitecaps and seagulls grieve
over some common but irreplaceable loss
while a high, disdainful frigate bird, a *ciseau*,
slides in the clouds then is lost with the forgotten
caravels, privateers and other frigates,
with the changing sails of the sky and a sea so
deep it has lost its memory of our hates.

XI

My climate now is the marsh, the leaden
silver water that secretes in reeds
or moves with a monody that happily might deaden
endeavour and envy and the waste of noble deeds
for reputation's sake, my frenzy is stasis,
like a shallop with a staved-in hull.
I fly like the slate heron to desolate places,
to the ribbed wreck that moss makes beautiful,
where the egret spreads its wings lest it should totter
on the aimed prow where crabs scrape for a perch,
all that vigour finished with which I sought a
richer life to this halfhearted search.
I am thinking of a specific site
that is Hunter's Cove, away from the road
and traffic, of a marsh in marsh-light
with charging dusk and the boom of a toad
in the reeds at the firefly-flecked night
and a heaven improbably swayed in mirroring water.

XII

The nausea of horror continued as he read
and wrote and read and wrote in the iron-railed
Spanish hotel with wrought-iron pergolas
in its inside courtyard, at how often he had failed
with women, in a bullfighting town, Merida,
its ruined amphitheatre ringed with silent olés
for the flourish of his thoughts, for the self-murder
of his pitiable jealousy. Time might deliver
him of his torment, Time that had gnawed at the stone and
eaten its heart. You, my dearest friend, Reader,
its river running through reeds and lights on the river
by the warp of a willow coiled like an ampersand.

Derek Walcott

DOWN THE COAST

I looked out through the freezing window, homesick. The idea of Manhattan, the stalagmite towers, faded into the distance of fantasy. There was not a stronger contrast than that fabled, metallurgic landscape with its rivers of molten lead and this real volcano with its infernal stench. The city's fantasies were mechanical, its liturgy of titles came from the ceaseless spin of machines, of spools and tapes and meters, thousands of stories poured from it, finished and eager to be consumed. Film, reel after reel, from the intestines of the city.

I could imagine, seated in an armchair, staring at a bush for a long time until it brought me peace. Its waxen green leaves and the shadow of the leaves and that would be all of the labour, no more needed than that, for a slow joy to begin. At the edge of that joy would be the faint reek that came from the volcano, a reek with health, with the curing properties of sulphur, not the white world outside.

In the dry season the pasture turned Flemish, a spreading tree that I had painted emerald green against the burnt whitened grass burst into leaves of pale gold as tan cows moored themselves in the parched grass or moved slowly on the wide field under a blue enamel sky. Only a windmill was missing to make it as brown and dry as an old Dutch painting. Could the Dutch ancestry in me be so shallow as to recognise something some bastard ancestor knew before sailing to the West Indies? Why assert only one side of my racial mixture? Wasn't the Dutch in me as valid as the African? And my other Dutch island, Manhattan?

And in the other island, a Christmas breeze from the mountains.

The road empty and cool, with leaves tossing in gusts. The river with the waterfall. Some figure moving in the deeper part of the pool under the waterfall. Gliding, a woman's figure, clothed in weeds with spread-out black hair. The natural life around the pool. A frog.

Cameras, lamps, reflectors, much machinery brought to bear on capturing the warts of a frog or the yellow eye of a blackbird, and the instant of capture both memorializing and murdering the subject, imprisoning it in a frame. There were no huge subjects in our pathetic history, no battles; no sieges and surrenders; intimacy was the epic, the intimacy of the fable, but the fable was more grandiose than history, in its width it surveyed with the eye of the blackbird, concentrated and enlarging events by concentration.

II.

In Santa Cruz valley, in Trinidad, on a crystalline Sunday it begins to rain. The natural history of Antillean rain has obscured fleets at anchor, carried landslides that have buried whole villages, as one did in my childhood in Praslin, the drizzle that riddles the scorched steps of this mountain hotel with its view of tree-choked valleys. This drizzle is the beginning of a fable, stuttering at first then growing more eloquent in strength, in incantation, its silver net catching the trees and sheeting the hot asphalt road; it goes back to the ecstatic fear of country stores, to the smell of cocoa, of kerosene, of river mud, the smell of patois.

A frog jumps out of Basho into a pool under the waterfall where boys are screaming and leaping. We shot that in a very primal video that still caught the frenzy of their happiness.

The steady, relentless, Asiatic rain isolates an egret on a rock, then just as quickly is over like a quarrel between two lovers, leaving a huge glittering wetness and the tricklings of its aftermath. The egret is gone and the light rages at the vacancy. This is the perpetual, recurring freshness that makes at least one section of the island paradisal. Now multiply these sections.

Why did I write "Asiatic" rain, when I am writing about my island, Saint Lucia, a large rock in the Caribbean archipelago? Because I am in Taiwan, preparing a prose address, and the rain is as heavy as it can be in the hurricane season, furious and blurring distinctions. The rain brings erasure and anonymity. Hills blur, trees lose their edges, the sea is horizonless and the "I" of the ego of the writer is like a solitary, disheveled palm tree standing isolate and miserable in the Caribbean rain.

On the island, when it rains like this, when windows steam, when the vermillion blossoms on the ground blown from the flamboyants are even brighter because of the wet, when the bushes are beaded and dripping cold crystals, when the sky is sullen but beautiful like a woman you have quarreled with but instantly miss, when the doves hunt for dry places and the sea is an even grey and the hills are even lusher than this prose, I say, to my quiet joy, This is Ti-Jean country; also that no one writes like this anymore except it is Edward Thomas, whom I love and who wrote so beautifully and sadly about this rain: "Blessed are the dead that the rain rains upon." There is an almost ecstatic sorrow in Thomas that defeats despair, an incredible toughness that is pliant, like the reeds he writes about:

> Like a cold water among broken reeds,
> Myriads of broken reeds all still and stiff,
> Like me who have no love which this wild rain
> Has not dissolved except the love of death,
> If love it be towards what is perfect and
> Cannot, the tempest tells me, disappoint.

The syntax, too, has a pliant pause in its invisible parenthesis, its held breath resignedly expelled.

While I knew that myth cannot be photographed, there were things I hoped to film: the rain suddenly exploding on a hot, bright day and as suddenly vanishing, leaving only the wetness as witness, the almost imperceptible arc of a timid rainbow, the look, like a horse's hide stained by the rain, of a meadow in the drought of April, the horse's whinny, and the repetitive gallop of those breakers called "white horses."

Rain, and the threat or promise of it, lured me to the high country, *en haut*, those hazed mountains that I could see from the beach, and in those mountains was where myth and legend and fairy tale were, but not as legend or fairy tale, as real trees and even roads, and certainly steep tracks with unpainted wooden houses perched on their small cliffs, and nettles and lizards. Every corner you pushed around meant another corner and then another on the baking asphalt and the heat-stunned leaves, the wires of the heat dancing with their cynical promise, whisking themselves away like a magician's cloth, but revealing nothing.

III.

When the big ferns begin you know you are approaching Soufrière. They grow at the edge of the rain forest as you climb and clear them and take the coiling corners of the road into the town that lies on the bay at the base of the Pitons, in the cleft of mountains where the springs of sulphur give off their healing reek and where steam coils from the volcano that exploded less than two centuries ago. There is one bridge over and into the packed, dense heat of the town, along the cemetery and the coast.

It was the second town of the island, one that I feared and hated in my childhood and beyond. It felt too dominated by the peak under which it huddled; it was, in my island, a different country. To me, people from Soufrière always spoke as if they carried a shared secret, and there was arrogance in that secrecy, but after all, they lived under a geological phenomenon: the soaring horn of the Petit Piton and the two horns made by the other Piton. To wake up every sunrise and go to bed every night under its implacable rigidity, its persistence that acquired a casual and driving awe, made them souls bound to its respect in a general bondage if you were born there, but in an imitation that could become anger at their inflexible thereness if you were not. Also many were the colours of the earth they came from, red, as we called them, hazel-eyed and volcanic, and sometimes you expected from them too, especially girls and women, the soft smell of sulphur, demonically sexual, brazenly secretive.

The Pitons themselves looked as if they harboured a secret, although their harbour did not have the dramatically picturesque design of the other villages along the leeward coast, Anse la Raye, Canaries, and Choiseul before the Japanese government ruined it in exchange for whaling rights. To me the harbour felt smoky and clogged, perhaps because the two peaks contracted it, so that there was not that exhaling width of horizon that you get in the coves and bays of both coasts. The sky was full of mountains and the mountains were tumultuous with forest. In them, the tree-packed mountains, there was the smoke of fables, mist from heavy rain, and the smothering vines of African superstition. In them there were not wandering, elegiac deer horned and drifting through the bush as in northern

Trinidad, but deadly snakes, fer-de-lance (iron spearhead) and regurgitating constrictors, some of them dangled and twisting in the hands of men showing them along the road where you would startlingly see the first Piton, its rigidity a contrast to the fanged and writhing reptile.

So this was always a frontier of alarming fears: the plunge of the precipices, the hugeness of the ferns, the thought of stalking or coiled serpents, and even the eternal roar of cascades over the rocks, the mongoose and agouti all steeped in the reek of sulphur. And out of the smoke, on the steep scrabbly paths to perilously perched houses and huts, came a language whose similes and guttural melody enfolded their released apparitions, incantations repeated by the Roman church, and tunes from Guinea and the Ivory Coast. This was not a country of sane Protestantism, of Methodist and Anglican and Adventist clarity, but one of smoke and mirrors—the smoke of La Soufrière and the mirrors from rain puddles and pools.

There were few flat places, no savannahs, which meant no cane estates with their feudal order, but dark crops like cocoa with its low, tangled trees from which the motley of leaves was as varicoloured as a Pierrot Grenade and where the fruit—gold, orange, umber, and crimson—looked false and waxen and which, when ripe, had a sweet cottony interior. It seemed to me a logical habitat for a creature I feared, bats, which in their winged accuracy of dodging objects at the last second were demonic, made for and maybe by the dead. Yes, he could come, lowering his horns, under the branches, in medieval array, camouflaged, cunning as the serpent; or there was the other figure, one drawn more from the folklore of the forest of Trinidad, a Pan-like figure, horned and armed with an old shotgun and a dented bugle, who protected the deer that were not there and who could handle snakes like a wrangler, whose rumours terrified hunters—the father of the forest, Papa Bois.

Between the haunted African night and the Caribbean glare Soufrière seemed to have its own dusk, even at noon, because of the supernatural aura surrounding it. It bubbled in the cauldron of the mountains, and it grew genuinely spectral when the steam of clouds hid the Pitons. I had been driven through mist that was no longer mist but the dissolving flannel of a fog that obscured everything, pieced everything out and shrouded vision for no more than two or three feet, as if the very climate had changed, as if this were not the road to Soufrière but an autumn or spring highway in the Sussex countryside, a fog that was hiding or held the spectre of a hare, as the fog hid its natural apparitions, a soft book that opened on unclouded figures, in which the imagination, or rather memory, seethed and appeared and disappeared with this litany of specters: Maman de L'Eau, Mother of Water, mainly river and waterfall and pool; Beau L'Homme, a child caught in limbo, its feet reversed, I think; or Douens, small creatures with hats like mushrooms, also known as the devil's parasols; Loupgarou (the werewolf), Gens Gages (souls bound in service to the Devil), and Soucouyants (succubi who drank your blood as you slept, the universal vampire legend), most with their own habits and incantations.

When we were small boys, my brother and I would climb Morne Dudon hill afternoons after school (before we knew radio and television and record players) to hear stories we demanded from our great-aunt, Sidone, who bewitched us easily with the intensity of her storytelling. Just as in Jamaica the spider Anansi became the folk hero for its mockery and cunning, Ti-Jean, a little boy, Little John, was the precocious hero of French Antillean fables. This is true of the French South, of Louisiana, and of French Canada. Ti-Jean was devoutly disobedient, he trusted and obeyed his own instinct, a green anarchist who was impatient with the laws and discipline of formal debate, of the design of logic, the conventions of restrictive religion; in other words, in his aggressive innocence there was revolution, and this boyish refusal, more energetic than Bartleby's, was a prophecy of independence in the rigours and customs of the colonial Caribbean. What he felt like not doing was right. The innocence of the small black boy did not contain William Blake's plea to insulting compassion, "and I am black, but O my soul is white," because to change his life and colour never entered his mind, since he was too young for envy, but it was Blake's innocence, in the political sense, that made Ti-Jean enchanting in his defiance. You did not fight what was bigger than you, i.e., The Empire, like his bigger brother Gros Jean, who is devoured by the Devil, by the repetitive assertion of his name and identity, nor argue with what had the resources to outwit you: the courts, the classics, "culture," like his second older brother, the lawyer litigant (the attorney of small papers) Mi Jean. All these came from the smoke and the rain and the wisps of fog on the hills and the sighing wind of wide, imprisoning cane, from the factory wheel and tired men walking behind broken mules in incredibly lush valleys and their women whose bones and beauty went so fast, as fast as fog in sunshine. I knew and feared these estates and the mounted white men you sometimes saw riding among the labourers in the fields, from the country buses of my boyhood, through Roseau and Cul de Sac, past the satanic mills of the sugarcane factory. They were Catholic and hierarchical while my Methodist upbringing sang of building Jerusalem here, but not if the Devil could help it. The church encouraged such servitude for at the end of it there was reward. The landscape was already paradisal, but not to the labourer, only to two young boys, my twin brother and I, who drank in the stories and chants of Sidone, her head now heraldic and sibylline, her voice the guttural of a cave or of a blackbird possessed by its own chortling. A voice that was a landscape, an island in itself.

All this I carried in me when I came to Soufrière to add my own shapes to its mist, my own fiction to what had created it. And my brother too.

When I began the writing and rehearsals of Ti-Jean as a film, all that was mythic and fabulous had to have a new reality whose basis, more than any other craft, of verse or paints, had to be credulity. There was no more enigma or riddle but a simple arithmetic of *it is true, it is happening*. Its tense is the perpetual present. The thought of metaphor irritated it. Only simile can be filmed, not metaphor, the two halves of separate frames placed or run side by side or one after the other stops at *this is like that*, since metaphor has no conjunctions. This is where film falls short and even shrivels from poetry. A film can be poetic but it cannot be poetry. Yet that was what I was determined to do. But, again, in what language?

✦

How much of Soufrière would be left before I finished the film? Already there was a high four-story structure next to the cathedral that would change the look of the square, and who knew what else was to come? Between my irritation and the new building there was the gap of centuries filled always by a serene cerulean sky with changing clouds, but what was below the clouds—the rusting corrugated roofs, the shacks, the lanes—had not changed and had not expected to.

For more than fifteen years I had been doing detailed, small paintings for a storyboard; every painting has its own language: Dutch still-lifes speak Flemish, a Gainsborough portrait has its own accent, as does a head by Dürer or Mantegna, or a portrait by Orozco. But as I painted those miniatures, the language I heard was St. Lucian

English, ungrammatical if you choose to call its Anglicized dialect that, or maybe English anyway, with a patois echo. It was when I began to rehearse the actors in the open on a steep hillside, in a crowded rum shop, that I heard their own language, these figures I had carefully painted, the vocabulary, melody, and gesture of characters speaking in patois, not in a translation that gave or hoped to give verisimilitude to their fable. The gestures in their own language were not essentially different, but in English patois they sounded like accommodation, if not translation. But who would understand if I did not?

And here was the heart of sadness, a choice that was not merely my own but the island's, a denial that was in fact a betrayal. "Bon Dieu" was God. God untranslatable in Greek, in Creole, or in English, but the sound of "t'auoviere" (*la rivière*) for river was wider and stiller in Creole than in English, which was in St. Lucian English "der reever."

Could I paint in Creole like a Haitian "primitive," not only in subject matter but in style, in the Egyptian style of flattened perspective and iconic profile, when my drawing had been brought up in the European tradition of classical depth and matching shadow, with an unalterable sense of narrative, a scale of proportion? Inwardly from boyhood I despised naïve drawing, but how could there be associations of magic in the logical, Protestant, or Catholic delineation of devils, imps, or angels in that rational context that contradicted mystery by concentration on the real? I also despised surrealism as too literary, but so much was lost when the actor's body moved in English, as if obeying stage directions.

The stage was in fact the medium for reality even more than film, which was supposed to return what it saw without comment. We believed immediately in the fiction that was being offered by a play as we believed in the opening wings of the book, the play, we were reading. The film only pretended to frame things; everything around the frame was frameable for the camera, not only the house but the bush around the house. The lens could not restrain itself, and in this way threatened to annihilate choice. In the bush of the Soufrière landscape, it framed one possibility after another, it created luck. What it held to bursting was joy. If the lens of the camera could have glazed over with that other film which beauty in nature brings, everything it saw would have jammed its mechanism with bliss and furred and blurred what stood before us like paintings realized into smell and sound: young black boys splashing in the pool of a waterfall, the waxen pods of cocoa against a green darkness, the roll and steam of the pocked, gaping volcano, and the swift shriek of a blackbird under the trees.

Then, too besides, as the phrase goes locally, it was drought, it was a fiercely dry season. The sun gutted everything. Driving to Soufrière I could clearly see the giddying crevasses over which the parched asphalt ran, the fire trees ablaze without smoke, and the hills gone autumnal, over whose barren outlines I could hear the echo of a young black boy singing, a boy who contained all our delight, in whom we placed our aged love and our untiring hope. And again, we loved him in what language?

✦

My brother, I write you this, that even gone you nod in thorough understanding, for it was that joy which guided our work for the theatre, the songs that tenuously survive translation. And these songs not only belong to the patois-speaking Caribbean, but to certain islands and to certain districts of the islands, and then to districts of those districts, from Piaille, from La Fargue, from the different *mornes* (mountains) and different *trous* (valleys or coves, from the word "hole"), and are to be sung in their accents...

In the eye of the camera, even a common video camera, this meant that everybody in Saint Lucia, particularly in Saint Lucia, had been translated. No, not only people, but the geography that they moved in. No script I had ever written was so close to home, a home that they breathed. Schoolchildren in blue and white uniforms climbing up a mountain road, boys shouting at each other, the polite caretaker who unlocked the church and let us in—they lived a formal other life in English, but the one they knew, as organic and natural as dasheen, was Creole to the depth of every prop and improvised costume, to a mortar and pestle for pounding breadfruit, cassava bread, and the odour of kerosene. I refused parallels and sources. I would not work with references. There had been none in Eden. Not that this geography was sublime or paradisal, it was Edenic in its rawness, it was recognition and naming in the sound of patois on the verge of an estate road and in the singing, particularly songs by Sesenne, who must have been a musical sister or daughter of Sidone. Sidone was from Choiseul, from a district with its customs nearly gone, I guessed. This is not nostalgia, this is creation, this is the conflict of the present, the start for me and I hoped the actors, the beginning of a different time. Vocabulary crouched in the bushes and scurried across a long shadowed road like a mongoose, too swift to be chronicled, too fast to keep an echo like the patois vocabulary. I wanted the whole film to be in its language, with subtitles perhaps, as a Japanese film has, or an Italian opera that nobody understands.

IV

O n the stage, especially in America, I had grown so used to failure that it had become a philosophy. What I dreaded more than a succession of flops like *Steel, The Capeman,* and the mediocre versions of *Walker* and *The Ghost Dance* was the roaring, treacherous pitch of a hit which, I felt sure, would be praised for the wrong reasons and which could convince me that I was a Midas who turned bread into inedible gold. I did not want to fail, but failure had a poignancy that success did not, and a contradiction was that as a poet I hated fame, but as a scriptwriter and playwright talent was measured by wealth, by the honour of becoming a millionaire because of my exotic, that is to say my racial, achievement against their odds. On stage in the Caribbean, in Trinidad, I had worked with a company I had founded that had and produced genuinely gifted actors, several of whom were gone from both stages, the one that the world is, and the one where we had rudimentary lighting and limited runs. The one I preferred, the rudimentary one, was like the world of film, by which I mean what an American director had called the common "fried chicken" accessibility of video.

These excursions on the twisting, vertiginous drive to Soufrière brought me the elation of another vanity, that when the film came to be shot, if ever that was to be, I would delicately lift the sinuous line of the mountain range after Anse la Raye, the river with its clattering bridge that took you to Canaries, along the road where men handled constrictors for tourists, then the frightening parched crests of the road that, before the huge ferns cascaded down, showed the incongruous sign in a taming English of BELVEDERE, as if it were in some English country drive with a decent castle to come. It was a quiet happiness every time, it was a returning benediction, without delight in the sca-brous poverty of the villages, but also without anger. The beauty was inseparable from, perhaps synonymous with poverty and my sense of celebration. Was that what I wanted, this degeneracy of delight in bleached, shingled shacks, in toothless, unemployed men marinated in white rum at ten in the morning and the girls who went quickly to pot, if pot is a crude metaphor for pregnancy, and if all the poetry came from another light, another literature?

Where was William Blake among the cedars and the *pomme-aracs* and the centipedes and the stagnant rivers mantled with scum since the last century? Where were Eliot and Pasternak in the sharp tang of copra that sickened me? And who wrote with a power equal to these breath-stopping views, a single sail out in the sea beyond Canaries, a frigate bird dipping and gliding, or the history in the eye of an iguana?

Academia would make this the old Caliban jig, but the reply was in water, with or without berries, and not saltwater but abounding, cascading, deaf water that pitches from rocks, water with one relent-less metre—poetry—and that was what I had always written in, despite or because of the failure of so many productions, accusations that my dramatic verse was either poorly, or pompously, or prosaically spoken. And this was not any country's fault, neither England's nor America's, but here like the vegetation my verse could grow.

It could become a tangle with the lianas of lines, and critics like overseers could ask me to trim it into a suburban hedge, it could riot or be as still as bamboo on a windless day, and my actors understood this. I had, according to the critics, an unearned, ambitious, and imi-tative fustian, and they judged it thus without knowing the melody of its origins. They heard American and English melodies for a different music they did not care to hear, much less learn. That is why I felt such delight when these actors spoke their language. That is why the songs spring from their roots more eagerly than with the foreign failures.

But the faces! The faces of those I had chosen and those I could choose from for the film. They had never been seen before, the camera had glided or paused, thought better of it, and gone on to the moves and dancing eyes of stars; they were a background frieze to jungle thrillers or beach comedies or Bond romances, cast as barmen, fisher-men, tribal warlords, or waterfront rummies; but here were faces on which the camera could rest, creased with a different biography, here were voices hoarse with indifference to their importance, faces with incredibly hollow sockets with luggage in sacks under their yellowed eyes, and these were the old ones. But often, near enough, in a fabric store, behind a counter, even filling a gas tank with a too-priapic hose, were beauties that had never been looked at except through the glau-coma of conventional beauty. Beauties with such breasts, adoration, who carried a green whiff of bush in the sun.

They had their music, folk songs with fine Creole poetry in them, but I had to find, in English, without mimicry, and without transla-tion, a verse whose metre and vocabulary would be organic.

The ochre cuts and excavations made by machinery that was wid-ening the road to Choiseul and Vieuxfort were organic with rubble and necessary devastation because the bush besieged and often defied the backhoes and grinding tractors. Once long ago, a twisted twine road along and above the coast had been the only one, and in my youth the better way to get to the town was by motor vessel or long canoe. Now the road was interspersed with country inns and parlours and was relatively well paved, but the mountains and settlements outside the town still held secrets and superstitions. People believed in curses and apparitions, and in their fables they relished twilight and the chimerical dark. I was told stories of the reality of those creatures that Sidone had told us of on her enchanting, frightening afternoons. I remembered the gentle ecstasy of fear that hid in the rough ochre roads, and in the foetid, dangling leaves of the dark cocoa. But this magic had to be metrically conveyed in another language from which enchantment could fade, English.

I wanted these untranslated faces for the film.

The violinist Ramon Poleon had the head of an African tribal chief in a jungle movie, solemn, sharp cheekbones, and an implacable brow, almost a cliché of racial dignity, with a smile like a pension; he had thorough hands and understanding eyes, was probably humourless, but the camera would bow to him before recording him. His expression was one of instant posterity.

In boyhood the expression for traveling by boat south of the capital was "down the coast," which had its equivalent of entering the deep and calm harbour of Ramon Poleon's face now, its crags and inlets, into a reflective wisdom. "Down the coast" was an expression that seemed to come from Conrad, and indeed to go down the coast—past the ochre cliffs with their deep green chrome water on a rickety motor vessel called the *Jewel*, passing long cargo canoes loaded to the gunwales with freight and customers, to offload those customers who came off at villages that had no pier or jetty, who had to balance themselves as they were guided into canoes that came out to meet them, or load them on to the *Jewel*—was the life of the colony from a Victorian travel book, a life thick with mountain mist from always threatening rain, from forests that felt unexplored, from men in responsible petty positions with both helmets and ledgers. My politics, my aesthetics, and maybe those of the island as

well were that archaic; they were not anachronistic, they were feu-
dal. The island was divided into huge estates owned by a few inter-
marrying white families, mainly French, and that was where my
Devil, a planter, supposedly came from, except that he was British
and despised his French colonial peers.

But he still gave orders to Ramon Poleon, to my French charac-
ter, and to the workers of his estate. Imagine the distances, Reader,
even the distance between the camera and whom it photographed,
imagine the distance between my memory and this pen, between
the boy I was then and, in adventurousness, the boy that I have
remained. Blake taught us the imaginative experience of child-
hood. To lose that innocence is to become hypocritically wise, that
is, adult. The critical faculty becomes cynical and therefore corrupt.
And the cynical whores out Imagination on the basis of Necessity.
Necessity meant selling out because of necessity. To be tempted
because that is what the Devil offered and what the rock-brown face
of the country violinist refused with his small smile. That smile of
refusal, of pretended ignorance, defended its music and the soul of
its actors. If there was no such thing as a soul, then any seduction
was not demonic but sensible. It was the reasonableness of profit, of
the market. It was where my own soul resided, close to the fiddler
and the chac-chac player, and those seamed and superior faces were
the apostolic succession of a faith that my gift had to serve, that I
felt I was chosen to preserve.

As the *Jewel*, with its choleric, asthmatic engine, traveled "in
periplum" parallel to the cliffs and bushes and sometimes salt-
whitened tree trunks of the coast, its rhythm and the reek of the
exhausted engine brought such elation, of the troughs of the waves
endlessly dipping then rising again, and then the astonishing rise

and steady approach of Petit Piton, and the slow turn of the *Jewel* into Soufrière harbour.

✦

We traveled by car now—on a good but vertiginous road that she said was more beautiful than the Corniche, when in my boyhood there was no real road into the valley and town of Soufrière, which emerged late from the nineteenth century—to a forested landscape that concealed hieratic fables in a fuming crater. The island was horned and fable imbued it with African and Catholic mythology, and the mythology of Empire.

For me, then, the town was nothing, quickly ended, with a dull, didactic square in front of a small cathedral where, as a Methodist, I was unwelcome, which meant I was refused its mysteries and its rites and processional banners. Its empire was in Rome. Its architecture at its most ambitious presented tall wooden balconies with mansard roofs and fretwork, like Castries, but fewer. I had stayed in one of those. I painted even when young, and in oils. I remember doing a small landscape and running out of white that I needed for clouds and squeezing my toothpaste onto a surface, knowing that it could melt or that roaches would eat it, but I was desperate to finish the picture, a phrase that was prophetic because I was desperate to finish the picture I now wanted to make a half century later with many small paintings for my storyboard. The church, the square, and the same French colonial building at one corner of the square had not changed since the colonial days, the Conradian days of "going down the coast," the days of Empire.

There was a new Empire now, more pervasive and vainer than

the Conradian one with its Administrator in white, with his white pith helmet and its plume. Those were the days of malaria and the visions of London that had never seduced me. Of innocence and fever, of bush baths and the yellow plums, *moubains,* that fell and piled up on the side of the road, and of the sickly mortal smell of that yellow flower I still can't name that loves cemeteries.

Cemeteries simplify, and so did the one at the edge of the town with its volcanic sand and bright canoes. The town was full of emblems of fear; I felt afraid of Soufrière. It was not like the other fishing villages down the coast: Anse la Raye, Canaries, Choiseul, Laborie, and after Laborie the exhilarating, lung-cleansing sweep of the Atlantic plain of Vieuxfort, with its long rolling breakers that were born on the coast of Africa, ancestral coast of Ramon Poleon and the country musicians.

Now we had passed from one shadow to the next, as the sun slides from the Pitons into another domination, supposedly freer, more benign, but into a new abandonment. Into tourism. Into the American idea of development, into hotels that dwarfed the beaches and once innocuous inlets. What I wanted to capture was dying, and there was not even the sadness of others in that truth. On the turning road over the village of Canaries, above the postcard beauty there was now, indestructibly, an obscene tiled advertisement for AMERICAN DRY WALL, which company has since blessedly gone bankrupt. But the disfiguring sign remains and remains American because it is advertising, it is freedom in its insulting anarchy, its contempt for the landscape from which it came. The other Empire would never have done that.

Some native businessman had gone to the heart of the Empire and come back American. He had ignored the copyright of the sign and had placed his billboard over the view of the bay at Canaries, and it was indestructible. Nobody wanted to, or could, do anything about it. Not the Tourist Board, not the government. There was no prosecution for the rape. In fact, a restaurant owner whose business overlooked the beautiful riverbed saw "noffing" wrong with it. It didn't do him "noffing," it did noffing to the whole harbour or the lovely circuitous road on which you could read the sign miles off, or to the people who had not had the privileges of our new Empire, that ease with which slaves accept new masters and for whom beauty was money as greed ravished itself. American Dry Wall (St. Lucian version) had its billboard for its perpetual movie. I had none. I had nothing but the memory of my brother who wrote plays about the patois people, and the memory of our Morne Dudon sibyl, Sidone. Nothing except dark school halls where we rehearsed and the love of the names of the colony that so rapidly, so spontaneously set themselves in song.

These songs, mimetically simple but with elegant melodies, grew the way trees grew overlooking some valley or hiding some river, trees with the wind in their throats, tossing their heavy leaves in gusting rain, and containing in their noise the roar of the cascade and its demon-haunted pools. I was attending the funeral of a dialect and its customs, the faces in which they are preserved in the rock-strong features of Ramon Poleon, or the still delicate and elegant features of the singer Sesenne. The tiles of AMERICAN DRY WALL were demonic but they foretold a future before which we were help-less. The sign could have been a billboard for another American movie epic, ablaze with defiant stupidity and forgettable, until the next blockbuster.

The sign needed stars, not actors, the empire's language and accent, not patois, it advertised the capital I would possibly never raise to make my little ignorable film. Poetry, when it dies, dies very quietly, it leaves a culture soundlessly, its fatal signs being its fading prosody, its blending into the empirical, democratic universality of the Empire's market. It has its metropolis, Hollywood, and it rules the intellect of an entire archipelago. It is a dreadnought. It is not a rusty vessel going past the ochre cliffs and bush along the coast to Soufrière and the incorruptible Pitons.

Perhaps, more than the finished film, I respected the need to make it. This need was from the philosophy of failure, for, from the lack of smell alone, of burnt grass, of baking rock, of a drizzle on hot asphalt, the film could not really be made, and yet this is true of all that we make, even those things we consider perfect, poem or painting or movie. These are better when they contain jolts and twinges of their own death, which our more immortal poems and paintings contain, and which is in the small, dark interior of the pews and altar of the cathedral of Soufrière, and in the sunlit, musty smell of a café in the empty afternoon.

So, what touched and slid up the walls of shacks and houses and unopened shops in an alley at sunrise, in its silence and in the humility of its radiance, was love. It was love that had or has endured so long, beyond my brother's passing and Sidone's, in the patterned shade of a calabash tree in the old dirt yard of a house near the streaked stones of the cemetery, a pattern of shadows that only changed when the sun changed its angle, and one that had lain dormant as the volcano, a joy that kept shooting its steam exultantly from the fissures of a heart that had cracked often but one that was seamed and whole with a steady happiness looking at the small hot town below me and the rain-packed mountains above the town so crowded with leaves and stories.

V

And oh, oh I could have done so much! We could have set out in the pearl light of predawn when the trees are still heavy and black and even by the shoal coves of Tapion Hospital you could hear the sea before you see it, and when you see it, after months away in a foreign season, it is happily the way you knew it—the waves coming in behind a coconut tree, thick, flourishing trees whose names you never learnt, a delicate, colourless sky that soon ripens with light. We would have set out in the Rover or the Suzuki, anyway a country car to catch the first hour of daybreak in the still dewy country, passing a silent man with a felt hat and boots and a haversack cradling his cutlass, the whole country in his eyes, in his formal, joyless greeting, sharing the daybreak with his pothound perpetually on a scent, at this early hour when everyone is kind, traveling evenly on the empty road up through the big ferns of the Barre de L'isle, and if it is the season, the orange detonations of immortelles, towards some intimate and remote location, into Papa Bois country.

But the film will never be made; still reality was not confirmed by the camera; rather it evaporated. The pearl-pale morning could not be completely recorded by the camera, not with the smell of the salt shallows or the leaves; its light did not move over the skin of your hand like the sun.

From the hospital window, as the light strengthened, I saw the bay with the yellow and green bungalows of the hotel cresting a small promontory, the deepening blue sea with the small triangles of sailboats leaning on the wind, and, moving motionlessly on the horizon, the sunlit hull of a tanker under puffy tinted clouds, and two men, still silhouettes gliding in a flat canoe. Then, through the window of my side bed the day developed its heraldic blaze, moving from convalescent to radiant health the weather of my paradisal fable.

We needed at least a million to make the film.

I knew how to paint this. I had been trying to paint all my life, from the days when I went out with my small equipment, out into the open, the lilac and purple bush near the ochre rocks at low tide and the curl of a lime-green breaker between rusty sea almonds, the inflexible purple line of the horizon, the comforting turmoil of massive cumuli, bleached canoes, and beating gulls, and the red shortcut in the hills where a mother lived with her three sons.

From a clear sky rain began to fall. Through the wires of silver drizzle the view was speckled with the tentative then surrendering sunshine. This was the weather of the film's country too, in the thick forests behind and above Soufrière.

To be up this early was to be forty or fifty years younger in the early manhood of the island and the lightening predawn smells that went with that, the first silken breeze and the first blue coming out of the thinning dark. The palm fronds defining themselves.

First the rain fell, or rather the drizzles in fine looping veils through which you could see the leaves fading and darkening until all the trees were this general blur, and as your skin cooled, it was as if the change of the temperature of your skin was a change of time and you were, but without longing for it, a boy.

Everything I saw in that first light said "Ti-Jean." The grapefruit stacked like cannonballs in their ceramic bowl blazoned the name. This was the other boy's voice that breathed warmly in my ear, "Make me. Make the heights at sunrise, make it very cold and the yam leaves beaded with dew or drizzle, make a frog leaping into a grove of dasheen, and make the church cold and closed."

VI

Afternoon in the harbour, the high white liners moored, flecks of buildings from the dark-green Morne, and behind the Morne the deep country under those serrated indigo peaks where the country music and the country fables hide under the yam leaves and in the harlequin-tatters of ripe cocoa. If you went now the road would be empty and hot, with jagged shadows, and some crazed car would tear past you with suicidal speed but the small brown streams that you would pass, all of them called rivers in Creole, no matter what their size, would look serene and as inaccessible as boyhood under a hard blue sky with inviolable white clouds. Names sing past and more names are coming. They are coming with the memory of kerosene lamps with their bright brass shields, coming with the smell of codfish in dark pungent shops, a female smell, coming with a language that has all its odours: of hanging onions and crocus bags full of who knows what from wherever. All Ti-Jean territory.

✦

The plunge of memory into Soufrière. We finish with the nineteenth century before we can make room for the modern, finish with narrative before we can be moved by abstraction; and better to be there, with the young illiterate faces with wide white eyes hungry for stories that terrify and delight in their terror, in the immortal enchantment of fables that the battered heart yearns for.

On the lawn the flowers fallen from the cedar are scattered like snow, the asphalt scorches and in some places melts, as we head out for high country, *en haut betassion.*

The drive around the dry, foam-based cliffs was exhilarating in the wind that came straight from Africa, passing bare thickets from which you heard the monotonous valve of the ground dove. This was my season, a multihued aridity from which sparse bush took colour—red, orange, yellow, rust—where fallen branches or even remaining ones were poised to crackle, its barren peninsulas scorched above a sea whose blue looked as if it could stain your hand.

VII

So the basics of drawing come from the fresh snow, defining roofs and window-ledges, peaked water towers and also the half-erased blur of the river and the scumble of the Jersey shore.

To have kept the story in me so long, longer than the grey sky has hoarded the snow, for over fifty winters, is more remarkable because there is no winter where the story comes from, only eternal spring, green as the fable as I look out at the first snow of the year, at the painted city, defined, like blank pages, but blurring now. Defined by the white spaces left on the paper or the canvas.

The powder along the windowsills, the grey stretched sky, birdless because of the cold, is all fairy-tale décor with Christmas approaching, and this same fairy tale of white-dusted streets and white tablecloths stretched on the roofs is the one told in the hot green islands, of benign snow and sleigh bells and roasted meat and ham glazed and studded with cloves and the fifes and drums of the masquerade dancers and the Devil, a black Santa Claus bellowing his chants with his speckled molasses imps responding. These silent sounds come out of the snow that has made a Christmas card of Greenwich Street.

Across the piled snow, the cold grey river and the sunlit flecks of the Jersey shoreline, down the serrated coast then across the Gulf is the island, incredibly green and sunlit with wood smoke moving with the same leisure as smoke from the winter chimneys or the bubbling volcano's steam.

Film cannot capture odours but I still hoped that everything would have its natural fragrance, in bloom and in decay; the old, unpainted wood of a small house in the heights, the sharp morbid smell of lilies off a track in the rain forest, mulch and rot and compost, the staining smell of varnish, the stinging odour of salt fish from the dark recesses of a country shop, the smell of blue soap, of spilled kerosene, of a stale mattress. I wanted all those to come off the skin of the film, to be its sweating body.

As for the credibility of the fable, its spirits stood at the edge of fantasy, not completely actual on manifestation, but dim in the then-fog of bewilderment and uncertainty, unfinished hallucinations, unformed fears, like when the ceremonies of an epoch are passing and sublime terror fades into literature, winged demons, and angels. This is when great literature comes, before doubt goes into eclipse with that radiant twilight that is the climate of Dante and Shakespeare, when the hinges of belief swing slowly open or shut, when the gods become anthropomorphic and men have hallucinations of divinity.

The central dilemma is where to place things, and that causes the distress. The things that are placed here—a bush, a fence, rocks in the sea—are placed here to be found not as at the end of a search, but to be regarded newly, not with their given names until they have earned those names; yet even when they are found and renamed with the same name they suggest that a new syntax be designed for them, another melody than the one they are named as. And, after that, where to place them? In film, which is odourless, which cannot carry the smell of wood smoke or the stagnant odour of a ditch or the fragrance of a warm drizzle on the hot sea, not to mention the smell of yams and *pomme-cythères* or a girl's neck? In paint, where there is no motion? In prose? In poetry? Always missing is that other thing which might have concluded meaning and which I suppose is life itself. The smell one wants is not of immortality, which is art, but of mortality, which is life.

In the meantime time races, jumping like a cricket on the wing, like a speedboat in the bay, as fast as clouds, and before you can halt it in the stasis of art, film, painting, poem, photograph, you are now a truly old man, and your young actors are no longer children but growing boys, their treble voices breaking, on the verge of shaving, "smelling their pee" as the saying goes, and the film recedes further and further, like a sail on the horizon or, more solidly, the tanker in the roadstead that fades into a phantom. And the year goes by and there is no sign of the money, and your yellow notepads fill up, like this one, with the sound of one perpetual groan, over twenty years of one infinite lament.

There is a lot more. This will be, might have been, may forever still be a film, a movie about a little black boy on an island who accepts a challenge from the Devil and outwits him.

You have to change your life. You have to give up the cowardice of safety, its nocturnal and matutinal fear and yield to the film. Yield? With what?

Everything is there waiting, ripe and innocent and bridal. No, the sexual parallel is silly. There is nothing anthropomorphic in the thick mountains and the hot roads and the fierce fire-coloured trees.

Do not metaphorise them, the palms and the hot pebbles on the road or the curve you take that plunges to the sea along the cliff's edge. Or the stink of sulphur, the dances of evil, and the spirits that wait to be called onto the set for the happy screams of your children once, but now for your grandchildren.

VIII

Since there is no such thing as reality, I found myself living in two fictions. One of the film, continuing to manufacture itself without money, the other of perpetual preparation that seemed only to end with death, my actual death or the slow dying of a dream.

There was an equivalent noise in the orchestration of the thick vegetation, an unheard harmony in the breadfruit's broad, operatic arias, the plunging, plangent lament of wind-tossed bamboos, the mute drumroll of a packed mango grove, the wind instruments of varicoloured cocoa. They were mutely deafening and always in the head. One woke to the unrolling of their thunder down leafy slopes, to the thrum of their woodwinds crossed by the bamboo flute of a bird or the scraping rasp of a chicken hawk, and the *shac-shac* of uncoiling snakes. It is to such eternal music that my daydream might die, and I was running out of breath to keep the lowering flame of a bonfire alive.

The open orange beaks of the ginger lilies were twittering "Make me, make me" to my clattering portable, and to the video camera "Take me, take me," as children used to do before the camera became common. The dry brush whose name I knew once put out its fall colours in the dry season, and our two seasons passed year after year, and all the sites and locations that I knew were common to the camera now, with the mystery and magic going out of them by repetition, which is the aesthetic of the Tourist Industry. The waterfalls were common and the trails, the volcano peaks became a logo, leaping from the postcard to videotape to a beer advertisement. The stories from a faded Africa were being forgotten. The ones who tried to preserve them were the country musicians, and I have already described the sculpted head and the bearing of one of them.

There were so many simple but exhilarating things to shoot. Do Ti-Jean crossing a river like the one below the rattling Canaries bridge with women beating clothes on the stones of the banks, and for the sake of joy let one or all of them be singing, or let the river be in wilder country, with its sand shoals and clogged vegetation, and let the women doing laundry, as you once saw, have their breasts bared, brown as the river in their nakedness. There aren't many real rivers, mainly streams and none moving that fast, but with luck, in certain places you might find one, and you'd camp there with the camera and do the boy crossing the river again and again to his challenging encounters. All in the somnolent glitter of the afternoon.

✦

Outside my bedroom's glass doors is the sea. Waves crest, whiten and break into spray and the spume dissipates and so many connected with the work have gone the way life does, the way that the light and the spurning wave does, pierced for an instant, or for the length of a song by Sesenne. On video I look at the transient beauties of the chorus dancing—long-limbed, supple, and elegant, with different features but each heraldic, French-African or straight African, Congo or Guinea, with an exultant Sesenne singing in Creole and the banjo ringing, the drum thudding its heart out, the country whine of the violin and the chac-chac like a steady rattle of cicadas.

Music pierces the membrane of their race, the colour that damns them from birth in the great cultures of a distant world, categories that make this a black film, therefore second-rate, a West Indian film, therefore third-rate, a St. Lucian film, therefore fourth-rate. But music dissolves this faster than poetry. Sometimes on Sundays, the whole country sang:

> He rose a victor from the dark domain
> and he lives forever with his ..... to reign.

The word I could not remember was not *sins*, but it fitted and produced a horrifying vision of a triumphant resurrected Lucifer, not of Christ. Besides, the hymn was Protestant, and nothing could be less Protestant or tighter than the small family in their small house in the hills, surrounded and besieged by their superstition and the doxology of saints. There was another vision, this time from Revelations: "Behold a pale horse," the Planter was its rider, a white man as pale as his horse, who owned the land around the hut, an expatriate Englishman of great firmness and delicacy, perhaps as consumptive as Keats, not a fire-breathing demon unless he had to go to work, which was to terrify his tenants. But in that fear was faith, a faith as far away as Africa was, and in Sidone's urgency to frighten us was that will to strengthen our faith. And both are gone now, Sidone as the teller, my brother as the listener, and while the light rises and dies over Soufrière, my task as their witness.

✦

My brother was dead and I had to think about my own dying, and I didn't think that I would have minded dying in Fond D'oux, Sweet Valley, with the flamboyants and immortelles in bloom, those flame trees that were planted as boundary markers on the cocoa estates, with the steady murmur of wind in the hill trees, and, leisurely circling, a few hawks. My brother loved them and wrote about them. And I don't know where we got such a furious love for these country simplicities except it was from the hymns and Collects of our Sunday services, because my mother did not go out into the country, but we loved it more than if we had been raised there, in Choiseul or D'Eau Baignant or a place we came to love late: the country outside Soufrière. But I felt that one could fade into death as easily as a leaf or as a rain puddle on a drying road.

I would lose smell, touch and sight and taste, like him.

The smell that, in the afternoon heat, the vegetation gives off: a smell of mould, smouldering, and if a sudden drizzle sprays the scorching asphalt, the smell of a flatiron singeing sprinkled laundry. He had wanted to make films too, and had written several scripts.

✦

Sometimes a dull light covered the countryside, as if the fabric of the fable was being washed out, and as if faith in it were rapidly and permanently fading, and when the simplest thing to do was to surrender enthusiasm like the sun. The asphalt was grey, the leaves seemed juiceless, either there was no sky or there was all cloud and endeavour felt colourless. That was the falsely benign climate of despair beginning, then one felt like praying for a little light to hold and for the march of radiance to resume, for the sun.

All that freshness would go out of the country. A different breeze as cool as air conditioning would blow across those vertiginous peaks that would slowly diminish in stature, in awe, and become backdrops to vehement, emphatic verticals: telephone poles, billboards, hotel structures, until the more important the primal wilderness became to development the farther they would recede into their local names, into flashes of desperate, despairing memory.

✦

I wanted to make its poetry flash like light off a buckle, like lightning flashes in broad daylight, without melodrama or a storm-threatening, brooding climate of evil, but open and free-striding strokes like little leaps of joy.

Then, disastrous news. The production has jolted to a halt. Too much money to make it even in 16mm. Less turmoil and in fact suddenly calm, at the end of March, at the edge of April, perhaps a new peace. A broad spring day in New York, cool light and the silence of the river from the apartment window. Temporarily, maybe, a promise: You don't have to keep scrounging and mentally hoarding for the film which is fading from the fantasy of being made. An interval of release, but longing whispers at the edge of the paper, You can't give this up. But I was grateful for the respite provided by disappointment.

But it was as if I always knew it, certain as death yet inexact; the script proceeded brokenly, flashing and petering out like a fever, or like the fever-coloured cocoa pods of the Soufrière estates, the motley and mockery of harlequins. I could feel my disenchantment like an

invisible badge as I walked through the streets of the Village or stared
from the wide glass of the window with its view of the river.

✦

Those streets that I had photographed, that vibrated in their vid-
eos, were fading with patience even if I had silently promised them
that I would come back with costumed actors and cameras, waiting
like women for an impossible consummation because there was no
money for that dowry and the money was too much. So one Ti-Jean
grew too tall and his treble broke and his innocence hardened help-
lessly as the months passed and certain blocked and planned set-ups
changed because something new—and anachronistic because it was
new—was built there, a shop from concrete blocks instead of wood, a
bus stop. The town of Soufrière was spreading outward like a vine, not
smothering things but clearing and consuming them, and I wanted
to halt time. The road to Vieuxfort widened into a highway, the forest
around it grew decent and understandable, little mystery left in it, and
sometimes billboards jumped out of the bush, startling you with their
fixed leer. The whole island might go that way.

Before it went, like Sidone's features, into forgetting, went with
the full-moon-lit nights of ghostly banana leaves and phantasmal fire-
flies (*bêtes a feu,* beasts of fire) into ordinary night, taking the sweet
terrors of childhood with it, I could be too old, too tired, to commemo-
rate it, the horned island.

Here he was at 77, an age at which directors were resigned or
dying, or resigned to dying, still hoping to make his first film as if he
were some unpredictable genius of 27. He had the disease, diabetes,
enough to intuit mortality daily, but he had the hopes and zest of that

twenty-seven-year-old. But now, daily also, hopes dimmed and the look of the island faded. New proportions shrank its intimacy. Hotels sneered, shortcuts were asphalted, the sense of discovery thinned.

✦

September 5, 2007

The ember fading at sunset into the horizon was my zeal, shrinking helplessly into night, from which other embers, the emerging stars, were little consolation, just distant echoes of my hope.

I thought the realized film would have made this preface superfluous, obsolete, but it serves its purpose, the preservation of the memory of an ambition, a prolonged dream. ♦

Edwin Frank

DECEMBER

1.

A heatwave in December. Blue
Luminous field of vision
Where the eye moves, dispossessed and possessed,

And you,
And the river, wide,
Almost in spate, and the tall

Black cedars, their broad
Pluming branches that front
The far cliffs, *contre jour*,

The whole cargo of dazzle
Turns too.

2.

This
Parenthesis in
The weather: the heather
Still pungent, the bees
Still busy about
Its pinched flowers—

        All blindly
Determined, enthralled,
As love is or
As justice—

      We meet
Stopped at the threshold
Of recognition, we meet
As always such bare

Figures of speech
Still trembling and
On guard.

3.

The accident of things: not what one had
In mind. Yet the flawed
Edges caught
In the daily combustion of light
Will flare, remain
Glamorous as
The singular tokens of
One past.
      (Outposted
Yucca, on the red
Hills, its handsome
Corolla of spikes,
Its creamy blossoms
So heavily perfumed
They stank; the neither
Ash nor silk
Of the empty wasps' nest held
In hand.)
      But who

Can believe it in fact?
—That the record might be
Made good in the damages
Sustained, preserve,
In spite of ourselves,
Some intimacy of
Conception won
From loss.

4.

But where a line is
A field opens, and they,
As if newly engendered
While we were looking away,

Cross over.
      Full-grown
Already, decked
Ostentatiously out
In loud
Chains, furs,
And whatnot—who are they?
Shamans? Big chiefs?
Pop singers? Perhaps
Nouveau-riche buccaneers?
But they have severed connection,
They have slipped aside now
Into elsewhere.
      We watch,
And they, who have fallen
Silent or gone
Too far now to hear,
Move off farther, grown vague,
Though in sight still, and yet
Ever more undefined,
Ever less anyone,
As they continue across
The small field of their common

Observance. Then stop.
They pick up something
And then they put it back down.
Then they move on as before.

5.

Then here, as it happens,
One is,
    Half-

Recognizing the other,
Like the unlikely brilliance
Of the winter sun in the woods,
Or the sparse grass sprouting
Up through cracks in the tar.
You put one hand on the wall

And it stays there. They stay.
Sheepsilver.
Muscovy glass. The lost names,
The abandoned uses, the common
Burden of the ground
We turn (one hand
Brushing the hair from the eyes)

Away from
       (Though what
Is it, goes on
Digging and keeps
Digging, turning the leaves up, the grass,
The dirt, to find
What? A lost shoe,
The taste of lime upon lips)—

Too much or
Too little. What's left
In any case is
Excessive:
       The shelved
Volumes of earth's
Parsimonious annals,
Its shuttered promiscuous core.

FALL

1.

Blue-eyed and brown
Hidden in shadow
Fall—
     Fallen
Gold gathers
Under the trees. What are
Their names? or those
Of the small birds flitting
Back and forth among the branches, in
And out, as quick
As flame, as sharptongued?

Why sparrows. Sparrows.
They were never juncos to me.

Blue-eyed
Hidden in shadow, you watch
Your birds plunder,
Your trees squander
The gold that gathers
As it falls to rise,
Kindling, into the air—

Your brown eyes also—

And the sky's single blue flame.

2.

Until
Sun drops, wind gathers
Cloud, hauling it off

To the beach, vague
Liminal zone
Called strand caught

Between here and there,
Coming and going,
Between and between—

Old dump:
Fish-hooks, heads,
And bones, clamshells,

Shoes bogged down in the sand
You turn
Away from, back

Toward dunes, push through
Dense undergrowth, skirt
Poison ivy, nettles,

And briars, to pick
Bittersweet for its bright
Red berries and bay

Laurel for its little
Puckered ones, like moons.
Orange sky.

No moon.
A fire-ring and
A beach-chair flipped on its side

In the white sand of the clearing
You enter, arms full,
And stop.

3.

Dark. It's cold,
With a sense of oldness about
The narrow wood-paneled hall—
                              Fall

Ends
    (In such
A vacation house

In the off-season, vacated,
With only a birch tree ghosting
A window's flawed glass,
And the sound of lakewater, churning,
Of the boat that knocks at the dock)—

Though there is someone who stands
There still, back turned,
Head bent towards a match,
And the other one who,
Hidden in shadow, holds back

Still waiting—who was it?—
Wanting to be in the dark.

ADDENDA

The something, the always
more to say
that remains to say,
to unsay, to gainsay

(forgotten
moonscape dwindling
to nothing in
the expanding

universe of
regret, which is where
one begins in the end
once more, in the facts

remaining).
Fall of night
and break of day.
Black on white

reversible
page of characters
like trees in snow
uphill, and down come

the hooded scavengers
slipping among them
stripping the bodies clean.

SENTENCES

1.

In the no place of your birth
there were only imperatives,
only the judgment already passed—

but who were you then
standing in place there
and watching, as from an ever greater remove,

as one stands for example
in the doorway waving
to the friend who departs

before turning away then
a little impatiently even—
who were you, ever,

if not I?

2.

As my body,
come into its own, extends itself
in activities, labors

to expend itself, finds
words growing, complete
sentences, subject, object, predicate, demanding

attention, becoming
indispensable till
they in turn,

fulfilled, dispense
with it, are done
with it, leave it

alone again, crying
for help, food, love,
exhaustion once more.

3.

Somebody else comes out to stand at the door
and see what there is to be seen:

hot summer night, the great trees,
shadows sweeping the street.

Lorri McDole

AS PATIENT AS DEATH

It's late and you've just finished watching a movie with your husband; you're tired but can't resist flipping to the news. You never used to watch the news, before you had children. Back then the world was as small as you wanted it to be: you were magic and could disappear, just like that. Now that you're a family, a bigger target, you *have* to watch—for protection, for ammunition. Now everything affects you.

You watch mindlessly for a minute, the noise on mute, and then up pops a picture of a boy, 19 maybe; old enough to be a man, but really just a boy. He's beautiful, someone's son, lost too soon (you know what pictures on the news mean), and you can't *not* watch for the same reason that other parents can't not watch: there's pain out there, and right now it isn't yours. Children are being lost, but tonight, yours are safe in bed. You purse your lips, shake your head, and turn up the sound.

While the reporter talks about the boy, you watch as his life flashes before your eyes. There he is in his volunteer fireman's uniform, there he is graduating from high school, there he is looking like he's got a lifetime left to live. You're a student of literature, collecting quotes like you used to Bible verses for prizes at church, and you search the boy's face, looking for "the fatal flaw, that showy dark crack that runs through the middle of a life," as Donna Tartt put it. You think how "destiny is not what lies in store for you; it's what is already stored up inside you—and it's as patient as death," according to Geoff Dyer. But this boy's face is too young for cracks; in *this* case, death has proved not to be patient at all. You look for reasons, portents of doom—anything you can salvage from this boy's story that will help keep your kids safe.

Now a balding, round-faced man is talking, the boy's father. With tears on his face, he hugs a friend at the funeral and says all of the things you expect a parent to say—such a loss, so much to live for—and then this: "The sad thing is, this is someone who never did anything wrong. This is a kid who had it all figured out." It's the punch line you've been waiting for: that not only will you never know what your kids have figured out, no one (not you, not your kids) will ever really have it figured out. That the distance between living and dying may be a lifetime of luck or, as in this case, the moment it takes to swallow a pill at a party. You already know this, of course, but you go through life looking for these epiphanies, little capsules of words *you* can swallow that will help you slip, once again, down the rabbit's hole.

But this story isn't over, because now the father's name appears on the screen and suddenly you're leaping out of your chair, sending the cat and your husband's heart skittering.

"I know that guy!" you yell. "I went to high school with him!"

Your husband pulls you down on the couch to comfort you, but you shrug off his sympathy. You're not thinking about the boy anymore, nor even the father (you didn't, after all, know him that well; he was a jock in school, while you were a brain, and you've only seen him since at high-school reunions). Now you're thinking about your friends and, mostly, yourself—at 18 and 23, 30 and (can it be?) 40. How you've all done stupid things over the years—driven drunk, tried some drugs, gone out with too many of the wrong guys—but were going to live forever anyway. How you've weathered the occasional shock of hearing about those who *haven't* (Lila and Wen and Rhonda). How you've gone from being old enough for peers to die to being old enough to have children who die.

But looking at this man on the screen, whom you knew but didn't really know, what grabs you by the throat and won't let go is how shocked you are that you didn't recognize him. How you can't believe that you are as old as him, that you might *look* as old as him. How you can't believe that you are old.

And you know that this is *your* fatal flaw, *your* destiny: you won't ever be able to untangle your fears for your children from your fears for yourself. You won't be able to stop them from getting old enough to die or stop yourself from dying. You know that's one magic pill you'll never find, even if you spend the rest of your life looking for it.♦

Carol Moldaw

NARCISSI

I like simple flowers best—
the mason jar of daffodils,
tin of mock orange, crock
of purple tulips carried in
the crook of a friend's arm.

I give ornate arrangements
to the nurses, to brighten
their station down the hall,
but the lilies' Lysol stench
infects the whole ward.

While tulips bow to exalt
survival, narcissi coxswain
the skiff of staples rowing
my stomach's fresh fault line—
nothing to do with birth.

Easier, at three, to imagine
bubbling up from nowhere
than from another mother's
tummy. "Can we pretend,"
my daughter asked, sliding

toward me in the tub. *Yes,*
if we know we're pretending.
Now, at six, bringing me
a poster-board get-well card,
she takes in my ratty hair,

backless gown, machine-
tethered wrist, oxygen tube
I'm scared to do without,
and keeps to her father's lap
until, sighing like a teenager

giving up her iPod, I bury
my IV and rip out the tube.
Closer, I breathlessly coax.
Whoever thought about
croaking? Not now, not me.

TORN SILK

for Janis (1958–2005)

Pearls set in bird bone
Ashes kneaded into clay
The sound of tearing silk
A dog trotting away

Women—especially beautiful ones—
hardly ever shoot themselves,
but the shot went clean through
leaving your looks so intact
Kimi thought you were sleeping off
a bender or some sleeping pills
until the line of blood in the crack
of your mouth led to a red
pillow under your fanned hair
and then the tacky feel of blood
her own shoes were tracking everywhere.

Ashes kneaded into clay
Stamped with a double wheel
A dog trotting away
The wind in a sudden whirl.

Your boyfriend heard the shot
but thought the stack of pots and pans
that you had washed had fallen
off the overladen dishrack, and he
spent the day hiking, hoping to avoid
another fight. But newly dead,
hovering, you know our reasonings
while we can only guess at why
you lit death's acetylene torch
once and for all burning off
the dross of need, sheen of strength.

Stamped with a double wheel
To help you on your way
The wind in a sudden whirl
A basket's coiled weave

We used to idle on the washed-out
riverbed's palimpsest of the river's
drifting course, tossing sticks
against the current, shaking off
misleading men like mislaid earrings,
the same mishegaas, swapping
prophetic dreams like raw gems
sifted from the silt of sleep, not once
suspecting the stealth bomb ballooning
in Bruce's brain, your life together
collapsed in the ruin of a synapse.

To help you on your way
Pearls set in bird bone
A basket's coiled weave
The sound of tearing silk

THE LIGHT OUT HERE

Our life looks trivial and we shun to record it.
                              —EMERSON

Looking up "taxidermy" this morning
in the same edition of the American Heritage
that you gave me, I saw a word
bracketed and asterisked in bright red ink,
something neither of us would do,
not even with a light pencil. My guess
is that whoever marked up "taphonomy"
had been browsing in *Moonlight Gems*,
where last week I found a fossilized shark tooth
for Sarah. Knowing so many writers
come here to work, like prospectors
sifting the same riverbed, I find myself
blocking out the clear golden light,
the freight train's honking baritone.

Instead, I brood, on the severed deer head
we found last fall, the fire five years ago
that cut an S-pattern through our field,
leaving tufts of grass untouched
amid wide swathes of char.
Things I haven't managed to get to,
like the pair of hummingbirds Sarah found
in the screened porch—iridescent,
green-gorgetted. ("One sad, one green,
one dead," she proclaimed.) I remember,
the female was crushed under an overturned tin tub
while the male had one perfect wing laid out
as if waiting for its Dürer. "Black-chinned,
not Calliope," you said, correcting me
as you passed the field guide: "I'm sure
they'll be in both our poems." Perhaps.

A bird may be as many different birds
as it has observers, but an image
can ossify in no time, and my birds
languished, quarantined in a quatrain.

But what I started out to tell you is
that the only javelinas I've seen so far
are in a curiosity shop's window,
fronting a display of black sombreros.
Two of them, as if trotting in place,
each on its own rock slab, one
not very convincingly baring its fangs.

Lloyd Van Brunt

*Oh hell Gus. I might as well type the poem here. I despise computers,
including the one I'm using. I'll probably die of apoplexy some day when I
have to check "OK" when I don't mean O.K. Of course, this poem was not
meant to be anti-American but anti-jingoistic.*

THE CANDOR OF JESUS

I watch school children taught the same old lies.
I watch them abused, I watch them "unitized."
I listen while two ugly redneck teachers
Shout at a second grader until she shakes.
Sobbing will do you absolutely no good.
They want the *you* in you, child, nothing held back.

And I say nothing, I'm the poetry man.
I say welcome to the world, kid, welcome to the world.
Learn to be an oppressor, not to be oppressed.
Get used to injustice, get used to pledging
The Stars and Stripes, a flag represents power.

You must "cross your heart and hope to die"
For the 13 soldiers killed yesterday—
Whether in Iraq or Afghanistan
The 3900 will never walk again
A long white beach with a wife or husband,
Or wake in a bed
Sleepy and warm and mussed with sex,
Sip a little coffee and make small talk
That is not small at all
To the only person to whom you can tell
What's hiding in your heart.

Yes, cross your heart and hope to die
For this one nation, "indivisible."
The asshole who wrote it meant to confuse you.
And forget about the candor of God Almighty
In his incarnation as Jesus Christ,
God at his most merciful.
That's the part of him they call a loser.

I sit in Moscow's cemetery
By the grave of Sophia Andreovna
And stare at her ringlets of auburn hair
Until I think she's caught me out.
Her hazel eyes accuse me of living
While dying is all she knows about.

*Gus, the last stanza might come as too much of a surprise, but it's not
uncommon for Russian children to be beaten to death. As the old chief said
in* Little Big Man, *that is all I have to say.*

Christopher Cahill

THE COARSE AIR

for Jim Jacobs

Such brevity, and the long slow decline
    from it, the evershining genuine impulse
lit still (how else?) but distant now, so distant
    that an instant's turn to look back towards
its little light, lamp in a wood of words and urges,
    hauls the heart up short, a halt that verges on pain
so sharp is the loss it offers, and again brings to mind—
    to the body itself, really, all of it, nerves wound through
the length to the tips and edges, blue blood coursing
    across the brain, the breast, the wrist, versing the system
(leaf, branch, and stem) in this moment's carryings on—
    and again summons, then, if that's better,
a rush of images, rushes, still, in motion, bitter, toxicant,
    deluding, silencing, of such a silence one can't do more
than stop, stunned, before them, after. In the end,
        of course, it all backs
    up, clotting the mind with what it's known—the facts,
        the lies, the dim
undone enactions, the sacrificial, grim, uplifting throbs of pleasure
    or humiliation—all this swells, dropsical, hiatal, the
        cincture tightens
and the weight of light which thought to brighten to
        preserve even something
    at least of this distends till it weighs nothing and is gone.
Before it does, before it's done, what else is there to do but take
    the moment "simply for the moment's sake" and nest within
the traces spun from all the time you've moved among before. Cup
    hands and sip from what's still falling, particles and free
complectionary flakes of air. Allow the day to gather
    or deliver—along with peregrines and double-tailed
swallowtails, *sauza añejo*, chain-winches, flash flood
        rubble, heat lightning,
    giardia, and road signs promising an ever greater distance yet
to go with each mile traveled—a set or suite of photograms

on cerebellal Cibachrome, a colored flood of thought
        that stems from long
unthought of lingerings, winding me from the
        pathrailing shadows in St. Stephen's Green
    sometime almost late in 1969 to the ceiling's present
        clean reflected shadowy
reflection: a row of balusters (wild pomegranate flowers
        that rail my balcony) filmed
    on the meltwater spread thin away from the stopped
        drain then cast
by the sun upwards and inside to rest and rustle above my
        head like ordinary Venetian
    light: the splay of it somehow calling to mind a girl
        in an ultramarine sweatsuit—
legs tucked neatly away for this my first look at her
        beauty, bright polish on her bare
        toenails, bright black hair,
mysteries of persistent desire, of despair even—
    who even as I write these words has or well might
have her crampons set lightly into the frozen waterfall
        at Ouray, Colorado, the tall ladderless
flume of ice she climbs like a ladder, less intent
        on the helmeted head of it, the downbent plume
at the crest, than on the momentary fume of air
        she's stencilled against just now, black hair tucked
under her stiff blue polartec cap, a just-fucked look
        softening the lines of her fine face (the book I wrote about
her so far out of her mind now I could have written
        it on water), consummate cheekskin bitten by wind,
            in her mouth a coarser breath
of air than what I breathe. She's working. My mind's a slate.

A mound of earth outside the Roman gate
        at Arles; a doddering sunsmitten sunflower on a
            roadside near Elizabeth,
New Jersey; a bout of flies above a hidden body,
        copperplating its unwritten
    epitaph on the air of Hole-in-the-Rock Trail or Lookout
Mountain; and this: one stone stacked on another until the stook
        cambers in the ancient midday glare, a fresh deity licked
dry by light, a stone mushroom grown by hand and left there
        as though to show a god sprent from this desert hot
            as the Western Cwm

with its windless radiant fields of snow, its coruscant
        sidereal embankments: the mind that dispossesses
itself so steadily under time might stay faithful
        to, might even abide forever by so bright
and bare an image of its own solitude, its heaven
        of utter simplicity, its where-there-
is-nothingesque pursuit of mere
        being, merer becoming. Gentians, bluets,
blue ballast in the sacred plenitude of life's unrecorded
                passing, each incarnation
        overwhelmed in time, each delicate puzzle: what
                Pushkin meant by "the cast
of her eyes"; the spidery veins of one wild iris; the way
        the sea is calmed
        and lightened by rain until the green shadow of that scow
set upon it like a long, low temple can hardly be called green
        anymore; the chrome gleam of the ceiling
at Ménerbes, so fat was the sun on its white or cream
        crude plasterwork, and how it shed down again on her
                ghost pausing at the lancet
to hold the scene in mind, the brightness of the day only heightening
        that other brightness—all of this recalled
in one free moment stolen from an afternoon I'd otherwise rather
        forget. All this and more. We'd hiked to the top, the three
of us, the trail up Deer Creek Canyon through ripped
        sheets of mist, and we'd stopped for a break, coming down,
at a stone pool fed by a horsetail waterfall, no rattlesnakes
        now though earlier something moved there then was gone.
On the lip we sat and shared some gorp and croutons,
                then waded under the singing
        water, so pure and cool in that baked air. She had a
                brace of pitons
strung on her bottle belt and with one of them she scored
        our three names into the lax red mud within the rim
of a single heart—one more scrip of marginalia on the great codex,
        one insignificant hieroglyph. Before
we left there the water had begun its disintegrant
        lapping on and over who she'd said we were.
And here's whoever I am walking home through
                Central Park as you crest at an elevation
        of 10,666 feet crossing Vail Pass in a blizzard, strewn
                seed of a cloud system
rending itself in two on the western peaks, and while you're cursing

a truck driver hard on your bumper what I've got in
    mind is this shore of blue
ice shelved out from the reservoir's granite edge; the
    stained evening air with no wind
to it, none; the tall apartments on the verges
    standing in light from a moon
stalled somewhere or rising still, the towered palaces:
    and then the whole of it merges
into a sort of scent—ageless, faint as death—and
    for once I have no words
for it, not a one, though my pulse is steady and my eyes
    clear, it's just that I can't
believe it's all mine, for now, ours, all this, all
    this then nothing else,
not one thing else. Not one thing else. Imagine.

Odette Heideman

MADAME SOLOMON

The day had started badly for Madame Solomon. In the morning, she had taken the seven o'clock train to Nice for her weekly browse at the antiques market held at the *Cours Saleya*. The usual vendors were there, selling antique linens, stacks of Provençal baskets, glazed pots, loose pieces of polished silver. For more than three decades, she had come to this market on Monday mornings well into October, not a week of which she came back empty-handed. At the market, Madame Solomon fingered some cloth and a few pieces of the silverware— items that she had by the drawerful at her villa. It wasn't until she came to the stand of a man she recognized but had never bought from before that she came to a full stop. Here was something to look at: a set of dessert plates, fifteen of them, thick terra-cotta, glazed in yellows and reds and blues, but the thing that caught Madame Solomon's eye was the pattern of thick black brushstrokes on them: twisted studies of grimacing faces. In the style of Picasso, she thought.

"In the style of" was very much Madame Solomon's taste. When they built their villa on the Riviera, the Solomons had been seduced by their architect's reference to Le Corbusier, convincing them that cheap concrete construction, construction that would crack and require patching on a yearly basis, was far more chic—"in the style of Corbu," as the architect put it, as if he had known Le Corbusier—than the tra- ditional materials of the area: stucco and stone and tile. When it was done, the house hung out from the side of the steep hill like a concrete barnacle, and they furnished it with items that Madame Solomon bargained for at the antiques market and elsewhere: in the style of a pair of Louis XVI chairs, in the style of an Eames bookshelf, in the style of a Bernard Buffet painting, in the style of an Eileen Gray rug, so that in the end, the style of the house was that it had no consistent style at all. Madame Solomon picked the plates up, one at a time, and examined them, back and front. No cracks. No signs of mending. The plates were in perfect condition.

"A very unique set, Madame. Reminiscent of Picasso in Juan-les-Pins," the man said. He looked at her, taking in the Hermès handbag, the gold of her watch, and the diamond ring, all three hanging heavily on her old woman's hand. "595 euros," the vendor said. It was a fair price for the plates, but still, as a local she didn't like to think she was paying tourist prices. She tapped on the stack of plates. "They are hardly Picassos," she said. "And it is not a full set—fifteen is an odd number at any table—450 euros is what I will pay for them and not a centime more, and even that is a lot. I know this market *extremely* well. Everyone here. I'll be back in an hour to pick them up."

But instead of coming directly back, Madame Solomon had a coffee and a croissant at the *place du Palais*. She paused all along the length of the square, following the twisting path made by the thread of vendor stalls, handling objects she wouldn't buy: a set of punched metal lampshades, five teacups with worn, gilded rims, silver spoons with ornate initials, the dense weight of an African servant boy painted onto a plug of lead. She had another coffee and read the headlines of someone else's newspaper. Two hours had passed when she got up and continued browsing down the line of stalls. She stopped to look at a tray of carved horn buttons. 450 euros was not such a bargain for the plates, she had come to conclude. The vendor would mark them down at the end of the morning when he saw that they hadn't sold. She was sure of it. But when she looked up from the buttons, the bright orange canvas of the awning overhead reminded her of the orange background of one of the plates—the plates she already thought of as *her* plates—and when she couldn't stand to wait another minute, she walked rapidly back to the stall. Immediately, she saw that the plates were gone.

"Sold," the vendor said, when he saw her, "at my asking price."

"But how could you have sold my plates?" she said. "I am a local—I come here every week. You have made a terrible, terrible mistake."

"*Mais, non, Madame!* There was no deposit. There was no formal arrangement between us. When you didn't return, I thought perhaps you were uninterested—that you would not come back at all, and so the plates were sold half an hour ago. To one of my regular customers."

"But I've walked by your stall a hundred times! For years and years," Madame Solomon protested. "For years!"

My beautiful reminiscent-of-Picasso plates, she thought. Sold.

"I am terribly sorry, Madame. They are gone. There is nothing to be done," the man said, and then he turned and began tidying up some papers at the back of his stall.

The whole of her train ride home was occupied with thoughts of the plates. When she closed her eyes, Madame Solomon saw reds and ochres, and even imagined that she had missed something in her rushed examination of the plates: perhaps among the black lines of the contorted drawings, there had been an actual Picasso signature. She tortured herself with the thought of it for another half hour, until the train arrived at her stop.

Le Trayas was the town which she and her late husband had adopted as their own, first as a place to summer with their son, Jonathan, and then as a year-round home. The town was one of many hill towns strung along the coast of Southern France—towns that had once been little more than a few houses clustered around poor fishing ports, transformed now into ad hoc retirement villages, with local signs that advertised real estate in German, Dutch, Russian, and English. Local accents were sparse in the town: the clipped vowels following hard on the edges of consonants that sounded stingy and tight compared to the schoolroom French that the majority of current residents had learnt, the local accents in Le Trayas found only now in paint-peeled pockets: at the gas station, or within the crumbling walls of a few nineteenth-century villas overlooking the railroad tracks. Madame Solomon's villa was located high on the hill, and she had a perfect Parisian accent. Her American father had made a large fortune in Shanghai in the 1930s, and when it was decided that she should learn French, a tutor was brought over from Paris to teach her.

At the station, Madame Solomon was the only one off the afternoon train. A man and a woman were standing on the platform in the shade of the station building, alongside a row of dusty blue hydrangeas. They were arguing about money. One was the Moroccan, Hassan, who was known about town as a layabout: a man, no longer young—roughly the age of Madame Solomon's own son, thirty years old or so—who lived with his aunt near the public beach, and was known to do small handyman jobs that local workers, flush with the building of low-market housing projects on the coast, were too busy to take on. He had the reputation of being not entirely trustworthy, although Madame Solomon could never remember exactly why. If Madame Solomon thought of Hassan at all, it was a thought of a sinewy man; of small eyes and troutish skin: brown and oily, often lurking suspiciously on the steps of the post office, or in the vicinity of the cashier's checkout stand in the town's one grocery shop. He was speaking with the stationmaster's wife. The woman was shaking her head, and saying "*Non, non, non!*" slapping her fist against the palm of her other hand as she said it.

The small car park was empty, save for Madame Solomon's car— an old Mercedes coupé that glittered white and boat-like in the afternoon sun. Hassan was on the road now, carrying his brown tool bag. Over his shoulder was slung a radio, and a string of high, whining notes of North African music were coming out from its speakers. As she passed him in her car, he lifted his head and put out his thumb, his hair falling in wild, sea-salted mats that touched his shoulders—a hairstyle that managed to look at once stiff and greasy. For a moment, Madame Solomon pictured the sour smell of him, his small eyes, and the general shiftiness of his manner seated next to her in the car. "No, no," she said out loud. In a swift movement, Madame Solomon rolled up her window and, gunning at the engine of the old Mercedes, shifted noisily into a higher gear, leaving Hassan in the middle of the steaming road.

It wasn't until Madame Solomon had clicked open her villa's automatic gate, maneuvered the Mercedes into the carport, calmed her frantic dog, Mitzy ("Oh, for heaven's sake, Mitzy! Shut up!"), and taken her cup of strong tea out to the terrace, with her newspaper and the mail, that Madame Solomon was able to put the business of the plates to the back of her mind. It was a beautiful day. She could see that. From her terrace, the view was like a postcard sold in the tourist shops: blue, cloudless sky, wide-open vista of the port and the Bay of Cannes, bordered by a hedge of cypress trees, and beyond the bay, the rise of white buildings at Cannes, and then the faintest outline of the French Alps. Madame Solomon examined the hedge. When they had planted it, the intention had been decorative: a sort of natural frame of the sea view, in the style of Somerset Maugham's garden at the Villa Mauresque that Madame Solomon had once seen photos of in a magazine. They had had the pick of lots on the hill thirty years ago, and had chosen theirs specifically for its view.

There was a postcard from Jonathan—the Japanese stamps and Kyoto postmark on it so large that they eradicated half of the written message, such as it was: "Think . . . O . . . Y . . . ," she read. This was followed by the great, loopy signature spelling out his adopted Japanese name, Youki—a name that Madame Solomon pronounced as "Yolki" or "Yiki," never quite understanding how the word should exit her mouth. Jonathan was an odd duck even as a child. At ten, he quoted Bishop Berkeley at the dinner table: *esse est percipi*, to be is to be perceived. When Madame Solomon said she didn't have the faintest idea what he was talking about, he explained that everything that exists is either a mind or depends for its existence upon a mind.

"I am an island," he said. "Or, alternatively, you and Dad are each islands. Let's say there's a coconut tree on your island, but none on mine. Therefore, the coconut would exist for you, but not for me."

When they pushed him to go the beach, he went, but instead of enjoying wind surfing and swimming like the other children, Jonathan found a few dull grownups—myopic and pale—to sit with under the thatched roof of the beach café. None of them went into the sea.

One summer morning when he was fourteen, Jonathan asked if he could have an old white bed sheet and some thread. He was going to make something, he said, and Madame Solomon found what he wanted. She hoped he was making a sail for a model boat, or a parachute—anything that would get him away from his books. All day, Jonathan stayed in his room with the door closed. When he came to the table that evening, Madame Solomon saw that he was wearing a white belted dress.

"What's that dress, Jonathan?" Madame Solomon asked him. There were large, clumsy stitches all along the edge of it, and its bat sleeves tangled his arms as he tried to cross them. He looked childish and ridiculous, she thought.

"I'm converting to Tenrikyo," he said.

"What on earth is that? Tenkro? Tenko?"

"It's a Shinto sect that focuses on attaining *yoki-yusan*—a joyous life on earth found through charity and abstention from greed, selfishness, hatred, anger, and arrogance. If you would call me by my Japanese name, Youki-san, that will be fine."

Madame Solomon said she didn't understand, and she truly didn't. She was a non-practicing Catholic and her husband was a non-practicing Jew. As a family, they had never belonged to anything—no church or synagogue, not really even a country: every few years they moved because of Harry's business—Hong Kong, Barcelona, Singapore—and so what exactly was Jonathan converting from? When they sat down at the table, Madame Solomon made a point of addressing her son by his given name; the name *she* had given him. "Jonathan, please pass your father a plate." "I forgot napkins. Jonathan?" "Jonathan, your sleeve!" And so on. She couldn't help it. She felt as if she were seated with a stranger, or a volume of Tenrikyo text, not her son. By the second week, the name Youki became the unwanted guest at the table—a guest to whom Madame Solomon was purposefully rude.

Harry Solomon began exchanging the delicate Venetian *apéritif* glass that he used for his dinnertime drink for a taller half-stein glass, and as the summer wore on, the half stein was replaced by a brandy

snifter, which he flooded up to its rim several times during the eve-
ning, alternating whisky with Armagnac, after which he would sink
into his seat at the dinner table, his senses mute and fuzzy: chewing
took all of his concentration, leaving little room for conversation. The
following year, Jonathan enrolled in a boarding school in Switzerland,
and after that, went directly to the Tenrikyo headquarters in Kyoto.
In the end, it was almost a relief when Jonathan left—all of his talk
of abstention from anger had the effect of making Madame Solomon
breed anger as if it were a dying species that she had decided to rescue.
After every telephone conversation with their son—awkward, grap-
pling endeavors where he talked about the deep satisfaction of belong-
ing—Harry Solomon girded himself with liquor to dull the force of his
wife's disappointment in the boy formerly known as Jonathan.

When Harry Solomon collapsed one morning—his liver bloated
and choked with alcohol—and died the next, his wife and son saw
each other for the first time in ten years. The director of the crematori-
um suggested that she say some words, or that perhaps a priest would
say some as the body was cremated, but Madame Solomon refused.
Instead, it was Jonathan who began singing, in Japanese, as the pine
casket rolled around the stage on an automatic rail system, and then
disappeared behind two velvet curtains.

Two o'clock in the morning: her son asleep in his childhood bed
for the first time in a decade, and herself, alone in the vastness of a
king-size California: *esse est percipi*, she remembered, and in the black-
ness of the room, she pictured the beds—Jonathan's and her own—
like floating islands, occasionally bumping into each other, with noth-
ing to say, and nothing—not anything, it seemed—to anchor them
together. She opened her eyes in the darkness, and stretched her arms
out as far as they could reach. But she felt only the cold, slippery cotton

of the sheets. Since then, there were only postcards from her son.

Her other piece of mail was a letter concerning her western neigh-
bor—a German woman who had never made any overture of commu-
nication other than a yearly letter via a lawyer in Cannes, demanding
that the Solomons' hedges be cut to legal norms—a certain Code 4798
that dictated the height of tree growth, a height which would allow the
neighbor, Madame Meister, a view of the Alps to the east. When Harry
had been in charge of the correspondence, the response to the letters
had been no response. The first letter arrived in the stone slot of their
mailbox soon after the sounds of house construction next door had
ceased. As Madame Solomon translated the letter for her husband,
she imagined they might cut a small window in the hedge. To be
neighborly. The Germans were on all sides: the Meisters, the Obers,
the Wöfflers. She had seen the names on the mailboxes. Madame
Solomon had imagined taking a few German lessons, and then per-
haps having a German *apéritif* party, serving Schnapps or Becks—a
sort of mini-Oktoberfest, Riviera style. There would be German card
games and evenings of Teutonic music: opera and marching tunes,
alternated with American nights soaked with Louis Armstrong and
bridge and Harry Solomon's liquor collection. That was five years ago.
Harry had laughed at the lawyer's letter, and then sworn at it, and then
tossed it in the garbage.

This year's letter from Monsieur Marteau: the hedge, the view, the
Alps. Madame Solomon took paper from her writing box.

Dear Madame Meister, she wrote,

*I received a letter from your lawyer who informs me that
you are requiring me to cut my cypress trees so that you can have
a view of the Alps. As in his letters from previous years, Monsieur*

*Marteau suggests that my trees are in violation of the allowed
property law governing the height of border trees: one meter 60
centimeters above the legal height of trees. What I have come to
understand in the five years of receiving these letters, never hav-
ing personally met you, is that what you really want is not a villa
with a view of the Alps, but my view of the Alps. The fact is, that
although you can have a view of the sea that is a beautiful one,
you cannot have the one that is mine. Rest assured that I will have
the hedges trimmed on both sides of my property—hedges that my
(late) husband and I planted thirty years ago—to the legal height,
so that you may have the view you are entitled to, by law.*

 With cordial good wishes to you and to Monsieur Marteau,
auf Wiedersehen,

—Madame Solomon, Neighbor (Voisine)

She placed the letter in an envelope, and addressed it to Madame
Meister.

"There," she said to Mitzy, who stopped licking at her paws when
she heard her name. "I'll bring it over myself."

Madame Solomon put a small quiche to warm in the oven, and
then packed a stack of old newspapers and two empty wine bottles
into a straw shopping bag. Deliver the letter (by hand), deposit the
paper and glass in the municipal recycling bins near the post office,
then quiche. She was putting the bag in the trunk of the Mercedes,
telling Mitzy not to worry, to not be stupid, to be a brave little dog
as she would be home shortly, when the second mishap of the day
occurred. As she was lowering the bag into the car, she stepped on
Mitzy's paw, causing the dog to bite at her mistress' leg, and Madame
Solomon to slam the bag down hard. There was a sharp crack and

Madame Solomon saw that one of the bottles had broken. "Mitzy, for God's sake!" she shouted, and the small dog cowered against the gate. Madame Solomon put the chunks of glass in a parcel she fashioned from a section of the newspaper, and slammed down the trunk door. "Shoo!" she said.

Mitzy whined and put her head through the iron railing, watching as her mistress walked the hundred yards or so to the neighbor's gate. Madame Solomon saw with distaste that a mailbox was installed at the center of a decorative metal ship's wheel the size of a small car tire. Another smaller wheel surrounded a marble doorbell and an intercom grate. Both of the wheels were painted a bright aqua blue. Madame Solomon could see her neighbor working at the bottom of the garden. She was digging a small trench between a stone pathway and the first terrace of an extensive cactus garden. The trough was narrow and deep, and the woman's head of cropped grey hair bobbed over it as she raised and lowered her arm without pause. Madame Solomon hesitated between the doorbell and the letterbox, but then she noticed that the German woman was wearing what appeared to be underwear: a pair of turquoise underpants and matching brassiere, triangles of sweat darkening the fabric under the woman's arms and all around the small of her back, above her bottom. Gardening in her underwear! Madame Solomon stuffed the envelope into the letter slot at the center of the ship's wheel, the flap of which closed with a heavy *thunk,* scraping against the tips of her fingers.

At the town square, Madame Solomon parked under the mimosa tree. Hassan was sitting, shirtless, on the steps of the post office. He was manufacturing a cigarette with pouch tobacco and a packet of cigarette papers. He looked up at the sound of the approaching car, and, seeing it was Madame Solomon, he remembered the heat of his walk up the hill from the station, and turned up the volume on his radio.

The smoke from Hassan's cigarette drifted up through the branches of the old mimosa. He was singing along with his radio and Madame Solomon winced at the sound of it. She took the bottle and the sheath of newspapers in one hand, and her handbag and the make-shift package containing the broken glass in the other, and locked the Mercedes. In front of the vast blue and green recycling bins, she hesitated, not sure if the broken glass wrapped in paper belonged in the paper bin or in the glass bin. It was then, with Hassan's eyes upon her, that she made her worst mistake. On the toes of her leather flats, she reached up and dropped the one bottle into the green bin, and then quickly stuffed the newspapers, the lumpy parcel, and her leather handbag into the long slot of the blue container, watching the purse—holding house keys, car keys, money, identification—fall, as if in slow motion, and disappear into the darkness at the back of the bin.

What tormented Madame Solomon in the following minutes was not the stupidity of having put her own keys and handbag into the bin, but the fact that the pile of newspapers inside it was not quite high enough that she could reach them. She peered into the opening. The light was unnerving and odd, the way the light underwater is unnerving and odd. Madame Solomon could see the outline of the purse—so darkly orange that it seemed as if it wasn't her purse at all—as if she were looking at somebody else's purse. The bag was sitting on top of the pile of newspapers, but it had slid to the back, behind the parcel, and when she reached in, with fingers strained forward until it was painful, she felt only paper.

She pulled her arm out, red and smarting in the armpit from the exertion, blood pounding in her ears. Crickets screeched in the square. The car was locked; the gate to her villa was locked; Madame

Solomon could not think if she had or had not locked her front door. The beat of her pulse and the noise of the crickets thundered to fill her head. She thought of the quiche in the oven, and of little Mitzy whining at the gate, and she felt suddenly the strongest urge to urinate. Summer hours in Le Trayas were over: the post office was closed until four o'clock, and the one shop as well. Her cleaning lady was not coming for another two days. For the first time since her husband's funeral, she felt as if she might cry.

She put her hand on her forehead and then over her mouth before saying to herself sternly, "Oh, for heaven's sakes!" She could use the telephone booth outside the post office to call the maid, who could be here within the half hour. What she hadn't thought of until she was halfway across the street was how she would avoid Hassan. He was sitting directly in front of the entrance gate to the post office. Keeping her gaze above Hassan's reclining body, Madame Solomon altered her course, stepping sideways more than forward, until she had figured in a wide, half-moon arc around the obstacle of Hassan. Even so, she felt his eyes on her back as she climbed the steps to the phone booth. She closed the glass door behind her and picked up the receiver. There was no dial tone. She depressed the cradle a few times. Still no dial tone, but now a shrill beeping bombarded her ear. Madame Solomon stared dumbly at the receiver until she noticed that a message was flashing on the screen of the telephone box. "*Inserrez votre carte téléphonique,*" it read. And her heart sank. She didn't have a phone card; she had never had a phone card.

Her head was throbbing when she left the booth. Hassan was standing in the path, between her and the road, and again she had to circumvent him, this time passing so close to his body that she noticed his shirtless torso: black hair and a horrendous smell coming out from his armpits, and the waist of his cotton pants hanging low to rest not so much on his hips as on his pubic bone. He both disgusted and frightened her.

"*Eh! Madame. Ça va?*" he asked, shooting his cigarette butt to the gutter.

"*Oui, oui, ça va,* yes," she said. She had a smear of black newsprint ink on her forehead and along one side of her mouth, and as she spoke, she pulled at the collar on her dress and marked that with the ink as well. She made a gesture with her hand—a sort of dismissal, waving him away and out of her way—and then turned up the road to her villa.

The road rose from the post office in a series of hairpin turns, each one steeper than the last. At the third zigzag, she stopped to rest. There was a clear view down to the port, a popular picnic spot with tourists in summer, tourists whom Madame Solomon often passed in the Mercedes, as they opened up their collapsible tables at sunset, put out their hampers, and ate their dinners—with silverware and china plates, wine and wineglasses, as if they had moved their dining room to this vantage point to see how the world looked when you saw it from up here. A small cluster of eucalyptus trees lay at the outermost point of the turn, and there was a worn wooden bench beneath it. Madame Solomon took a seat on the edge of it. Nothing else occupied her mind now so much as the urge to empty her bladder. She felt almost intoxicated by the desire: slightly dizzy and lightheaded, with a band of pain pressing low and deep into her pelvis. She looked down the road. It was empty except for old Monsieur Hubert's dog, who was rooting in the scrub at the roadside a hundred yards away. The breeze was blowing the dog's hackles up into a stiff line along its back.

A small stone barrier in front of the bench separated her from the gorge below, and she saw that a faint path had been worn into the side of the hill. Madame Solomon followed the path with her eyes. It was the width of a pair of shoes, and strewn with balled-up tissues, ice-cream wrappers, and toll receipts. A few yards further on was an old goat-herding hut. There was no roof over the building, and two of its stone walls were crumbling into the ground. With small steps, Madame Solomon approached the building. Two enormous bushes of wild rosemary had taken over the entrance of the hut. She pushed the branches aside and saw there was a clearing at the center of the bush. Here, there was more refuse: tissues, a torn condom package, the string of a tampon trailing off under the dry leaves. Madame Solomon lifted the hem of her dress up and around her hips. She squatted. Through the branches of rosemary, she could just see the turn of the road. There was no noise from the crickets, only the rustle of dry grasses that put the thought of stale weeds and grass snakes into Madame Solomon's mind.

She tried hard to concentrate, remembering suddenly a violin concert she had attended with her father as a girl of 12. At the inter- mission, she insisted that she go to the toilet by herself. The ladies' room was out of order, and she joined the end of the line to the men's room, which wound around and down the hallway. Men and women moved forward to take their turn in the single stall. As she came closer she heard the sound of the stall door closing, urine releasing, toilet flushing, door reopening. The closer she got, the more she felt a twist in her stomach. When it finally came to her turn, she sat on the toilet, two strips of toilet paper separating her legs from the plastic seat. She thought of the strangers standing outside the door, waiting for her to give up the seat, all frowning or scowling, listening for the ring of intermission's first call with one ear and the ring of her urine against the toilet water with the other. She pictured in her mind the long, snaking line of people who had come before her, and then the line of people still to come, shifting from one foot to the other, looking at their watches, shaking their heads, swearing silently at whomever was taking their sweet time in the one functioning toilet in the whole damn hall, and still her urine would not come. She left the stall finally, to be greeted by a procession of sullen glares. In the red-carpeted hallway, she dawdled, hoping that her father might come and take her by the hand and order her to go in and use the toilet, but he did not come. She waited until the last person relieved himself before going back to the toilet herself, and, the sound of it mingling with strains of Bach's *Concerto for Two Violins in D Minor*, she let her bladder empty, then as now, in a single effulgent stream. There had been no toilet paper then either.

Madame Solomon was still squatting when she heard the sound of footsteps. The ground about her feet was dark and splattered with her urine, as was the hem at the back of her dress. She half stood in the bushes, looking out for a sight of who was coming, and she felt the cloy wetness of mud and urine sticking to the backs of her calves. Hassan was rounding the bend. Every few steps he lifted his head and looked about, as if he were searching for something.

Old Monsieur Hubert's dog was now trotting behind Hassan, with his long pink tongue dangling to one side between two curved incisors. Madame Solomon crouched with her knees bent and her hands resting on the front of her thighs. She watched the man and the dog drawing closer and closer to where she hid, the odor of her own urine coming up to prick the lining of her nostrils. Now the other two were very close to where Madame Solomon cowered: maybe five or six yards away. She could see Hassan set down the radio and his tool bag.

He lay down on the wooden bench.

The dog was sniffing again at the roadside, and Madame Solomon watched as it began picking its way down the path to the ruin in which she stood. It was a large shepherd breed with a studded collar around its neck. The collar bit into the thick mat of black and brown fur covering its body. Around its muzzle, the fur was grizzled and sparse. It panted heavily in the heat. Each time it came to a scrap of refuse, the dog opened its mouth to let its tongue out to lick at it. Every few steps it lifted its leg, and a drop or two came down to mark its territory: a male dog. Madame Solomon held her breath as the animal approached the entrance to her hut. Her throat was dry and she covered her mouth to stifle the choke that was rising in it. At once, the dog stood motionless, his tail and ears rigid: he too held his breath and listened. Madame Solomon watched him turn his head, cocking his pointed ears to hear all that there was to be heard. His eyes were ringed with grey hairs and she could see that the whites of them were no longer white, but yellow. The irises were clouded and glassy, and the old dog moved his sight slowly back over the terrain near the hut. From where she stood, Madame Solomon could smell the sourness of his breath so strongly that it made her want to cough, and behind his lolling tongue she could see that his mouth held several brown—almost purple—rotting teeth.

When he saw her, his breathing stopped entirely and he drew his tongue back into his mouth in a single snapping movement. His body lowered into a crouch and he raised the sides of his jowls to show the sharp points of his brown teeth. Madame Solomon sank to her knees and a whimpering sound came up from her throat. Behind the dog, she could hear music from Hassan's radio. Slowly she reached her hand to the dog.

"It's alright," she rasped. "I won't hurt you."

The dog stared at her eyes, and emitted a low belly growl. His yellow eyes narrowed and he raised his lips to show his teeth again.

"Please," she said.

With one leap, the old dog fell upon her, letting his teeth cut into the soft flesh of her palm, which he shook as if in a terrible greeting, before letting go and fleeing through the opening at the back of the stone hut.

Madame Solomon let herself fall against the stone wall. She pursed her quivering lips. Her mind was dazed—as if it had skidded off a road and landed upside down in an unfamiliar place. She looked at her hand and saw a pattern of tooth-marks engraved in the palm of it. The indentations lay in two bands, one above the other: on the lower one, a castellated impression rose and fell unevenly, and left the skin purple, but intact; across the upper band, however, the dog's jaw had cut two jagged tears, and Madame Solomon gasped when she saw it, as the blood crept out to drip off her hand. Two bright splashes of it spread down the front of her dress. Madame Solomon held her hand away from her body as she looked around for something to bind it with. There was nothing on the ground but soiled tissues. She felt in her dress pockets with her good hand, and found a small handkerchief. The hand was starting to swell, taking on a fullness that seemed to puff up and billow like a yeasty dough, rising even as she looked at it. She wrapped the cloth over the wound but found it was too short to reach all the way around, so she loosened the narrow belt from her waist and wound it tightly around the wrist of her injured hand and then around its swollen palm, causing a spear of pain to shudder up her arm.

The pain in her hand was something white and solid, and when she closed her eyes, she could see it clearly—a searing rod slicing through the meat of her palm—and more than at any time before in her life, Madame Solomon wanted to be back in her home: her living room, her blue chair, the terrace and the view; she would gulp down a brandy snifter of whisky, like her husband before her: to sit and not participate. She straightened her body and looked in the direction of the bench. Her grey dress was now spotted with flecks and clumps of drying mud and blood. She held her right hand tenderly to her chest. There was no way to get back to her villa without passing Hassan, so she would just have to pass Hassan.

Madame Solomon came back up the dirt path to the road. Each step was a jolt to her hand, which meant that each step required her utmost attention, and so she did not see Hassan stir and then sit up on the bench until the bench was directly in front of her. She blinked. She didn't have to speak, she could just walk past him, she thought. She didn't have to explain anything to this Moroccan man. There was nothing and nobody to say that she should.

"*Madame*," he said. "Eh, *Madame, ta main. Il y a un problème?*"

Each word out of his mouth came out as if through a mangler: *Madame* became *Mdim, main* became *min*. Madame Solomon could barely understand a word he was saying. She stared at the tattoo at the center of his chest. A word was inked across the brown skin in a faded black. The biting pain of her hand; the heat of the unending day; this oily man who was like a bad smell from which she could not seem to escape: all of this converged upon Madame Solomon like a thick plastic bag. If the pain in her hand had begun as a searing rod, it was now fifty rods, like spokes on a wheel, each one of them reaching up and into her throat to stick in it as she tried to speak. No, she said. There was no problem.

At the fifth and final switchback before reaching her villa, she came to a community gate. Madame Solomon entered the code on the keypad at the side of the gate, and as it swung open, she felt a small relief: this was where the Moroccan and his stalking would stop. From here, she could see the concrete walls of her villa; she could hear Mitzy's shrill bark somewhere low at the bottom of the garden. The unpleasantness was almost over, she told herself: a few more steps and she would be able to run cold water over her smarting hand, wash, change her clothes, and sink into her blue chair on the terrace. Drink. It was only when she heard the sound of the gate opening again and then the terrible sound of footsteps and Hassan's music dogging her once more that she remembered: the gate to her villa was locked and the keys were at the back of the blue bin.

Thirty paces or so behind her came the trudge of Hassan's sandals, and in a moment of panic she continued walking—past her own gate and over to the smaller of the ship's wheels next door, just as Mitzy arrived in a state of frenzy: long strands of her white hair caught up in her teeth as she whined and barked through the iron bars separating her from her mistress. If Harry had been there, he would have climbed the gate. Jonathan, too. When Madame Solomon looked back at the height of it, the wrought iron molded into spiking curlicues all along the top, she felt suddenly weak and small, as if she were a child again. She knew that climbing the gate herself was quite impossible. The whole situation was impossible: the excruciating pain of her hand, the approach of Hassan, whom she had slighted for years and years, and again just that morning, and the impossible thought of ringing Madame Meister's bell, to whom she had hand-delivered her own rude letter that afternoon.

The German woman was still in her garden, working on another irrigation trench, this one closer to the gate. Madame Solomon saw now that she was wearing not underwear but a blue bikini, and it fitted closely over narrow, tanned hips and muscled arms. She was older— and much prettier—than Madame Solomon had seen earlier. Madame Solomon pushed hard on the button at the center of the ship's wheel, starting to cry even as she did so. At the sound of the bell, the German woman looked up, but instead of running up the steps to the gate, she ran down them to her house, taking them two at a time. Madame Solomon could see her neighbor's shadow behind the frosted glass window of the villa's front door. A flat voice, panting slightly, came out of the intercom panel in the small ship's wheel.

"*Ja?*" it said, as if it were talking to an object—a chair or a table that had been deposited outside the villa's gate.

Madame Solomon pressed the intercom button and said, in French: "I am Madame Solomon, your neighbor. I have placed my keys in the recycling bin at the post office."

She made a gesture when she said "keys," twisting her good hand to the right and then to the left. It was a difficult thing to explain: should she speak about the blue bin? The glass bottle breaking? The dog bite and the walking up? And the stalking Hassan? And Harry's death? And Jonathan's name change? Should she speak about the letter and the hedge? And the beginning of this awful day, when she was cheated of her rightful plates at the market, should she just start there and explain how she came to be standing here, asking for something? She didn't even know what she was asking for. She held her puffy hand up in front of the gate for the German woman to see.

"By accident," she said. "I put the keys in the bin by accident."

She didn't have the language to explain it in any other way. The only common ground they had between them was the hedge, and so she pointed at that and pressed the intercom button again.

"I will cut the hedge. In my letter, I said I would cut the hedge," she said, enunciating each word, understanding even as she said the words that a line had been drawn a long time ago, and she was now on one side of it—on an aged battleground from which there was no graceful retreat. She felt like an island: a dumbstruck, deserted island. She looked down at herself, conscious suddenly of how she must appear to this stranger neighbor: the large white collar stained with newspaper ink and red dust, the dark splashes of dried blood, the red clots of mud, and the sweat: all of it hung on her, beltless, like a dirty grey sack.

"*Ich bin,*" she said. "*Ich bin!*" She didn't know the word in German for neighbor. "Your neighbor," Madame Solomon croaked in English into the center of the wheel, holding up her hand. "*Votre voisine!*" The shadow moved behind the glass, but no more sound came out from the blue wheel.

Hassan was standing at the gate when she turned back to face her villa. She put her good hand out to steady herself on the railing of her gate. He pointed to his chest and from this distance she saw that the word tattooed across the center of it was "*Fraternité.*" He pointed to his chest and then pointed to the gate, motioning a looping gesture over it and to the door of Madame Solomon's villa. She nodded, wiping tears into the ink and red dust on her cheeks—making its own sort of mud in the mixing. A moment ago she had been humiliated and fearful, but now she just wanted someone else to take over. She wanted someone else to climb over the gate and get her back inside, so that she could collapse in the cushions of her chair. She nodded at him vigorously, and said, "*Oui,*" in a trembling voice. "*S'il vous plait.*"

Mitzy was growling and snapping in the direction of Hassan,

looking back at her mistress for encouragement. With some difficulty, Madame Solomon linked her arm through a loop in the iron railing to make a chain around Mitzy's neck from her side of the gate. Hassan lifted himself up and over the railing in one catlike movement.

The door leading into the kitchen was unlocked and Hassan pushed it open. There was a smell of burning coming from the oven and he turned it off and pulled out the black disk of quiche with his fingers. He threw it into the sink. Glass-fronted cupboards hung off of the walls in the kitchen, containing stacks of colored dishes—more dishes than he had ever seen in his life. He walked past them and through the living room, noting the large Sony television on the stand in one corner, and recognizing a stereo system he had seen on a bill-board advertisement in Cannes. He looked for the intercom box on the wall. None of the furniture in the room matched. Hassan could see through to the dining room, the flash of shining silver candlesticks crowded along the mantel, drawing his eye: there must have been fifty of them, maybe sixty, he thought.

The intercom box was next to the front door, and he pressed on the buzzer until he heard the gate slide in its track. He walked out onto the terrace. Below him on the hill, he saw a gradation of houses: row after row of them, leading down to the sea. He studied them until he found his aunt's house: it looked small and insubstantial, and precarious—as if it were teetering on the side of a cliff, jutting out over the railway tracks. He had never seen his aunt's house from this angle before, and he couldn't get over how different it looked—shabby and white, like a grub that you find in the dirt.

Madame Solomon came to the door, her body bent over at the waist so that she could keep a hold on Mitzy's collar. She saw Hassan swing his arm out in a grand sweeping movement towards the sea, as if he were introducing her to her own view on the terrace. A few hours ago, this gesture would have seemed outrageous, but now she didn't care. She wanted to give him something, this Moroccan standing on her terrace—a reward of money, but her handbag and her wallet were sitting at the back of the blue bin. She asked him to wait, and pulled Mitzy into the dining room, where she grasped two of the silver candlesticks with her good hand. When he saw what she was doing he shook his head. "*Non*," he said. She was a pathetic figure, he thought, an old woman who should go home and live with her son—in England or America or wherever she was from.

When Hassan had gone, Madame Solomon washed her hand and bandaged it, but she was too exhausted to bathe and change her clothes. After that, she sat on the terrace for a very long time. Trains flew past and through the town and away. The wind pulled the old cypress to the side, so that the hedges looked like thick green curtains framing a view of the darkening sea. Eventually, Madame Solomon heard the sound of people eating on their terraces: forks clinking against knives and the soft murmur of dinner conversation. She couldn't remember what she and Harry and Jonathan spoke about when they had last sat down together for a meal. What had they ever talked about? She went to the kitchen, holding her swollen hand up to her chest, and got the telephone. Pulling the cord of it tight across the whole of the living room, she carried it out onto the terrace. She dialed the number, and cleared her throat so that she could speak, the last of the sunlight sliding past her to flood the grey walls of the house, so that they reminded her of something else: something shiny and unplumbed that her shaky mind couldn't find the name of. She held the receiver with her one good hand and sat down on her chair. The phone was ringing somewhere in Kyoto and she heard the foreign tone of it buzzing off and on and off and on, as she tunneled deep into her memory to find the image that the wall reminded her of. Something rounded and fragile. Something pale and gelatinous, like the shell of a quail's egg or the innards of a snail. But not quite. And then she came upon it, not deep at all, but resting on the surface of her memory: the wall was like the inside of the blue recycling bin, with its hollow, unfamiliar light—the emptiness of it, the silence.

"Youki?" she said. ◆

Dion Farquhar

SEARCH ENGINE
(for Matt)

Riveted by anything that moves
and speed and size and noise, each a plus—
fire engines, ambulances, foghorn-
honking sixteen-wheelers his pantheon
of pleasure. *Cuk, cuk,* he'd point with drool and glee,
levitating from his booster seat.
After trucks came contrails and helicopters,
flying monsters and instant objects:
guns, skyscrapers, and trains—
made of Legos, Zoobs, and Gears,
K-Nex, Magz, and Lincoln Logs
Traded virtual dangers for real.

Then years of *'speriments* and *po-shuns*—
always fearless, everything fair game:
baking soda box on end, half-squeezed lemons,
vinegar bottle bone dry, an arcane amber slime
bubbling in the missing Tupperware
under the bathroom sink, starting to stink.
I mixed cleaning spritz, Gatorade,
and lemon juice, admitting to the muck
he's made, maybe hoping to germinate
a mutant superhero breathing fire.

Now hammering, nailing, jerry-rigging
a boat, a fort, a box—much unsupervised sneaking
of treacherous tools: saw on the bathroom floor,
duct tape on the table, nails embedded in the carpet,
shed's a mess, garden a swamp from trying to flush
out a mole and the saved wood's screwed together,
half a plastic pretzel barrel a jagged sail.
Two-by-four hull thumps to the bottom of the tub—
it's still a great galleon he's made.

Fourth grade he used pencil and protractor,
drew complicated fantasy machines with pulleys
and levers, his Machines for the Future
Honorable Mention in the Science Fair.
Two years later, perfect little pixel
in the matrix, he plucks the new digital
out of its box, grasps the tiny silver thing:
mode, sub-menu, analog stick, he spouts,
parents marveling at the engineer
he's become, wondering what's next.

SHIFT

skepticisms
alternating qwerty
pound it out libra
scales tipped classic nails
libera nos first
person epidural
unstoppable as
ruse epizootics
avian joiners
lights stop pedal pink
cycle buds crossing
signs lying curves stop
ambush *mother* concrete
bunker buster
fellows dreaming sad
abstract follow-through
dazzle metaphor
deliver waiting

SPAM.1

Mass on side in blow
art and brown not thick
left hemisphere trauma
its point virtual
monthlies not avocado
but ripened cheese
like another postponement
of the housing court case
not snake the support
it bit on poison
ship its sharp hook steel
to sing the history
imperious if I'd been
the measure of you
were the double of something
or else the measure
not of celebrity
or kingdom come
lay out some lines
like secrets silence
exacerbated
photogenicity
the calculated
climb *and* conjuncture
the right mentors
a solid mass
always productive
the means and the relations
cry wolf she was shot
by a priest on a blind
date pretending to be
Plato's secretary
of state in a box
at the theatre,
before East Village
gentrification
are you really wanting more?
this knowledge, too, depends
on a said to be qualified
in some specific way

in most, indeed in almost
meritocracy
this is not true,
for we may say
that all affections,
or nearly all,
no one of these is

.

George Franklin

BREAKTHROUGH

I.
Under slurred trees
Communing the wind
In cool bent rushes,
Each to each, a plotted
Row, they planted a line.
A ladder to the sky!
It fell & tracked its steps
Like clues to other clues
Across the earth;
They spaced a row of poles
Beside the rails in paced
Harmonic time, staked out
The speed of sound.

II.
A bullet hole:
A web of glass:
An X, a cross
Of black masking tape,
A dressing for the wound!,
A crude divided sight
& a hanging blind;
An O, a swaying
Loop on a string,
Hypnotic.

III.
The surface is broken/
The window distorts.

      Imagine the attempt
Was on *my* life!, the Silver Bullet
Lodged in a dream.
Assassin!
Your face is imposed

On edgy, shifting landscapes—
A maze, a confusion of order,
A progress of vacant lots.
I stare into my eyes
Through a film of dust.
This is no frontier.

This pane is a picture frame.
Light is caught in the clefts
Of the web. Its matching edges,
Exposed, would cut.
One tap,
And the puzzle flies apart.
The face has fallen from the glass,
Flashing stored lightning.
The pieces are transparent—
Each justifies its image.
No clues remain.

But now, the glass intact,
Trees bend from ear to ear—
A rural passage!
Cracking back a scruff of bright leaves,
The portrait is a verdant blur,
Humming from frame to frame.
A green ghost smiles from his slide
At a god of inspection,
Whispering in the hollow
Before the next station,
Whispering of victory & speed.

Imagine the attempt was on *my* life!
The grid falls like a wish—
This pane is a picture frame,
A vain self-preservation.
Acres of malls and revolving signs,
The emblematic commerce of destruction.

IV.
This is no frontier.
No clues remain.
Under broken branches,
Rung by rung,
Neither climbing nor descending—
Slowly, the ghost is crawling
With his collection,
Out of this offering,
Out of these bright splinters,
To make, to worship
Just one, one perfect image!
The glass is intact;

The tracks
Are ragged with glass.
Imagine an open space,
A terminal past,
A moment transfixed— & follow.
These hands can neither cut nor carry;
This intoxicating blood
Is a delusion.
                    The ghost
Assembles a shattered window;
His face has fallen from the glass;
The mirror is blank. After it,
He cannot form himself/
The image justifies nothing.

V.
No vista out/
The inner scheme's revealed.
Across the aisle—
Inverted on the vibrating pane,
Rattling in its brackets,
Exposing the tunnel's wall—
Gamblers rifle through cards
& chew cigars.
I watch my own face watching
Them on the glass, chilled
By frigid air from a chromium vent.
—Betraying no emotion,
Surveying each other's stares,
They flick their ashes
Into empty cups.

      A sparse smoke skims
The window as I breathe,
Trace tentative designs,
Then wave the surface clear
With the palm of a hand.
The gamblers expectantly
Tap their cigars, then
Drop the burnt-down stumps
To the floor;
They're ground underfoot
& split like burst cocoons.
—One touch of the glass!
You'd think your heart had stalled
But under a pulsing haze,
The clefts still seen,
These pinned
& glassy veins suggesting
Wings—a frozen ascension!,
Stopped at summer's height/
Few clues remain…

VI.
A bullet hole;
A rush of black;
A face crossed out;
A circle, an arc,
A divided image—
Out the other side.

VII.
Rattling over trestles,
A bridge where two rivers meet…
The sinking sun is caught in an iron cage;
A brand of warm black bars, mirage!,
Grows soft, impressed
On slowly moving water—
It is not broad; it is not deep.
Sing out the meager confluence! America!
You've caught my breath. The shadows
Are far below: they shock.
They neither split nor move
In the turgid flow, but bend &
Arc, like waves, in place. Across the rivers,
Lining their banks: from mazes of plants
& wasted generations, rising—
Plumes of unessential smoke…

Remembering, remembering/
Words that will not fit the puzzle,
Abstracted in a dream;
Meanings I would have carefully made
& coded my own image

        Exactly & unbreakable to say:
        Only this rage is essential,
        This brutal falling out—

Now nothing fits;
No gesture fails to divide;
No reunion. —Rooms that I remember—
        (Sing out a random specificity!),
        Bars of an invented song;

Harmonics locked into an inner dissonance—
This world that will not fit the last,
No increments: detachment

Utter as birth/
  The ghost assembles a shattered window.
  After it, he cannot form himself…

Remembering, remembering.
Attempting some new song of self-release!—
  The gesture leading past itself,
  Tending the moving air with expression,
  The gesture that never arrives…

Separated autonomic sounds—
My pulse rose when you dropped your line;
You spoke. I strained to answer.
  The pieces are transparent.
  Each justifies its image…
I heard myself
Against those sheets, folded
With a perfect backbone line
& lay, deceptive, deathly still,
Fitted in the brutal trace of sleep—
A frozen river, splintered,
Unreflective…
  I would broadcast these waves!,
But they are broken.
I shiver on the riding fringe of hope,
Invoke a cool suspension,
& subside,

  Awaiting definitions…
  The coil of attention is wound;
  The room is attuned.
   Unlock the river!
  Hack it & haul it away…/

The river is not brittle enough.
The shadows cannot contain it, & slide
With the sun. Reflecting a sky its currents
Cannot move, yet making a constant
Of motion, this speed cannot

Be broken; its images are safe.
The bridge will span its lengthening print
While just upstream occasional clouds engage or
Disengage, too separate still to herald
A coming storm. The shadows
Are far below: they shock.
But one could fall beneath them, deep,
To the dark unfeatured force that feeds and drives.

VIII.
The sky comes apart/
The storm slides in.

The overlapping river
Spills its print,
The bridge's black skeleton
Sunk in a richer earth.
—Who stirs

Within your skin
Like a prisoner?
In a clearing two ghost merge
While from a rumpled bed
You rise,
You occupy the world you displace,
This insubstantial weight,
This moving air,
& hunger for a soul,
An alien birth,
The will to will a real hunger,
A hunger greater than self. O,
Do not read faces
In fluent clouds,

Unprecedented forms
The mind invents;
The sky erases all thought,
& names you Impossible.

Winding around a vacant eye,
The storm leaves a sun-flooded core.
Rooted, a drifting stem of light

Grows down
From a movable source.
It catches, & will not release

These leaves,
Whining beneath a tidal sky,
Shaking out bright gusts of rain,
Sending a random code
Before each thrust;

Conducting
Shock after shock
Before one arrival,
Iron tracks
Slide humming past the banks…
Under high wires, a road appears;
One glance, & I traverse it.
I drive the middle of the strip,
Quick seconds tick,
The center split-line fades
& reappears,

A broken tape:
Pass: clouds collide.
The sky is a smooth stone,
An early face,
Itself/

LUXEMBOURG GARDENS

I.

To adopt a musing, but not a musical tone;
To select with great care the most dignified disguise;
Cobalt blue sky, decaying leaves,
A something
                leaden in the air,
Poison, which if taken
In small doses
Over many years, armors the salvaging blood.

II.

Marbling the silence above my head,

Wholly unoriginal,
Frozen to a blank regard, imprisoned
In secondhand gesture, held
At remove,
             when, when will you drop the weight
             you cannot sculpt?

O, statues that circle the fountain,
My eyes are sunk stone.

III.

Your single pose
Must shoulder the swollen sun

        remaining

That the shadow of your hand,
Outstretched, might circle the sleeping world
& the dark touch come

        to free you

Of the dread of yourself, withheld
In the body's delay.

How shall I contain you?

How shall I release you?

Too deep, too heavy in memory,
The thought of you drives me clear of myself.
I could tell you I love you,
Arriving alone. *I fear*

the shadow I have become.

Shall I wrap you in absence,
Clothe you in dark?

The sun is an orphan swaddled in light.

The water is still
At the fountain's white lip. I will wear
My own waiting, in waiting
Will change. With obdurate sympathy,
Now I will change;

I will study the red clay beneath my feet;
I will learn my own weight

in forgetfulness,

The path to the center
That leads me away.

IV.

Drawn out
By a gesture I cannot free,
Dark hand that travels through me,
Pulls me back
To the stillness of its frozen command

When the sun
Is on the horizon's rim, when stone
& gesture flare as they meet
& find a brief radiance deep in the sky

O, then will I see?
Then, then will I carry you as myself
Before all the shadows
Gather as one,
Dark body that sheds itself for a dream?

V.

Ascending the set of marble stairs
That lead to the terraced periphery,

The circular track where the joggers pass,
The wall that bars the horizon,

The gate, I see the red clay
Of the tennis court floor, shirred

In deep streaks where the players had lunged;
A passionate convention kept them there,

Inhabiting an awkwardness fully won.
On the farthest court a last game

Still flares, defying the failing light
To remain. Remaining,

I hear the crossed strings resound,
Proclaiming a hidden pressure

With each blocked shot, each volley
Finding my ears

With exquisite delay. In silence,
The lagged eloquence of shock,

I place my hands on the sun-stung cage
                    & feel the deep coldness in my palms

& draw my face to the iron mesh
That vanishes with my nearness.

Revealing the arc of the guiding hand,
A spun ball jars the frozen tape

Tied at both ends to a trembling height—
Lost, for a moment, in that web—

O, I am the slightest change of that web.
Step back & the prison must form again

But the prisoner bears the sudden change,
The echo of blood at the bolted ear.

I turn, & step at the contrary tide
Of strangers crowding home through the gate,

Irradiations drawn dark at the sun.
Before them are shadowed tiers of stone

& statues held fast in their gravity.
Behind them high opposite buildings rise,

Banked windows of fire that burn in my eyes,
The spark that catches the opened heart

To radiance, constant, within,
Though the panes go dark. Now, now

These walls cannot hold me: I stay,
I pass through, & know not the night

I awaited—I pass through alive—
But the threshold I cross by being here,

Horizon wherever my two feet light.

VI.

I turn, resuming the grace of myself,
Inhabit the body, the moment that flows...

O, others in the park,

In this closed space, hurrying past
To thrust outside, to be
Outside the gates, still
You are trapped in your city, then
In your rooms, then
In your dreams
        Of an end
That would thwart all arrival,
A mask of stone—

        Suspended in baffled reach,

Forever deferred,
While your shadow must guard
The inner gates,
        The threshold
You struggle to leave behind,
Blind to what reaches you even now—

        When, when will you see
That your world means you,
That the hand that guides you
Is your own?

Return!
Be the hand of fire
Constantly
Tripping the latch of your heart...
O, let our eyes catch!,

In rays each to each,
Constantly weaving a world between—

Let all our moments blaze in that web!

Come, let us put on life, a new sun
Consuming the night & its wasting dream.

VII.

Here, where the steps are bathed in red light
& the untended roses lapse low in their bed

You descend, growing lighter with every step,
Exploring your own, your human time,

Tending the fire that blooms in your chest,
Each breath a bright gift—to let go!, to let go!,

O what you withhold in yourself hides the sun
In distance that dies with your own neglect—

Each scattered petal awaits your changed eyes
& every moment must gather you back

Until you are present at every pore
& what seemed most distant remembers you

& the whole scene composes the face of your love,
The living face that burns through the mask.

VIII.

We could have gone the long way around;
We could have circled the outside wall

But enter, as to a scene prepared,
Where light, in breaking, extends itself
Articulate on a sudden shore

        moment by moment extending us

In voices that cannot suffer
Our speed, in waves of arrival, broken,
That part and withdraw.

        What must I cross?

I would speak to you;
You could have gone the long way around;
You could have circled the outside wall;
O, we have come farther
Than ourselves,
        know more
Than the breach of our histories,
That shut in a moment
        to open a world—

Let the statues surrender their burdens;
Let the leaves fall.

        Let others
Remain on the branch awhile,
Receiving the slightest shift of the wind,
A stirring without direction
Or coming from all directions at once,

Absorbing the children's cries by the pool
That leap from the fountain within my heart,
That enter, as to a scene prepared,
An invitation

      too open to bear;

Where is the host who attends me now?
Here, in these eyes that burn through my own.
Believe me, move against me, I will stay;
I see you, move against you,
We will stay

      one man,

The only revelation we can know.

Jeffrey Gustavson

NATIVE HAZARDINGS:
Asymptotes of Poetry

What never wasn't? I think you know. It is a faith and it is a gamble, a face no mirror and a surefooted kid no projectile. If you pushed out of sleep today, and plan to tomorrow, you probably have it, will probably take it, or even definitely, definitely. Even money definitely probably certainly. Frustrations shram us every direction, every dimension, but here we still. Are. So long as that sun, our sun, our multitudinous planet's tireless sustainer, abides. To shram is to benumb with cold.

1. Poems are written, but those who write them aren't "writers." Mostly you're not writing, if it's poems you're after. Mostly you're crossing out or erasing, in your mind, at least, as you go along. *The words aren't words*, and they're never quite good enough, never enough the opposite of wrong. It's all animal, vegetable, mineral, and then pathways for the energy—all you can manage.

2. A poem doesn't gradually come into focus, it's just suddenly there, like a hummingbird.

3. Exhilarating resolutions of miscellaneousness into coherency. Could be changed, but why would you? Just go on to another improvisation.

4. Who am I to give advice? Just do what you like, do what satisfies yourself. Does it make any difference what other people think? It's always easier to theorize than to go out in the weather of your life and make something there. Do whatever you want!

5. The use of it is in the afterlife.

6. Let's all cast a vote for our favorite poem! May the best poem win!

7.   Squint at it, turn it upside down, like painters do.

8.   Staying up late is one way. If it seems like a good idea.
     But it doesn't matter, you can always revise later.

9.   It doesn't matter! Nothing will happen if it doesn't work out.
     Just don't worry about it—everybody, after
     all, knows how to worry just fine.

10. Life is expression.

11. The lyric impulse is always the purest, but it's easy
     to fool yourself into thinking you've adequately hon-
     ored it. If some part of you doesn't despise your own
     most lovable qualities, the danger is magnified.

12. Any given poem implies a whole swarm of anti-
     poems, the Devil's bids for entropy. The better the
     poem, the more easily it might not have been.

13. Poems are happiest not being compared with anything
     else. What they are that nothing else is—after all, they
     have to like listening to themselves for a long time.

14. There are no poets, only poems.

15. Snake venoms are vastly more poisonous than they need to be.

16. Poems are suffused with a sort of thanatognostic sub-
     junctive, a monk's mood in the welter of life.

17. Haughtiness in an old bathrobe!

18. Poetry is like physics or chess—a minority pursuit.

19. Everyone has a notion satisfying to themselves of what poetry is.
     Look at the way people use the word, in diverse realms—"It was

sheer poetry," etc. There can be poetry in driving a fork-lift.

20. If you don't like someone's poems, don't read them.

21. You can prepare yourself, but that's not always enough.

22. The mind experiences itself directly, the way
a hiker experiences the weather.

23. Analogy is always the seeking of a genuine likeness,
one that it could conceivably gratify Nature to have
recognized, like the similarity of seawater and blood.

24. A lot of the time poetry is an exuberant ultracrepidation.

25. A poem is poetry incarnate.

26. You can't will a pile of words into being a poem, but
between any two words there is a poetic charge of some kind.
If you think you're getting near a poem, it may be
you are. We like poems, ultimately, because we're
animals, not because we're such rational beings.

27. I've never known a poet who didn't read a lot.

28. You only have to write one poem, and that
poem will write your other poems.

29. Poetry is whatever anyone says it is.

30. Each poem inhabits a particular microclimate.

31. Don't forget to breathe!

32. Poems must be ready to face intense opposition. They
probably won't have to, but they should be ready.

33. A poem is a protein: as it assembles itself, a more
and more comprehensive matrix of exclusionary forces
builds up within it, increasingly narrowing the range
of admissible additional elements, till at last it matures
into the only possible antithesis of all that it
wasn't meant to be.

34. Poems are held together by a sham tyranny, a tyrant
willingness to submit. Poems want to be understood without
being obvious, loved not for their originality but for their
meaning, so that in admiring them you're admiring yourself.

35. You can't accidentally write a poem.

36. It is a sign of immaturity to be impatient with
aphorisms but a sign of littleness to detest them.

37. Though there are as many definitions of poetry as
there are people devising them, there is something
they all have in common, and *that's* what poetry is.

38. It is much harder to like a poem than to dislike it.

39. The ego is the poem's navel, not its whole body and self. Your
poems don't belong to you but to themselves. You can't just
write anything you please—the poem has the final say.

40. A poem is a campfire.

41. If a poem has no heartbeat, it's not alive. If a
poem has no heartbeat, it has nothing at all.

42. The vowels are married to the consonants.

43. The thoughts in a poem are refugees—displaced,
frightened, unwanted, desperate, needy, friend-
less. The poem is their only haven.

44. We all know what any of us knows.

45. All poetry is local poetry.

46. The poetry isn't in the words, just as the tennis isn't in the racquet, the balls, the net, and the court.

47. Receptivity to poetry comes and goes.

48. Mountains, the sea, and the moon—what else is there?

49. Poetry is always looking for an opportunity to make itself visible, even though it's the opposite of pushy.

50. Two friends of mine were once driving in western Montana late on a winter afternoon, after a day of cross-country skiing, when they saw a mountain lion leap in three bounds across the road in front of them—"It looked fifteen feet long, you know, the way something does when it's moving," Nan said— and disappear into the trees. Nan has lived in Montana most of her life, and it's the only mountain lion she's ever seen.

51. Rivers of the unsaid flow around the words of a poem.

52. Good poems push bad poems out of the nest.

53. A poem is an adventure.

54. Distinctions between parts of speech blur a little in a poem.

55. The subsurface connotations at play in a poem should retard it as much as they advance it—the goal is an unstable stasis. Or: all the ideas in a poem should cross the finish line at the same time.

56. You can make up any rules you want.

JEFFREY GUSTAVSON NATIVE HAZARDINGS

57. Materials and abstractions are like opposite sexes.

58. Let society judge and weigh, since it will anyway.

59. A poem is an antivenin.

60. Poetry is free for the asking.

61. When I was young, I thought the crucial word
    in Blake's proverb "Sooner murder a child in its cradle
    than nurse unacted desires" was "unacted,"
    but later I realized it was "nurse."

62. There is an irreducible strangeness at the heart of a poem.

63. Poetry is duly grateful for any and all theories of poetry,
    and will not choose favorites. Any sincere theory pleases her.

64. No path leads nowhere.

65. A poem has the permanence of a cloud at best.

66. A poem isn't afraid of anything.

67. Poems set out to make things right.

68. There are only a few emotions—and they're the same
    for everyone—but the moods of this Earth
    are indenumerable.

69. Grammar is a branch of ontology—the world is the measure.

70. Bohemianism has its place, but a little goes a long way.

71. The totality of poetry is a peaceable kingdom, lion with lamb, etc.

72. Poems that don't tap the deepest aquifers of
sadness are doomed to insignificance.

73. Poems ingiddied by theory lack purchase.

74. No amount of trouble is too much.

75. Every poem represents a divide.

76. It's never a good idea to encourage someone to write
poetry; the only ones who should do it are those who think
of it for themselves, who have no choice. Likewise no one
should be forced to read it, either. There's no percentage.

77. Poetry thrives on neglect.

78. If you want to write poems, forget about prose. Prose always has
designs on the poet, approaches with bit and halter in hand.

79. Let them go!

80. If you leave behind just one poem, you've done your part.

81. If a poem doesn't speak to you, it's not your
fault and it's not the poem's fault.

82. Some patterns in life endure by accident, but not many.

83. Use the language as if you invented it, because you did.

Douglas Rogers

THE BAIT

Every night at 10 o'clock, when my mother has taken a book to bed, my father, a farmer and game-lodge owner in the hills of eastern Zimbabwe, gets his shotgun out of the cabinet, slides a cartridge into each barrel, and goes to sit with it in the garden chair under the giant fig tree facing the front gate. He's keeping guard.

The bait is in the tin roof shed to the right: two heavy barrels of unleaded fuel fresh in from Mozambique—a rarity and a fortune these days, as in demand as a South African visa or a reliable currency dealer, one who won't rip you off or shop you to the secret police.

"They stole it before, they'll try again," he told my mother.

"And what are you going to do when they come?" she asked.

"Shoot them," he replied, a little exasperated. "What do you think the gun is for?"

He'd bought the fuel soon after the thieves stole his last two barrels, along with all his tools, on New Year's Eve, and he made a good show of letting the workers on the farm know he had a new supply. He had John Orange and John Old offload it, watched Rosie the maid see them carry it to the shed, saw Sydney the young barman clock it as he walked past the gate down to the backpacker camp at the bottom of the road.

Word would get around. It always did. This was Africa, and you couldn't stop talk. They had the oral tradition, after all. *The oral tradition!* He chuckled to himself as he sat there. *What a cunning thing. So open to interpretation.* When your history wasn't written down, who knew how it changed in the telling? How it was modified, improved upon, exaggerated over generations? It just became storytelling after a while, didn't it? And everyone had some bullshit story about how they really owned the land and how they were here first.

He thought back to the robbery.

It wasn't so much the theft of his fuel that had enraged him. It was the tools. *Who steals a man's tools? Take anything but leave the tools.* He had been lost without them these months. His wrench was gone, the new spanners he had bought in Pietersburg, even a shitty old pair of pliers. He had been unable to fix the pump for the borehole, the grill on the coffee roaster, the leak in the geyser in the roof.

The timing could not have been better, too. On New Year's Eve, the one night in the year they were sure to be out. What a start to the year it had been! As if he didn't have enough shit to deal with. There were the squatters—"new farmers," they called themselves—across the road who'd slaughtered all the zebra and antelope he'd stocked the farm with. And there was the Section Five, that document from the government: "We hereby inform you that the above mentioned land has been allocated for resettlement."

The place was falling apart before his eyes. But there was no way he was just going to *give* it to them.

He felt good with the gun on his lap. A ripple of moonlight pressed through the leaves of the fig tree and shimmered on the barrel. Next to his tools, this was his favorite possession in the world. True, it wasn't the best weapon to have in the circumstances. That would have been the FN FAL, the Belgian-made automatic he had during the bush war in the 1970s. *Now there was a gun!* Back then, when they had the chicken farm across the valley, he would ride shotgun with it in the car as my Mom drove my sisters and me to school, eyes peeled in bush for "terrs"—terrorists—ZANLA guerrillas who would attack the farms. At night my parents would sleep with it next to the bed in case of an attack, and in the morning, unload the magazine, check that the barrel was empty, and start all over again. And somehow, all those years, when everything was being shot up and blown up around us—including our neighbors—we had miraculously been left alone. What could explain that? He reckoned it was the gun.

Of course, when the war ended, in 1980, he returned it to the police. *Idiot*, he thought. But how could he have known, 25 years ago, that he would one day need it for another war? Instead, the shotgun was the only weapon he had left, and it would have to do. It was a beautiful vintage 12-gauge and a good hunting gun. He knew that. But could it do the bigger job?

A fruit bat flapped over his head and swooped over the front lawn. Crickets chirped out a ragged chorus. He liked being out here on his own. He heard a lone bus on the main road that ran along the southern boundary of the farm belch its way towards Harare, the capital city. There was a time when that road was busy, the country's main link to the ocean in Mozambique 400 miles to the east, but now so few people could afford fuel that it was quiet and almost deserted during the day. And who wanted to drive at night?

Soon his eyes had adjusted to the dark, and his hearing became more attuned. He heard voices drifting over from the camp, voices he was starting to get familiar with the more nights he spent out there keeping guard. The backpacker camp was half a mile beyond the front gate, past the long grass, the avocado trees, and the umbrella thorns, but it might as well have been on the front lawn, so clear were the voices. He recognized John Old's baritone; the cackle of Mrs. John, his toothless wife. Some of the staff, before they had to lay most of them off, had thought she was a *n'anga*—a witch. He hoped against hope that she was one. He liked and trusted her more than the others. And he could do with a good witch.

He wondered, as he listened, why it was that African voices seemed to carry so far in the darkness, seemed to float as naturally in the inkiness as the wood smoke and the shards of weed grass. Did it have something to do with that oral tradition of theirs?

He tried to picture the scene down there. They were either in the bar getting drunk or around a wood fire by the compound, drinking and smoking *dagga*. He could smell the *dagga* from here—a green, bittersweet tang, mingling with the oak of the wood smoke. He wondered if the weed was from his own crop, the plantation he had started with John Old behind the house. People were doing anything for money these days, and he was no different. And he wondered what *dagga* tasted like. He'd have to try it sometime. Perhaps his son would roll him a joint one day. He was sure I would know how.

The last light in the house went off behind him. My mother was going to sleep. The light from the cottages on the hills to the north blinked off, too. Mrs. Herrer in No. 3, an 80-year-old Afrikaner woman, the best cattle farmer in the valley in her day. Delaney in No. 11. And at the bottom of the hill in No. 8, Harry Venter, his latest tenant, the most recent white farmer to lose his land. *Old Harry. What a bullshitter.* The man claimed to be friendly with the Vice President, claimed she could get him his farm back. Now that he'd like to see!

Still, he was glad these people had homes, and he knew it was because of him. When he bought this farm, when his kids had all left home, there was nothing on these hills but bush and stone. And in five years he and my mother had created a small empire: 16 cottages for rent, each with wide verandahs and sweeping views of valley; the backpacker lodge with its chalets, swimming pool, and restaurant-bar that once pulled in tourists from the world over. They had named it Drifters, and the guidebooks the travelers carried with them all wrote well about it. They had had some wild parties at the camp bar over the years. It hadn't really been a business at all; it was more like an extension of their home.

And now? Now the cottages were refugee camps for dispossessed whites. And the camp? *Jesus,* he thought. It was what it was. It made them money, but it also made them embarrassed. He tried not to think about it. Then he thought about it. Maybe they should start renting chalets by the hour? The whole country was whoring itself, why shouldn't they cash in? He made a mental note to suggest to my Mom the next day that if the marijuana side-business didn't kick in they should start renting chalets by the hour, formalize operations, so to speak.

It must have been well after midnight now because the voices were gone. The moon had ducked behind the Chikanga Mountains, and even the crickets were quiet. Now he didn't feel so comfortable. Did crickets usually stop chirping? Was that normal? He hoped the fruit bat would come back, and he wished he'd brought a blanket. Maybe even a flask. The kitchen was behind him; it would be easy to go inside and make some hot tea. But what if they came when he was making tea? What an idiot he'd be then. He stayed put.

He thought again of his suspects. It could be John Old or John Orange, but he doubted it. They would know he would accuse them first up—which he did—and besides, he didn't think they had it in them. Too old. More likely it was John Old's son. He had seen the little bastard down at the compound a few days before, skulking in the bushes. Like every other kid in the country he was unemployed. And how did he buy those new running shoes?

But most of all, he suspected the Political Commissar.

Now there was a bona fide bastard. A fat, lowly party official, he had appointed himself headman for the area and claimed for himself the farmhouse of old man Fritz Barnard across the road. He was too low on the ruling party ladder to be given a car, but high enough to be given a farm, and therefore, like all middling-to-average people everywhere, all the more dangerous. With his long grey raincoat and leather briefcase, he would stand on the road in the mornings and ask my Dad for a lift into the city, where, he was unembarrassed to say, he had a "town house." That was how it was. The bastard had *two* homes! My father could easily see himself shooting the Political Commissar.

His arms were growing heavier now. The leaves and branches of the fig tree seemed to sink warmly around him, enveloping him like the blanket he wished he had. He could barely keep his eyes open now. His head was heavy, too. Slowly his grip loosened on the gun.

The noise came from the bushes beside the front gate. He woke up with a start. Had he fallen asleep? What time was it? *Jesus.* Someone was out there! He gripped the gun, leaned forward, trying to keep silent while adjusting his position. It came again. A light rattle of the chain-link fence. Someone *was* out there! His heart pounded, the sudden exhilaration making him dizzy. He saw two red eyes in the darkness, staring straight at him. He stared straight back, trying to focus, easing the gun up to his shoulder now. It was happening! They had come back! At last, it was payback time!

He saw it as clearly as if it were day. It was a giant full-grown antelope, a magnificent bull eland with tall twisted horns like acacia branches grazing in the long grass beside the fence. His heart was pounding. *Jesus. An eland.*

He had bought a herd of them years ago when the camp and the cottages were being built, along with some zebra and impala, but he had not seen them in four years. He thought the squatters and the war vets and the Commissar had wiped them all out. They set wire traps made from his farm fence they ripped down; they hunted them with their mongrel dogs; others they just shot. He and my mother would hear gunfire in the middle of the night, and in the mornings find skinned carcasses in the hills. He had presumed the animals were all dead, but now, right here in front of him, one had showed itself.

It stared at him with those magnificent sad eyes, and he stared straight back. He had never felt so much pity for a mere animal before, and yet so much love for one, so much elation that something out there—something *else* out there!—had managed to survive.

The animal bent its neck, chewed more grass, then looked up at him again. It seemed to be nodding at him. He wanted to nod back, but he didn't want to scare it. Then the creature wheeled away and loped off into the long grass, past the avocado trees and the umbrella thorns. My father watched it go. For the first time in months, the rage he had inside him seemed to have gone. He felt light-headed and dizzy.

He walked back to the house. He set the gun by the dresser table and rolled into bed next to my mother. Maybe now he could get some sleep. ◆

Jane R. Oliensis

HISTORY OF RAIN;
OR, THE UMBRELLA MUSEUM

Rainy Dilemma

First, a dull grey cloud hovered above the car,
drenching the suitcases, out up on the car rack.
All our favorite summer things mother'd packed
so carefully: sun dresses, floppy sun hats
for the little girls, lace stockings for special occasions
on terraces, fragrant creams for Agnes—
oatmeal, honey, the beautiful open sandals,
plastic water pistols—purple, blue, green—
for Tim (he was in that phase) for eventual dueling,
and all Matty's ridiculous floaty toys.
Then the glum cloud came in. Sobs. Choking grief.

Soon we were all, per Dad: *sobbing wet.* Mother:
This is no time for a joke! The windshield wipers
tried gamely to wipe away all traces
of the Albigensian heresy of grief.
What's grief's pure faith? But mother, for the first time
The last straw! And in the car. It's gone too far!
broke down and tumultuously cried.
The thing was it had rained inside the house
for two years, enigma to dazed plumbers.
They tapped their musical pipes and left, perplexed.
Had something burst? And where? And when? *Sorry,
Mr. O. That's alright, Joe. Thanks for trying*
to soft-pedal the rainy tune on our stricken piano.

First Measures: Umbrellas

We tried umbrellas. Agnes' was raspberry pink
with bright orange stripes like that verandah in Hungary
the hotel with the bees who liked strawberry jam.
Agnes liked elegant hotels, jam pots, butter patties,
the rituals of breakfast, father's lazy coffee.
Tom's was lightning green, with prowling tigers,
Rain-forest safari, adventure's ecstasy.
Mother's was pink with happy yellow suns.
Dad's had high monsoons, rain on blue ocean,
Pygmies doing a rain dance, rain relativity.
Mine had grey stripes like a stylized fountain,
the yellow stone restraint of a classical column.
Matty's, I don't remember. Ballerinas, I think,
yes, pink tutus, arabesques, leaping quarter notes.

It got so we could do just about everything,
and with a certain grace, holding our umbrellas
in our left hands: get dressed, play the piano,
drink coffee, butter toast. Even have baths.
or read the newspaper. Father: *Rain sermons, rain symphonies.*
This must be the rainy season of our lives.
But mother couldn't bear the sweet *plink plunk,*
quiet crying, rain ballet, rain choreography.
(I loved the sweet, soft rain, wooing April
with fecundity, summer's slap-happy rain, carefree,
even the sigh sigh sorry for itself sort.)
Telegrams: the choir of helpers bustled in,
scores under their arms, music stands, batons.
They'd conduct our rainy melody, *make a harmony.*

Visits: 1) Aunt Mabel

First Aunt Mabel, mother's oldest, horsy sister.
She had never married. She loved riding
her blue bicycle down Paris' broad avenues,
Excelsior. She whinnied at father's jokes,
her laugh the happy gurgle of a faucet
after a winter stiffness in the joints.
Mabel preached books about the spring and change,
lugged three or four with her. *As grief's interesting...*
no—voilà, chère Lily.... Though the green sap hurts,
embrace your change. Some days, my life's dull prose,
as dishwater. Then voilà, it's elevating poetry,
Duel with the rain, this challenge. Don't just stick
the same old pins in mother's pin cushion.
Can't say I envy you. Kisses. She flew off.

Father's Eyebrows: 1

First, they were like the sweet white arcade
outside the commissary's dusty office—
that little town in Spain, the perfectly square square.
Evenings, a little merry-go-round would spin
with a gay music. Courtly cantering. *For carnival.*
Carne, flesh. They celebrate the physical
here, teased Tim. How could they? I wanted to weep
for the imperfections of the poor old world,
dying happily. *The world isn't ideal,*
I almost whispered to Matty. Silly goosey words!
We had to wait two days for a purple stamp
on our passports, a man with drooping mustachios.
Chicken on a spit, wistful smoke and stars.
That arcade had a rhythm you could count on.

SECOND MEASURES: MOTHER'S STRATAGEMS

For goodness' sake, Agnes said, when the rain crew came.
She was map-making, coloring continents.
Tim was graphing mathematical equations.
I was queen of daydreams. My straining heart,
stifled by the snowdrifts of homework, sank.
Mother's choice, an innovative, modern machine
like a giant pink-and-yellow straw,
with lots of guarantees, would *surely work*.
It gulped up the rain happily but soon self-shredded.
Not *sufficiently flexible*. They'd *mismeasured windows*.
The pieces fell, all one afternoon, on the second-floor landing
like rain, sighed Agnes regretfully. *Pink and yellow
rain,* shrieked Matty happily. Tim tackled her.
Mother luckily was away. We swept up the sad debris.

The next looked like a robot with a sieve
on his head. (He *was* a robot.) His name was Harry.
He ate his meals with us. His fork clanked up
an awful racket. Mother frowned. We weren't to notice.
He was kind and comical. He danced the polka,
an antidote to rain, *the upside down of rain,*
according to Harry. Matty polkaed, too.
One Sunday at lunch, the rain stopped suddenly
with a lurch. Two hot sultry days, then normal.
Harry stayed on six more days *for good measure,*
dancing faithfully in the hall upstairs. Matty cried
when he left. (So did I.) We waved goodbye
from the gravelly driveway. Sweet Harry.
Two gala parties. Then the rain came back.

FATHER'S EYEBROWS: 2

Harry was expensive. (So was the giant straw.)
Father ho-hummed it would have to be enough.
Mother's radiant smile, overcast, dimmed.
Father's eyebrows grew higher, jagged like the peaks
in the postcards of Mt. Fuji they sent back.
And snowier. Two each. Then they were home!
We were staying at our cousins', the cheerleaders.
What extravagant splits! How the silver baton spun
like the bright moon, bosom friend I preferred—
O, why? That spring, we took the family trip
to Omaha (I think it was)—it was beautiful—
to see the famous reservoir of tears.
But nothing cheered us up. Dad said our schoolwork
suffered from the sad choir we'd become.

To think, mother said, *I loved rain as a girl,*
fell in love with your father in the rain.
But this is different. Her weeping filled the house.
Dad's brows arched higher—almost above his head—
high as the Gothic arches in French cathedrals.
Dad said those arches lost their human scale.
Tim called them *mere abstractions of arches.*
Becoming etherial, they seem to disappear.
Matty worried Dad's would disappear forever.
Rain, dear, rain. Surely you've seen rain before.
Where is your patience, the flexibility I . . .
Mother's smile trembled, shakier, went out,
like the fireflies in the cousins' garden, bright
with them. Evenings, they taught us badminton, croquet.

VISITS: 2) AUNT AGNES AND UNCLE SVEN

Then came Aunt Agnes, mother's youngest sister
(She was beautiful and fashionable!)
and solemn Uncle Sven. He handed around
wooden construction toys. (He liked to build things.)
For Agnes a swing, a doll swing for Matty,
and for me, a little desk for dolls,
with a miniature, old-fashioned inkwell,
where dolls would sail their paper boats at school.
Dolls were mischievous, back in the Old Country,
dreamed up out of a corncob, bit of wood,
eh, Aggie? She tossed her honey-colored hair.
We were a regular conference of sawdust
what with the planing, the drilling, and the sawing.
Mother and Aunt flipped through their stylish reviews.

Then: *I've always liked this house,* began Uncle Sven
deliberately. *But now I like it especially. Free showers!*
Now there's a labor-saving device. Quite an idea!
We all fell gravely silent. In a corner,
mother and Aunt Aggie were sipping tea
under our most elegant (gold-fringed!) umbrella.
We weren't to mention the rain under any circumstances,
nor even allude to it. I couldn't breathe.
My nuisance of a body felt so heavy
the way witches must have felt who curdled cream
when, lead in their shoes, they sent them dunking.
Then (worse!) Uncle Sven began a hissing
like mother's favorite teakettle before it sang.

The hiss grew louder, like a tropical rain
dusty islanders had waited weeks for. Then goofy guffaws
to the refrain of *dear me, oh my dears.*
Dearest Agnes, my darlings, forgive me. I couldn't help it . . .
and Uncle Sven was whooping with delight,
containing what had been uncontainable.
Then there was a laughing like snorting, laughing like wheezing,
laughter like a waterfall, like a sigh,
like a jack-in-the-box popping open suddenly,
a brown-paper sandwich bag bursting with glee,
an uproarious symphony of laughter—
Dear me, dear me, forgive me, and all the tears.

CONCLUSIONS

After that visit, we all felt much better.
Eventually, the rain just went away,
the way things do, sometimes, even if you can't say why.
Like Tim's teasing. I almost missed it (not really).
He was shaving, Aunt Mabel sent cologne. He was dating girls!
Matty fell off Agnes' swing next summer
and broke her wrist. (She was still too little.)
These were our mishaps. Mother's teakettle
started whistling again. I came to cherish
her fragility. The radiant smile
which gave us so much comfort, brave stability,
hid her secret griefs, dear vulnerability.
Our parlor became the local umbrella museum,
open on Tuesdays, afternoons, for tea.

Joel Hinman

THE MINUTEMAN

To begin at the end, the last time I ever saw my father, both of my parents had come down to the train station to see me off to college. It was a stark December morning and we stood off by ourselves on the platform, stamping our feet against the cold, my father and I with our eyes fastened on the spot at the north end of the station where any second the Minuteman would appear in a blaze of glinting silver to take me to New York for the flight to Europe. In other families, such a departure might have been the occasion for an outpouring of tender affection, but in the year that followed my younger brother's suicide, my father, mother, and I had become even more protectively shy with our feelings. We each thought it was a sacrifice we made for the others.

The year had felt like a minute.

Only an hour earlier, I had been packing in the bedroom of my childhood. I had my duffel bag open on the bed and was just slipping in a last paperback when I noticed the house had fallen silent and for the briefest moment I felt myself remembering the child I had been in this room. A boy who had been frightened of the elm branches scraping the window, who had seen terrors in the darkest parts of the closet, who had lain sobbing on the bathroom tiles over some perceived disappointment or failure. But just as the memories were beginning to unfold in my chest, I caught sight of myself in the long narrow mirror. Staring back at me was a figure out of literature, a young Raskolnikov, with jeans tucked into motorcycle boots, and a long sweep of hair that he kept tucking behind his ear. He had on a red cowboy shirt under an army topcoat bought at a flea market. There were spots along his jaw but he looked like someone who went through life taking long strides, answering only to himself and a few others he thought his equal.

I studied myself and tried to think of something that might commemorate the start of my journey. To make for an auspicious beginning, I wanted my declaration to include "manifestation" and "avatar," words that had the right kind of suggestive power and resonance, but as much as I struggled, I couldn't construct anything sufficiently portentous. Nonetheless, by the time I was stomping down the back stairs with my duffel bag, my mind was so filled with a sense of my destiny that I barely noticed my mother as I passed through the kitchen and out the back door.

I saw my father standing in the driveway next to the family station wagon. Behind him a privet hedge ran along the top of a low stone wall until it ended at the gate of the drying yard, a place that had seemed enchanted in my childhood but now seemed abandoned and empty. Even though I had seen my father only the night before at dinner, in the daylight I faltered at the sight of how much he had aged. When I was growing up, my father had always embodied physical strength. He had the broad chest of a rower, someone I thought of as pulling himself through life using the muscular power of his upper body, but since the death of my brother, everything had fallen. The soft clay of his face had sagged, leaving his eyes exposed and vulnerable. His sandy hair has lost its color and lay lifeless on his skull. He had the traumatized appearance of someone who had undergone surgery. His face was puffy, the skin mottled along his neck and across his cheeks. For me it was an affront to see the way my father was suffering. We fought, disagreeing about everything, but he was a good man. It seemed unjust and indecent that he should be turned out to live his remaining life without the peace of faith or hope, his spirit crippled and beyond repair. We were alone for a moment and I wanted to find something to say to him that would give him relief, but my thoughts were becoming confused. Somehow I couldn't figure out what to say and my eyes stung and instead I reached for the car door and threw my bag inside. He looked up from whatever he had been thinking and we stared at each other across the roof of the car, both of us frozen, before I broke off contact and crawled into the back seat after my bag.

As we drove away, I slumped against the door, looking out the window and listening to my mother chatter on about the neighbors whose homes we were passing. They were people I had known once. At first, the houses lay at some remove from the road at the end of long rolling lawns, but then when we turned onto Red Farms Road the houses seemed to take a step closer to one another and the lots were smaller. Then again, after we came to Fern Cliff, the houses shuffled even closer, losing their outbuildings, then their porches and gables until by the time we reached the freeway all the buildings had been jammed together into rows of condominiums. The long series of roofs looked to me like the bones of a snake crawling over the hills. The way it had changed, I would not miss this country.

I was going to Leipzig to study German Metaphysics. Even as a child, I had been independent and thought it necessary to see things for oneself. I had never relied upon other people's versions of how things were. And what needed personal verification more than metaphysics? So when we were hurrying across the floor of the train station and my father called out the track number, I had to stop, go back, and see for myself. I looked up at the board. The train was on time.

In a single file we threaded our way around the pools of water in the passageway under the tracks. It had been cold the night before and the homeless had sought refuge in the tunnel. The air reeked faintly of urine. I heard my father make a low sound in disgust. There was nothing to do but breathe through our mouths until we reached the double glass doors which were so milky from handprints and spittle that the stairwell beyond seemed out of focus. Then up the stairs we went, again in single file, my father leading, until we came out onto the platform, where the sun shone brightly and the air was as clear as a bell jar.

There were twenty or so people waiting for the train. My parents and I moved away from the others, something we did almost without thinking. Even when my brother was alive, if we went to the theater as a family, we stood off by ourselves during intermission. It was not out of a concern for privacy, but rather the notion that being overheard was somehow imposing on strangers. Our idea of generosity was to deny ourselves. I put my duffel bag down and looked for young women among the passengers. I positioned myself so I could face my parents and yet keep an eye on two attractive college girls who, I noticed, were already acting self-consciously.

My mother asked, "You have your ticket?" She had turned towards me and had slipped a finger under my coat button, pulling on it to see if it was about to come loose. She used the corner of her thumb to pluck a stray thread. She patted the lapels of my jacket so she could keep her hands on my chest. I saw her begin to scowl at the condition of my coat.

"It's a Goodwill coat, Mom, " I said. "Goodwill."

My mother frowned, but nodded. She was having trouble looking up at my face.

"You're sure you have enough money, son?" my father asked. Even after he finished asking the question, his lips continued to move.

"I'm O.K., Dad. "

I was aware that the air between us was trembling with anticipation. We were saying goodbye, and despite our assurances that we would be together in March, it was one more departure coming so soon after the first.

I looked off up the track. When I turned back, I noticed how my father's face, with his cheeks and jaw freshly shaven, seemed overfilled with moisture. And how my mother's recent haircut, which was shorter than her usual cut, now made her appear so delicate and unprotected. I felt a twinge of longing and a sense of suddenly wanting to stay home to help them.

"Well, we'll miss you," my father said, his voice hoarse and dry. He glanced at me before covering his mouth.

"I know, Dad. I know," I said in reassurance.

We stood silently on the platform. It was one of those moments in which I felt the absence of my brother more than the presence of my parents who stood right in front of me. We had survived the year, but only slowly was life becoming bearable, and sometimes it was seeing each other that served to remind us painfully of our loss. Then there was the long low whistle of the Minuteman, and I felt my heart quicken. Something thick rose inside me and I began to feel an overwhelming and dizzying sense of failure that I had waited too long and now there was too much to say and nowhere to start. Then something came to me. It wasn't even a thought, yet it seemed to come from a great distance away, traveling along a compressed and narrow track before suddenly opening violently and washing through me. I could not at first put it into words, but it was an understanding that all the fear and anger and confusion that I had felt, and that my parents and I had shared out among each other, was really nothing more than just our mangled form of love. It was all we knew in my family. Simultaneously, I had a strange sensation that none of us was really older than the others, that the death of my brother had not aged us, but instead had left us all somehow unformed. We were equal in how little we understood what had happened to us. I looked at my father and saw how his shoulders were stooped and his suit bunched up under his overcoat. I saw how my mother's lips were pursed and yet drawn tight across her face. My hands were shaking at the end of my coat sleeve. The beating of my heart sounded like a man walking on a wooden floor. Shifting my feet, I brushed my coat against my mother's.

I turned as the train emerged from behind the red sandstone building. It came at us riding on its own cloud of steam and smoke, with its single light flaring a silvery white. Against the background of old buildings, the train seemed to have such size and immense power that it reset the scale of everything around it. I felt flooded with hopefulness. My father, mother, and I stood quietly, stepping back as the train pulled in, a gust of air brushing our faces. I squeezed my eyes shut. I heard my father trying to say something over the rushing sound of the train. Then the people all over the platform began moving forward. I looked at my parents, who seemed small and lost against the crowd that had begun pushing towards the train. I watched the anxiety in their faces, and yet, in that moment, seeing them together, I realized that they had each other and that my separate life was just beginning.

I turned to my mother. "Mom? Take care of Dad."

My mother's hand came up encircling my arm. People were already crowding the steps leading up into the train.

"Dad…," I started. I could see the confusion on my father's face as he tried to decide if we should embrace. Awkwardly, he seized my hand in his. Then with his other hand he gripped my elbow as if trying to steady himself. Then we were stumbling towards each other and our shoulders came together until the top of my head was pinned against his shoulder. His face was hot against my neck and there were tears on my father's coat. My shoulders were shaking under my army coat. Leaning against him, I said something to my father, though even a second later I could not recall what I had told him. It was as if some part of me had quietly appeared, but only for a moment before disappearing forever.

"O.K. then, Dad," I finally managed. I could feel my mother's hand on my back and her dry lips against my cheek. I felt the weight of the duffel bag in one hand. I wiped my eyes as I struggled forward. Then there was the handle and I was pulling myself up into the train.

I stood in the aisle with my bag. Up ahead people were arranging their suitcases in the luggage rack. When the time came, I lifted the duffel bag and slid it into the overhead space. I glanced down the aisle, remembering the college girls I had seen. My heart was still lurching around in my chest and I had to choke the feeling back. I tried to think of the journey that lay before me. It was only then that I turned to the window. My parents were there on the platform, both waving to a window far down the car where they thought I was seated. The train began to move, and I watched my father and mother wave until they were out of sight. ◆

Michael Ruby

INNER VOICES HEARD
BEFORE SLEEP

11

At the White House
You just can't
You're not supposed to

Why isn't he?
Here

The highest

And he's said nothing about the future of America
And the implications

There's no point in interviewing

JC said
You can only take one man
(These are good)

You don't really know
Are you doing it right?

There's no legend
Oh
Hired

If we do what we said
Five or six strong republics

He did a demonstration
Of nobody yet
With the money
Assistance learning

Struggling sufficiency
On the Driscoll booby head

It just passes through watching television

Well
He's making canapes
The smoke

Better criticism
…reads his ass off

He makes time at the end of it
To play synagogue

The Baltimer

As eyes against him
Well, let 'em
Hades

I'm not enjoying the feeling in my body
Or swing

All kinds of teachers and throwbacks
We might have thrown you into the fire

He's a lighter—
Teachers
Then school systems

Based on this one
Goin' for his future

I don't want to nurse you out
Some of which we've already decided

I just can't focus
Can you screw its—
Goose
The histories
First theme: I'm going to have to do it

Soap
Soap kills

The basketball cable
The total in my voice

If he tied you
You tied me

Could you tell me what the name of the kangaroo poodle
is?

Unless you tell me what to do
I'll write you down

They are nuts
His book's out

By me
Beautiful days
Sure

Haunted
That word
Please
The luxury

Build up one guy
Backfires other days

So he can
He can

He has another fancy brow

The outside chances are insignificant
What we're doing for doom's sake

Do you hear the speed of it?

Who say yes?
Who say now?

His 'stituency
Another vote for Sloater
Sloater

This hour
Reasons were down 2%

What's the issue?
What?

Face the wind with me
And the smallest de-tails

I don't know how you do it
It's not easy
It's not easy

46

This one
The position was a nice one

…hails from there

The yellow tag, and you can use three words

And I think retrospectively
We can turn our cheeks again

50

Take you somewhere else
Now, to step over them

Oh God, I shouldn't have been so pleasant
The West Bank is more interesting

Tulips, however
On the pleasure
On the history
On the eleventh

I guess so

No, he's not the thinnest
Not thinnest

It may not be advisable

Can you get a license for that

And I was

...developing in southeastern France
And their neighbors—

It may make the two parts more—
—They certainly don't

Once you're there, of course, it's been there

Peterson
A uniform position
Peterson's in

Whatever you want is fine with me
If you want presents, as I said

No matches on Sunday night
On Nissan
Cuz everyone's new

The house sleeps all night

Lynch knows it's his, not Peter's

...any historical sites anymore
By $50,000

Who works on it

So don't work on it
…gives a better clue
And it comes from the secret

51

They're the biggest eyelashes in your life

Last night
Just last night

Now it's going forward
Get up and set the gears

You must be doing something wrong

The minute the upheavals

Skip it

When you're watching one person

Sorrow classes
They're tomorrow

If you get closed up

Who's the next one who's gonna do it
By the time I noticed
Now my wife doesn't even notice
No more cigarettes
That would be momentous
Imagine that

But you have to keep on

To let music in and everything
Or leave us alone

Statue
…on probation

You know it sounds funny…

Singing
I think it was physical

Not many minutes, I know that

I was thinking of doing something for you
Like the Winter Garden

They were going to appear in order
The 25th of January

But I found a different place

Which is, of course
Which is, of course, record labels

I didn't know that
I thought we were friends with everybody

Everyone claims—
And they have no desire to desert themselves

However, that will end

Airplane aneurisms, which aren't ours, huh

Plenty of clothes, for the obvious reasons

Such luck as we entrust the almighty
And I told you no
Of any size
But I'm not gonna do anything

And then, there's all the communication

Got a bit of law on our hands

Along a different—
A juvenile delinquency

We need a tillion civilians
I want you to take over their hardware store

You know what he said really loud
Can I tell you what this makes me feel like

One a vacation
From the family of friends
A mistake

How do you know all this
How do you know this

54

Your illustrious ones
Your glorious ones

And you can't get everybody
No, you can't get anybody

…is American
Up and down

Now it's the dark waters
That you like waters
Done right when you shouldn't
One second

You know, this one is the best
To know this one

A record
Of what there was to learn

And went there 20 hours a day
And she got away with it

Anna Steegmann

MEIN HARLEM

Harlem, even at its worst, has always been good to me. The first friend I made in New York after leaving my home in Germany lived in Harlem. We met in 1982 at an audition at La Mama. I was excited when Dana Jackson invited me to her house. She lived with her mother in East Harlem, not far from where my favorite writer, James Baldwin, was raised. In my German guidebook, Manhattan ended at 96th Street, and foreign visitors were warned not to venture beyond because they might not leave Harlem or Washington Heights alive. But I wasn't afraid of Harlem. I already knew Harlem from James Baldwin's novels, short stories, and essays that I had read in the German translation.

As soon as I emerged from the No. 2 train at the corner of 125th Street and Malcolm X Boulevard, the air was full of danger and menace. The only white person on the street, I held my head high and walked with confidence east for a block, then turned right onto what Baldwin had called "wide, filthy, hostile Fifth Avenue." I looked for the grocery store's Jewish proprietor who had given the Baldwin family credit, the shoe-repair store's Negro proprietor, the Buy Black street-corner meetings, and the Holy Rollers Baldwin had described. I hoped to find the Fireside Pentecostal Assembly where James got his start as a youthful preacher.

Instead I found blocks of abandoned and burnt-out buildings that looked like Germany at the end of World War II. Street vendors aggressively hawked their wares and Black Israelite preachers pontificated to their street flock. One of them, looking extraterrestrial in his shiny silver headband and belt, suddenly spewed hatred in my direction: "Whites are the incarnation of evil. God will wipe out all the Christians and Muslims. Only we are his chosen people." I walked faster. Shady characters lurked in doorways. Young men offered me drugs. A good number of people had collapsed on the pavement, strung out on potent liquor or drugs. I was relieved to finally arrive safely at Dana's home.

The Jacksons' residence was fortified like a medieval castle with window gates, burglar bars, slide bolts, deadbolts, and impressive-looking high-security police locks. Dana explained that they had been broken into plenty of times: from the roof, the backyard, the basement, and through the kitchen window. Once I passed the security barrier, I found three elegantly furnished floors, an entire brownstone just for Dana and her mother. There were bay windows, a graceful parlor, shiny parquet floors, fireplaces, and a library with thousands of records and books. Miss Jackson could have started her own radio show with her outstanding R&B collection.

Dana's mother felt sorry for me, all alone in New York, so far away from my own mother, and adopted me for Thanksgiving, Christmas, and many Sunday dinners. On my first visit, I stared in disbelief at the abundance of food, the visual and olfactory feast spread out before me. The rich burgundy tablecloth was covered with plates, bowls, terrines, and glass candlesticks. There were three plates for each of us, rolled-up linen napkins, and a confusing assortment of cutlery. Unsure about what to do with all those knives and forks, I waited for Miss Jackson to start. She wore a chic flower-print dress that clung to her curvaceous body. Her hair was done in the latest Jheri-curl fashion and the bright orange of her lipstick and perfectly manicured nails matched the colors of her dress. So different from my mother, who always wore an apron or a housedress, never a stylish dress like Miss Jackson. My mother hated make-up. She had been indoctrinated by Hitler's youth organization for girls. *A German girl is a pure girl. A pure girl doesn't smoke or paint her face. Only whores do.*

"Child, are you hungry?" Miss Jackson asked me. Then she folded her hands neatly in front of her chest. "Dear Lord," she said, "thank you for all the blessings you have bestowed upon us. And thank you for bringing us this nice visitor from Germany." Overcome, I turned beet red. I was twenty-six and no one had called me Child in a very long time. At home, saying grace was simply going through the motions, mumbling the words without thinking. Miss Jackson made up her own prayer. She spoke like a poet and infused each word with deep emotion. An atheist since fourth grade, I was ready to join her flock.

I was taken with Miss Jackson's grace, hospitality, and her amazing culinary talents. She introduced me to new foods: black-eyed peas, mustard greens, okra and best of all sweet potato pie. Her collard greens looked and smelled similar to my mother's *Grünkohl*, but tasted so much better. Her smothered pork chops were the best I ever had. I found that black people, like the Germans, devoured pigs' feet, ham hocks, and tripe. What we called *Saumagen*, they called chitlins and maw. Our drinking habits, however, were worlds apart. The Jacksons did not drink beer or wine with dinner. They drank ginger ale with their meals and strange alcoholic concoctions before or after.

Miss Jackson taught me about Black history, about Harlem as "the capital of Black America," the excitement of the Civil Rights Movement, the riots and the devastation caused by drugs that followed. "The middle class moved to the suburbs and left nothing but poor people behind. Harlem turned into a slum." A supervisor at AT&T, she purchased her brownstone on East 122nd Street during that time and was very proud to have made it on her own. *Smart women buy low and sell high.*

A legendary beauty, Miss Jackson had enjoyed many suitors in her youth, but never married. She had banished Dana's father, "the sperm donor," from her life. He drank too much and "was a heap of trouble." She had a steady boyfriend, but would not let him move in with her. *Why buy the cow when you can get the milk for free?* Hank, the owner of a trucking company, was a perfect gentleman. He took her to fine restaurants, Broadway musicals, and weekend trips to Atlantic City. For her birthday, he bought her serious jewelry. He let her pick out his clothes at SYMS and agreed to have the rims of his hats taken in, since he, a native of South Carolina, looked "too country" for her taste. I thought of Miss Jackson as a feminist icon and tried to follow her advice: *Don't let a man treat your ass like a comfort station.* My mother, afraid to be on her own, had stayed in a loveless marriage with an irascible husband. She could have learned a thing or two from Miss Jackson's chutzpah.

In Berlin I lived in a spacious, sunny apartment with a beautiful desk and hundreds of books, but in New York my room was as sparse as a prison cell. Leaving Harlem, the warmth and comfort of the Jacksons' home, was tough. I was not looking forward to my dingy Alphabet City sublet. Emboldened by all the whiskey sours, I rejected Dana's offer to walk me to the subway: "Don't worry, I'll get a cab."

There were no yellow cabs in Harlem, but I was hoping for a livery cab to come my way. For a long time I waved my arms frantically, but all the cars passed me by. When I got fortunate and one car stopped, the driver, a mean expression on his face, sped away as soon as I tried to open the rear door. Some time later, as pathetic as a dog caught in the rain, I rang the Jacksons' doorbell again. Dana smiled at my foolishness, then escorted me to the street, and hailed a cab. The drivers always stopped for her.

When I was nine, the newspaper brought disturbing images into our living room. Young black children marching through the streets of Birmingham had been knocked unconscious by blasts of water jets and mauled by German shepherds unleashed by the police. Feeling sorry for the little girl my age in the picture, I became a champion of justice for black people and sent a letter to John F. Kennedy. I begged him to do something about the grave injustice in the United States of America. Later, in high school, I joined a radical students' group and got arrested for plastering the town with flyers proclaiming *Solidarität mit dem Schwarzen Panther.*

I admired many black artists. Miles Davis and Sarah Vaughn, Langston Hughes and James Baldwin. Black people seemed to possess a greater capacity for emotion and compassion. In Germany, I had been surrounded by anger, envy, and bitterness, but sadness was a forbidden feeling. You pretended that everything was fine, that you were brave and tough, that you didn't need help or sympathy. You let no one know that you cried yourself to sleep at night. The concerts of American blues musicians I attended as a teenager showed me a different way of being in the world. Champion Jack Dupree, Big Joe Williams, Sonny Terry and Brownie McGee, Joe Turner and all the others made it O.K. to moan and grown, to wail and cry. They made it O.K. to be human, warts and all.

In 1986, I married a handsome black man who had moved to New York from Baltimore. He owned his own fashion company and lived in a posh seventeen-story doorman building on the Upper West Side where he was the only black tenant. Many evenings, attempting to return home from his SoHo store or a downtown party, empty taxis sped by us. I remembered leaving the Jacksons' house and not being able to get a cab on 125th Street. Those drivers must have been retaliating for all the times they, their mothers, or their sisters were left out in the rain.

When Miss Jackson passed away I had no reason to go back to Harlem. The two cassettes she made for me became my most sacred possessions. (Twenty-five years later, in the age of CDs and iPods, I refuse to retire my Walkman, so I can visit Nathan Jones, "The Rubberand Man," and "Mustang Sally" whenever I need to lighten up.) Dana and I drifted apart. She sold the house and moved to the East Village, took on a pen name and supported her artist's life with the money from the sale. Her investment paid off. She became an accomplished playwright who portrayed the black/white divide in her writing and performed her work in a raw and unsettling manner. The public and critics took notice. She was a finalist for the Pulitzer Prize and won an Obie Award for her one-woman show. I did not stay with theater. I got a real job as a school counselor instead.

The school was located in Flatbush, a predominantly black neighborhood. It was the height of the crack epidemic, and the devastation caused by drugs, the danger in the air, reminded me of my first visits to Harlem. But the inhabitants of Flatbush, immigrants from the Caribbean islands, not only looked and dressed differently from their African-American brothers and sisters but had a different cuisine and spoke a different kind of English.

Inside the school, teachers and students were safe from the gang wars and shootouts in the streets. We did not venture out to get lunch at the roti stand for fear of not making it back alive. Most of the students were Haitian. Gladimir, age ten, was my favorite. He had lost his mother to cancer and was mad at his father for bringing his girlfriend to live with them while his mother lay dying in the hospital. Gladimir's fantasy was to be adopted by me. We'd live happily ever after in a big suburban home, drive to the mall in a station wagon, and go on camping trips. He was disappointed that I didn't own a car or a house like the white people on TV, but stayed my biggest fan. He called me the light-skinned lady and told his classmates: "Ms. Steegmann, she's not white, she's German."

In June of 1998, my friend Agnes, a veteran of all sorts of house-and-garden tours, asked me to join her on a tour of historic homes in Hamilton Heights.

"Hamilton Heights?" I asked. "Where is that?" I was afraid it might be in Westchester or Long Island.

"In West Harlem, between 135th and 155th Streets, Edgecomb Avenue to the Hudson River."

"In Harlem? Are you sure?"

"Positive. It's an area where well-to-do and famous black people live."

Agnes, born in Haarlem, Holland, had a special fondness for Harlem. She took all her visiting cousins there. I had never heard of a Harlem beyond 125th Street, but let her talk me into joining her for the 10th Annual Hamilton Heights House and Garden Tour. As soon as we got off the A train at St. Nicholas Avenue, she started to lecture me:

"The street was named after our Dutch patron saint. Saint Nicholas was the masthead of the ship that brought the first Dutch colonists to Manhattan Island."

"When was that?" I asked.

"In 1669," she said, beaming with pride.

I was stunned when we turned left onto Convent Avenue. This

was a jewel of a neighborhood. There was at least one church on every block. The picturesque houses in an eclectic mix of styles, with their high stoops and charming stepped gables, reminded me of Holland. The roofs with their towers, gables, dormers, and chimneys were exceptionally exuberant. Inside, the buildings held treasures like parlor floors, Corinthian columns, fireplaces, marble mantelpieces, and mahogany railings with delicate latticework. The double master bedrooms with their twin dressing rooms and matching his-and-hers marble or wooden vanities were an enchanting time capsule. These beautiful homes were occupied by black professionals, interracial couples, and white gay men, many of whom were employed in the arts. They lived next to Dominican immigrants and welfare recipients. I had not encountered neighborhoods in Manhattan with such a mix of class.

Curious, I asked a gay white lawyer: "How do you like living here?"

"We love it. It's marvelous."

"But is it safe?"

"Don't worry. This is mostly a middle-class neighborhood."

None of the immaculately dressed people streaming out of St. Luke's Episcopal Church turned their heads when a very tall, white, platinum-blond transvestite in hot pants crossed the street. For a moment, I felt as if I had never left the West Village. I recalled my friend David, an art dealer, who had recently passed away. In the fifties, he had moved to New York from rural Pennsylvania. He found the gay balls in Harlem exciting and inclusive.

The grand finale of the tour was our visit to St. Nick's Pub. Once we walked down the steps under the red awning, we found ourselves in a delightful dive. The red-checkered tablecloth felt sticky, so we opted to sit at the bar. The bartender, around sixty-five, with an impressive wig and too much pancake make-up, flirted with all her male customers. Many of them took an interest in us. Bayard Jones, old enough to be my grandfather, bought us a drink.

"Look at the photographs on the wall. Miles Davis, John Coltrane, Charlie Parker, they all hung out here in the old days," he said.

"You're kidding," Agnes and I said in unison.

"What about Billie Holiday?" I asked. Billie, a gardenia in her hair, looked melancholy-lovely, in the faded photograph on the wall.

"Billie got her start here," Bayard said. "Remember, St. Nick's Pub has been in business since 1940."

How I wished I could have met Billie Holiday here at St. Nick's Pub. I imagined her getting off the stage, sitting down next to Bayard, and ordering herself a whiskey. The barmaid, who had overheard our conversation, came over.

"St. Nick's is the oldest continuously operating jazz club in Harlem," she said.

"And it hasn't changed a bit," Bayard added. He turned to me. "So, how do you ladies like Sugar Hill?"

I finished my second beer and declared enthusiastically: "I love it here. I think I could live here."

Agnes rolled her eyes and crinkled her nose at my foolishness. "You'd be back downtown in no time," she said.

My marriage to the handsome black man did not last. I found a handsome Ukrainian man instead. Living downtown with my new love in one room (for eight years!) choked my creativity. I had given up on theater and then I gave up on writing, too. My English wasn't good enough, and my German wasn't great any longer. I had lost the fluency and elegance of my mother tongue. Anyhow, how could I be a writer if I didn't even have my own desk?

We could not afford to rent a bigger place. We could not afford to buy a place either. Not anywhere below 23rd Street, our preferred stomping ground. I agonized every time I wrote the monthly rent check. *One thousand two hundred and forty-eight dollars.* Friends told me how lucky I was to have found a rent-stabilized apartment in the West Village, but I wasn't so sure. In Berlin, I might live in a gigantic Art Nouveau apartment for the same rent. I worried that I might not be able to stay in my beloved New York in my old age. Most people couldn't even afford Manhattan in their prime. Many of my friends were seeking more favorable surroundings elsewhere. They moved to Pittsburgh, upstate New York, or back to Europe. Theater and dance companies, painters and sculptors were all leaving New York, and stockbrokers happily snapped up their lofts. My first apartment, for which I had paid $334.56 rent in 1980, was now on the market for $775,000.

I yearned to own a home, to have my own desk, in a way some women yearn for a child. It was irrational and all-consuming. Miss Jackson had told me over and over: *Only a fool pays rent.* At forty-five, I did not want to live like a college student any longer. I haunted stationery stores and bought inkpots, writing paraphernalia, and decorative objects for a desk I had yet to own. I started to investigate foreclosures, the only way to realize my real-estate dreams on my salary. In November 1998, in the week before Thanksgiving, *The New York Times* advertised a few places in Harlem. The agent on the phone was suspicious. "Do you know the neighborhood? Have you ever been to Harlem?"

I fell in love with the duplex he showed me. Overlooking

St. Nicholas Park, within walking distance of St. Nick's Pub, it had spacious rooms, a separate office (a space to put a desk!), lots of light, great closets, a laundry room, and storage for our bikes in the basement. Most of all it had good karma and promised me the life of a civilized person. A writer maybe?

My husband refused to look at the gem I had discovered.

"Harlem is a slum. You want to move to a crime-ridden area?"

"It's a neighborhood in transition and nowhere near as bad as you think," I pleaded.

Ivan grew up in Newark, New Jersey, and had witnessed the 1967 riots. He had seen his parents' house lose value; he had experienced white people's fear and their ultimate flight.

"There's nothing going on in Harlem. We'll be away from all the action. I bet you can't even get a baguette or a decent bottle of wine in Harlem," he complained.

He was right, but I begged, pleaded, threatened, and finally got him to come up to Harlem. As soon as we left the subway station he was pleasantly surprised by the wide boulevards, the architectural gems, and the friendliness of the people. Just as I had expected, he fell in love with the apartment, too.

We bargained M&T Mortgage Corporation down, borrowed money from my mother, and scraped together the ten-percent-deposit of the $95,000 sale price. When we moved in February of 1999, good things started to happen right away. Bringing down the garbage for the first time, I met our super.

"Hi, I'm Angela. They call me the Clean Nazi. I really appreciate how you separate your garbage. You do a great job tying up your recyclable newspapers and cardboard boxes," she said.

After my initial shock of witnessing a black woman calling herself a Nazi, I answered: "Hi, my name is Anna. Thanks for the compliment. I'm from Germany. Recycling is a religion in my homeland. You might go to jail if you don't separate your brown from your green and white glass."

"My kind of country. Welcome to Harlem. How do you like it so far?"

While I stuffed my laundry into the dryer, we talked. Angela, who was from Trinidad, didn't mind white people moving to her Harlem. "We have too many people with poor breeding the way it is now." Our conversation turned personal. We found out we were the same age.

"I hope you don't mind me asking, but are you menopausal?" she said.

"I stopped menstruating a year ago."

"A drag, isn't it?"

"I wake up at four every morning and can't go back to sleep."

"Do you take hormones?"

"No, I believe in really good-quality dark chocolate."

"You're my kind of woman."

On my next trip down to the basement I brought her some of the *Novesia Goldnuss Schokolade* from my mother's C.A.R.E. package. Angela inspected the green-and-gold wrapping, the see-through window revealing dark chocolate with gigantic hazelnuts. "Hmm, that looks different," she said as she ripped the package open. She put the first piece in her mouth and closed her eyes in blissful surrender. I have never had sex with a woman, but Angela looked positively orgasmic. I felt like a voyeur watching the chocolate and hazelnut dance around in her mouth. Finally she opened her eyes.

"Good Lord, this is divine. I'll throw my Hershey's away for this. What makes this so good?"

"The right kind of fat. Nothing but cocoa butter. No fillers and additives," I said.

Angela licked her lips. "How can I make it up to you?"

"No need," I said. "I just wanted to give you something to take the edge off those menopausal mood swings."

Then I threw the bright yellow Ikea bags with my freshly laundered clothes over my shoulders and made my way up the stairs.

"Wait a minute," she stopped me. "Do you have any plans for Saturday night?"

"No, not really."

"Want to come to my birthday party? We'll have a male stripper to entertain a crowd of menopausal woman."

Of course I wanted to go.

H arlem amazed me in many ways. Downtown, I had become invisible to men. At forty-five, no one stared at me, flirted with me, or complimented me any longer. The store clerks called me Ma'am. In an entire year, the only man to hit on me was a smelly homeless guy who sat across from me in the subway.

"You are some fine babe," he said.

"Thank you," I replied. "I appreciate that."

Stepping outside in Harlem, I could always count on male attention of the "Hello, Gorgeous," "God bless you, Sister," "Have a marvelous day, Lovely Lady" variety. Some men broke out in song at the sight of me in unshapely sweatpants, my hair unwashed and untamed. Once, waiting for the bus, a black BMW stopped in front of me. The driver, a black man in his twenties, decked out in hip-hop attire, rolled down his tinted window and said with tremendous urgency in his voice:

"I have to get to know you!"

"Don't waste your time with a woman old enough to be your mother."

"Wait a minute. You are married?"

"Very much so."

"Happily married?"

"I'd say so."

"Listen, he doesn't have to know."

Not everything was that rosy in Harlem. Couples aired their relationship drama under my window at four in the morning. Drivers parked their cars, opened the windows, turned the music all the way up, and forced everyone to listen to Mary J. Blige. There were plenty of examples of bad parenting: mothers who cursed at their two-year-olds and fed them Pepsi and potato chips. The cheerful children's birthday parties in the park started with hundreds of balloons and large tables loaded with fried chicken, potato salad, and all kinds of delicacies, then continued half the night. The deafening rap music made me feel as if the loudspeakers were in my bedroom. Ignoring the rules, people barbequed, stank up the entire block, and left enormous heaps of garbage. High-school students murdered the daffodils in the park. On my way to the subway, I passed a mural: *Owning a condo on 116th Street doesn't make you a Harlemite.* It told me I wasn't welcomed by everyone.

I did not dwell on these negative aspects of Harlem life. I chose to overlook the abandoned buildings, the old man living in his car, the empty garbage-filled lots, and liquor stores where I had to make my purchase through a bulletproof window. Most people were welcoming. Our white friends felt it, too. When they parked their cars too far away from us, our neighbors gave them proper directions and reassured them: "Your friends live three houses down. Don't forget to turn off your lights. Don't worry, we'll watch your car." Some of our European friends fell in love with Harlem, too, and moved uptown.

I enjoyed practicing my high-school French with my Senegalese neighbors. I took pleasure in the soothing view of the steep and rocky slopes of St. Nicholas Park, the early-morning sparrow concerts, and the children on the swings shrieking with delight. At night, I looked up at City College's Shepherd Hall in all its illuminated splendor. I walked on St. Nicholas Terrace, startled by the magnificent view of the Harlem and Bronx skyline. I passed by the Y.M.C.A. where Langston Hughes had stayed for seven dollars a week when he first came to New York to study at Columbia. The Harlem pace was slow and gentle, like a European city's. One day, marching at frantic Manhattan speed, an older gentleman scolded me: "Don't rush, young lady. It's not allowed up here."

Strolling through the City College campus, I admired the five Collegiate Gothic buildings. A sign explained that they were built with Manhattan schist, stone quarried from the excavation of the subway tunnels. The grey stone buildings were decorated with terra-cotta ornaments and hundreds of grotesque figures, which seemed to represent the fine, applied and mechanical arts. Shepherd Hall was the most spectacular of all the buildings. The security guard was kind enough to let me in without an I.D. I was enchanted by the work displayed by the architecture students. The Great Hall was an awe-inspiring cathedral-like space. It must have been at least four stories high. I looked up at the splendid stained-glass windows, and not watching my way I bumped into a professor. "Marvelous, isn't it," he said. "Just imagine Mark Twain and Albert Einstein lecturing here." He rushed off before I had a chance to ask him about it. How lucky he was to work in a space like this.

Maybe I could be a college student again and return to that time of promise and hope in indefinite future possibilities. My alma mater, the *Freie Universität Berlin*, had been built by the Americans after World War II. The university was spread all over town. Many of the buildings were shabbily constructed and already rusting or falling apart when I was a student. This time around, I'd study in a much more splendid temple of learning, a college with a real campus. I looked up to the mural showing Wisdom looking down on Alma Mater and the Graduate. In that moment, when I contemplated my life's journey, Miss Jackson whispered in my ear: *Ain't nobody holding you back but yourself.*

I fell in love with a charming desk. Made in Indonesia, it had an exotic aura and seemed perfect for a travel writer or well-traveled writer. Graham Greene, Bruce Chatwin, and Rudyard Kipling would have loved it. I really couldn't afford it, but treated myself to it anyway. Once I had my own desk, my love for writing returned. I wrote a story, "The Wrong Country," and on a whim sent it off to the Cornelia Street Café. A week later, I found a message on my answering machine: "You know, your piece is quite brilliant. We have an opening in three weeks. Would you like to read?" I saved the message for the next three months and was devastated when my husband accidentally erased it.

At the reading, middle-aged women, Angela among them, applauded enthusiastically. Invitations to read at other venues followed. Encouraged, I applied to the creative-writing program at City College, and was accepted. Three years later, my story had swelled to a book of two hundred twenty-five pages. When *The New York Times* accepted one of my essays for publication, I took it as an omen and left my job as a school counselor.

Now I teach freshmen at City College the finer points of writing.

Last fall, I even taught a class in Shepherd Hall. *Make room for the Lord to work his magic,* Miss Jackson used to say. As usual, she was right. I don't have to leave Harlem any longer to go to work. I just climb the stairs of St. Nicholas Park, where youthful contenders challenge senior citizens to games of speed chess, and Mexican and African-American boys play basketball next to each other, but not with each other.

Eight years after moving uptown, I still delight in Harlem. Uplifting gospel music spills out of the churches on Sundays. Old people at the bus stop tell me about Harlem in its heyday, the Mother's Day celebrations, First Communion processions, fabulous dances and musical performances. A retired gentleman at the Showman's Lounge (in business since 1942) invites us to his sister's house for Thanksgiving. I often treat myself to lunch at The United House of Prayers for All People. Their cornbread and meatloaf is almost as good as Miss Jackson's. On my way over, the plaque at the Lionel Hampton Houses reminds me of how much the people here love and admire their artists: *God gave me the talent. Gladys gave me the inspiration.*

I am amazed by the countless hair salons. Many stay open seven days a week until late at night. Veronica's Beauty-Rama is my favorite. She has won the KISS 98.7 Choice Award for Best Beauty Shop, made first place at Hair Battle Royale, the Ladies Avant-Garde Hair competition, and many other hair shows. In the store window, her plaques sit next to photographs of her prizewinning coifs. They show women with green, fire-engine red, and blue hair, hair with rhinestones and glitter, hair sculpted into elaborate creations that remind me of peacocks and Mardi Gras revelers. Getting my bangs cut (for $3, as opposed to $15 on the Upper West Side), I study Veronica, all dressed in purple, with purple hair and false purple eyelashes, as she performs her magic on other illustrious customers. I'm amused by the signs posted throughout the store: *If you can't grow it, Veronica will sow it; In this salon we provide many services. Recess time for your kids is not one of them; Let God take care of it.* Miss Jackson would have loved it. Smiling down from heaven, she gives me the thumbs-up: *The Lord has turned your setbacks into comebacks. Bless your little heart, Child.* ♦

CONTRIBUTORS' NOTES

B.J. BUCKLEY, who once roller-skated from the top to the bottom of the Guggenheim Museum, has been a Poet in the Schools throughout the Rocky Mountain West for over thirty years. She has been the recipient of the Joy Harjo Prize, the Rita Dove Poetry Award, and a Wyoming Literature Fellowship, among other awards. Her most recent book, with co-author Dawn Senior-Trask, is *Moonhorses & the Red Bull*, from Pronghorn Press (Greybull, Wyoming). She lives in the Bitterroot Valley of Montana, in a small cabin with no electricity or running water, with three dogs, a cat, and her sweetheart.

CHRISTOPHER CAHILL is the author of a novel, *Perfection* (L'Age d'Homme, Paris). He is the editor of *The Recorder: The Journal of the American Irish Historical Society*. He lives in New York City, where he was born.

ERICA CICCARONE, Connecticut born, lived in New Orleans for several years, where she attended Loyola University. After realizing she could not be sustained by the heat of the Marigny bar life alone, she applied to New York M.F.A. programs and ended up at The New School Creative Writing Program, where she had the divine privilege of working with David Gates and Shelley Jackson. She now lives in Brooklyn, wrestles with post-M.F.A. poverty, and teaches English Composition and Literature at three New York colleges. Her nonfiction has been published in *A Gathering of the Tribes*, *New Orleans Review*, and *Econoculture*. "Pit" is from her working collection, *Symptoms of a Greater Sorrow*. She is currently battling her sister for rights to that title. She also dreams of developing three small chapters of her Western, *The Authentic Life of Bonnie Durham*, into a novel. This is her first published piece of fiction.

MARTIN EDMUNDS is the author of *The High Road to Taos* and co-wrote, with Lavinia Currier, the screenplay for *Passion in the Desert*.

DION FARQUHAR is an ex-New Yorker living in Santa Cruz with the love of her life and their twin teenage sons. Obsessed by her formative experience of the '60s and repudiating nothing, she is finishing a novel set in the '80s in New York. Her poems have appeared in *Otoliths*, *3 by 3 by 3*, *Rogue Scholars*, *Main Street Rag*, *Perigee*, *The Argotist*, *City Works*, *Hawaii Review*, *Painted Bride Quarterly*, and other journals. Her chapbook, *Cleaving*, won first prize at Poets Corner Press in 2007. She teaches at Santa Cruz and Golden Gate University.

The writer known as ELENA FERRANTE was born in Naples. Though one of Italy's most acclaimed contemporary authors, she shuns public attention and keeps her whereabouts and her true identity concealed. Her previous novels available in English are *Days of Abandonment* and *Troubling Love*. Europa Editions will publish *The Lost Daughter* early in 2008.

EDWIN FRANK is editor of the New York Review Books classics series and the author of two chapbooks, *Stack* and *The Further Adventures of Pinocchio*.

GEORGE FRANKLIN has a book of poems, *The Fall of Miss Alaska*, coming out in the spring from Six Gallery Press. He lives in New York City.

CARLA GERICKE was born in South Africa, raised in a diplomatic family, and has lived and traveled all over the world. She moved to America in 1996 after winning a green card in the lottery. Carla is the recipient of various awards and scholarships, most recently from the A Room of Her Own Foundation. She is earning her M.F.A. in creative writing at City College of New York, where she also teaches. Her work has appeared in *Inkwell, Pindeldyboz, Promethean, Word Riot, Route Magazine,* and elsewhere. Carla lives with her husband and three cacti in a rather dodgy loft in the heart of Chinatown, where she is completing her first novel.

ANN GOLDSTEIN is an editor at *The New Yorker*. She has translated works by, among others, Primo Levi, Pier Paolo Pasolini, Alessandro Baricco, and Erri De Luca, as well as Elena Ferrante, and is currently editing the Complete Works of Primo Levi in English. She has been the recipient of several prizes, including the PEN Renato Poggioli prize and an award from the Italian Ministry of Foreign Affairs.

JEFFREY GUSTAVSON is the author of *Nervous Forces* (N.Y.: Alef Books).

GAIL ALBERT HALABAN lives and works in Los Angeles and New York. The Robert Mann gallery represents her fine-art work. The work in her last exhibit was from her project "This Stage of Motherhood," examining the lives of a group of women in New York. She is a graduate of Brown University and has an M.F.A. degree from Yale University. She is the 2007 Photography Fellow for the Design Trust for Public Space for which she is working on a series of changing New York views. Her editorial work can be found in *The New Yorker, People* and *New York* magazine.

ODETTE HEIDEMAN—born in San Francisco, raised in Tokyo, London, Cannes, and northern New Jersey, married in Stockholm, lived in Paris, Amsterdam, New York, and now the eastern beach land of Long Island—is a citizen of everywhere, which is to say a citizen of nowhere. She is the author of a nonfiction book, *Babylore,* and has written for *The World of Interiors* and the *Washington Post.* This is her first published work of fiction. She teaches fiction workshops at the Writers Studio in New York.

JOEL HINMAN was a film producer for over twenty-five years before turning to fiction. Currently he teaches fiction and poetry at The Writers Studio, in New York. He is working on his second novel and a collection of short stories. In the last year he joined the Board of the Institute for Mediation and Conflict Resolution in the South Bronx, where he does community mediation. He is married and lives in New York City.

ELIZABETH MACKLIN is the author of two collections of poetry, *A Woman Kneeling in the Big City* (1992) and *You've Just Been Told* (2000). Her translation of the Basque poet Kirmen Uribe's *Meanwhile Take My Hand* was published this year by Graywolf Press.

LORRI McDOLE lives in a suburb of Seattle with her husband and two children. Her work has appeared in various magazines and anthologies, including *Brain, Child, A Cup of Comfort for Writers*, and *400 Words*. She was a finalist in the *Bellingham Review*'s 2007 Annie Dillard Creative Nonfiction Contest and has essays forthcoming in *The Rambler* and *Eclectica*.

CAROL MOLDAW's lyric novel, *The Widening*, will be published by Etruscan Press in the spring. She is the author of four books of poetry: *The Lightning Field* (winner of the Field Poetry Prize), *Chalkmarks on Stone, Through the Window*, and *Taken From the River*. She teaches in Stonecoast, U.S.M.'s low-residency M.F.A. program, and lives in New Mexico with her husband and daughter.

D. NURKSE's most recent books are *Burnt Island* and *The Fall*. A new book is forthcoming from Knopf in 2008. In 2007, he was elected to the Board of Directors of Amnesty International–U.S.A.

JANE R. OLIENSIS lives in Italy, with her family, three dogs, and two cats. She is the director of Humanities Spring in Assisi, a summer program for high-school students interested in poetry, art, ice cream, and the classics.

SAMEER PANDYA has published stories in *Narrative Magazine* and *Other Voices*. He is currently at work on a novel.

DOUGLAS ROGERS is a Zimbabwe-born journalist and travel writer based in New York City. He is a frequent contributor to *The Guardian, The Daily Telegraph* and *Travel & Leisure Magazine*. His book, *The Last Resort: A Memoir of Zimbabwe*, will be published by Crown in 2009.

MATTHEW ROHRER is the author of five books, most recently *Rise Up* (Wave Books). He lives in Brooklyn and teaches at N.Y.U.

MICHAEL RUBY is the author of two collections of poetry, *At an Intersection* (Alef, 2002) and *Window on the City* (BlazeVOX, 2006). *Inner Voices Heard Before Sleep* is the final section of a trilogy called *Memories, Dreams and Inner Voices*. The first section, *Fleeting Memories*, is being published as an ebook by Ugly Duckling Presse in Brooklyn.

ANNA STEEGMANN, born in Germany in 1954, has lived in New York City since 1980. She worked as an actress and psychotherapist until making writing her priority. She has published academic texts in German and English. Her poems, stories, essays, and translations have appeared or will soon come out in *The New York Times, The Absinthe Literary Review, Boomer Women Speak, Dimension², Promethean,* and *[sic]* as well as several German newspapers and anthologies. She teaches writing at City College of New York, where she received an M.A. in creative writing. She has written a memoir, *The Wrong Country,* her first book in English.

JOE TULLY is a native New Yorker who has served as a partner at btldesign, a branding and interactive agency in New York City. He continues to work for select clients through Joe Tully Design. He is also working on a memoir, *Second House From the Corner,* about growing up on Long Island in the '40s and '50s, his Irish and Italian heritage, secretive parents, HIV/AIDS, and coming to terms with being gay.

LLOYD VAN BRUNT is the author of *Delirium: Selected Poems, Working Firewood for the Night,* and seven other books of poems, as well as a memoir, *Hardpan.* Over the past decade, he has been working on fiction, and has completed two novels.

DEREK WALCOTT's books of poems include *In a Green Night: Poems 1948-1960* (1962), *The Castaway* (1965), *The Gulf* (1969), *Another Life* (1973), *Sea Grapes* (1976), *The Star-Apple Kingdom* (1979), *The Fortunate Traveller* (1981), *Midsummer* (1984), *The Arkansas Testament* (1987), *Omeros* (1990), *The Bounty* (1997), *Tiepolo's Hound* (2000), and *The Prodigal* (2004). His books of plays include *Dream on Monkey Mountain and Other Plays* (1970), *The Joker of Seville & O Babylon!* (1978), and *Remembrance & Pantomine* (1980). He is the founder and was for many years the director of the Trinidad Theatre Workshop. Among his many awards are an Obie, a MacArthur grant, a Guggenheim, the Queen's Gold Medal for Poetry, and, in 1992, the Nobel Prize for Literature.

CYNTHIA WEINER's work has appeared in *Ploughshares, Open City, The Sonora Review,* and *Pushcart Prize XXX.* She is the Assistant Director of The Writers Studio in New York City, and is working on a collection of short stories.